Date Due

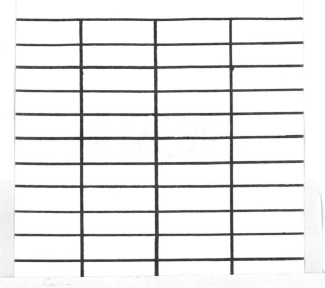

AURORA

AURORA

New Canadian Writing 1978

EDITED BY

MORRIS WOLFE

DOUBLEDAY CANADA LIMITED
Toronto, Canada

DOUBLEDAY & COMPANY, INC.
Garden City, New York

1978

ISBN number: 0-385-13646-3
Library of Congress Catalog Card Number: 78-1227

Copyright © 1978 by Doubleday Canada Limited

"Pat Frank's Dream" is excerpted from *Sunrise,* by Matt Cohen,
and is printed by permission of The Canadian Publishers,
McClelland and Stewart Limited, Toronto, and by permission
of Harold Ober Associates.

Printed and bound in Canada by the Alger Press Limited
Design by Robert Garbutt Productions

FIRST EDITION

ACKNOWLEDGMENTS

I'm extremely grateful to Rick Archbold and Betty Corson,
my editors at Doubleday Canada. Their support of *Aurora* was
enthusiastic from the beginning and their advice invaluable
throughout. The book became as much their pet project as it
was mine. Barbara Track of Doubleday spent long hours,
including Saturdays, acknowledging, cataloguing, and
returning submissions.

CONTENTS

Introduction   1

GUY VANDERHAEGHE
    Man Descending   5
BRIAN DEDORA
    That Signified   17
GEORGE WOODCOCK
    Such Is My Beloved   19
    Black Flag   20
SUSAN MUSGRAVE
    Flying the Flag of Ourselves   21
    It Is the Night   22
    Break-Up   22
    Wedding Song   23
    Sleeping Together   24
    I Did It to Attract Women   26
IRENA FRIEDMAN
    Dimitri: An Unfinished Portrait   26
GAIL FOX
    The Coming   34
RONALD BATES
    Un homme de quarante ans   36
KEITH GAREBIAN
    Adam Meeting Eve   37
    sleeping with th grass   37
    ths lust ium in luv with   38
JOHN HIRSCH
    Reminiscences   39
T. D. MacLULICH
    Prologue: Columbus   49
    Two Canadian Poets   51

AL PURDY
Writer-in-Rez   53
FRED COGSWELL
A Respect: For a Poet   56
JOHN GLASSCO
Canadian Poet   57
MIRIAM WADDINGTON
Lady Blue: Homage to Montreal   58
HENRY BEISSEL
The Sniper   60
How to Build an Igloo Into History   66
bpNICHOL
from *The Martyrology: Book V*   69
RUDY WIEBE
In the Beaver Hills   71
ELDON GARNET
i am red green colourblind   80
a hill gently sloping down   81
DARLENE MADOTT
Bottled Roses   83
JOHN REIBETANZ
Melba Sheppard in Her Garden   103
Will Travis: Blacksmith   106
Andrew Whittaker: Local Preacher   107
GREG HOLLINGSHEAD
The Sound   110
JOYCE CAROL OATES
Small Miracles   120
ROBERT BRINGHURST
Six Epitaphs   121
KENNETH SHERMAN
Lepers   122
JOYCE MARSHALL
The Escape   123
DOUGLAS BARBOUR
a waiting   133
for phyllis webb, 12.5.74   134
Jack Chambers — 'Nude' 74-76   135
the poem & the policeman   137

HANS JEWINSKI
!:-;; My Theme   138

JIM CHRISTY
New Living Quarters   140

RAYMOND SOUSTER
Wild Pitch   150

DON BAILEY
Offhand Comments   151

STEPHEN SCOBIE
Deputy Bell   158

CHRISTOPHER LEVENSON
Spiritual Exercises   173

DAVID HELWIG
Notes for a Ballet   174

DAVID MACFARLANE
Words for two dancers   175
Lines somewhat in the manner of Ovid   176
The routine of significant activity   177

WILLIAM LATTA
The Logician as Poet   178

TIM INKSTER
The Printer Addresses a Fop   179

GLORIA OSTREM SAWAI
Mother's Day   180

FLORENCE McNEIL
Family Dinner   193

RAY SHANKMAN
Wedding Poem   194

MARGARET GIBSON
Aaron   195

BARRY DEMPSTER
Uncle Claude   198

MATT COHEN
Pat Frank's Dream   199

FRANCIS SPARSHOTT
The Naming of the Beasts   207
Nympharum Disjecta Membra   208
Reflex   209

GEORGE RYGA
    Beyond a Crimson Morning   210

RALPH GUSTAFSON
    The Magi   227
    Country Walking   228
    Allhallows Eve   229
    Canada Still Life   229

TOM MARSHALL
    Summer of 'Seventy-Seven   230

Notes on the Contributors   234

AURORA

INTRODUCTION

There is more good writing being done in Canada today than at any time in our history. And there has never been a larger audience for that writing than there is now. *Aurora* is a paperback magazine that provides an annual showcase for the best previously unpublished work we can find on whatever subject, in whatever form, by new and established Canadian writers. This first issue contains poems, essays, short stories, and excerpts from longer works by forty-six writers, a dozen of whom are being introduced to a wider readership for the first time.

There has been nothing quite like *Aurora* in Canadian publishing. In 1944 Ralph Gustafson's *Canadian Accent*, a collection of mostly new stories and poems, was published by Penguin; it disappeared after just one number. In the late 1960s Roy MacSkimming persuaded Clarke, Irwin to publish *New Canadian Writing*; it appeared twice, each edition containing two stories by three short story writers. More recently, Oberon Press published /several editions of *New Canadian Stories*. But Oberon's annual collection now consists mostly of reprints of the best stories that have appeared in "little mags." I have long felt that the time was right for a Canadian publication patterned on the more eclectic U.S. paperback magazines, *New World Writing* (1952–59) and *New American Review* (1967–77) — a place to which the general reader could turn to get the kind of sense of the state of Canadian literature that *The Tamarack Review* used to provide. Happily, Doubleday Canada agreed with me.

So did Canadian writers. Over eight hundred submissions were received in response to the announcement of the first edition of *Aurora*. More than half of them were from Ontario; next came British Columbia, Alberta, Quebec, and Nova Scotia. There were some surprises. Judging by the submissions, the most fertile literary soil in Canada today is to be found in Alberta, especially around Edmonton; proportionately there are more writers in the book—eight—from that part of the country than from any other. In contrast, the work of only one writer east of Quebec City is included. Submissions from women outnumbered those from men by three to two; but three-quarters of the writers in *Aurora* are men. It's surprising how little experimental material was submitted. The best of our experimental poets, bpNichol, is represented here by a fairly traditional excerpt. The only prose piece in the book that can be described as experimental is Greg Hollingshead's "The Sound."

The experiences one has as the editor of a book such as this can be fascinating—and amusing. The father of an academic contributor, eager that his son be published, sent me a letter informing me that his boy came from good stock. To prove it, he enclosed his own entry in *Who's Who* and informed me that the paternal side of the boy's mother's family was *probably* descended from the Scottish House of Stuart. Another man wrote saying he hoped I'd give his poems special consideration because he'd "bought and read many Doubleday books." A woman phoned late one night to ask what I'd thought of her story. I told her truthfully that I couldn't remember it, but that even if I could, I wouldn't tell her until all submissions were in; this was, after all, a competition. She said she hadn't known that; if she had, she wouldn't have contributed. It wasn't nice for people to be competitive. Would I return her story immediately? A member of the League of Canadian Poets assumed that my letter inviting submissions meant that all work submitted would automatically be included in *Aurora*. When she received *my* rejection letter, *she* rejected it, returning it to me with a note scrawled across it, saying: "You must learn better manners. You asked *me* for material!" Another contributor brought a poem into the Doubleday office and told a secretary that it was really a song he'd composed for Liberace. It couldn't be appreciated unless it was heard; he proceeded to sing it to her.

But there is no greater pleasure for an editor than being the first to read a fresh and lively bit of writing that's so good it can't be put down. You want to call out to anyone within hearing distance: "Hey, look at this!" Susan Musgrave's poems made me feel that way. Stephen Scobie's fine story "Deputy Bell" not only made me want to call out, but made me wonder again about the attraction the Billy the Kid legend has for Canadian writers. Philosopher Francis Sparshott says poetry is "a continuation of philosophy by other means"; his own poetry is more haunting than any philosophy I've read. John Hirsch, a Hungarian by birth, is the only Canadian I can think of whose love of this country is such that somehow it isn't corny when he confesses to kissing the ground in Vancouver on returning to Canada after several months in Japan. John Reibetanz's sensitive dramatic monologues explore the feeling of community that only a people with deep roots can have.

Keith Garebian's delightful parody of Bill Bissett will gladden the hearts of the two Conservative Members of Parliament who recently attacked the Canada Council for giving money to Bissett. In Garebian's poem Bissett admits "i havn't made pomes fr years"; he uses his grant money "to pay off luvrs nd dew sum/balling." George Ryga's eloquent evocation of modern China, "Beyond a Crimson Morning," offers fresh insights into that country. Readers familiar with the prose of Margaret Gibson and Don Bailey will discover that their first published poems in *Aurora* are stylistically and thematically a continuation of their earlier work. The excerpt from Matt Cohen's forthcoming novel *Sunrise* reveals a delicate sensibility at its finest. George Woodcock's two poems show an increasing introspection as he begins work on his autobiography. Douglas Barbour has quietly become one of Canada's finest poets; his "Jack Chambers — 'Nude' 74–76" is especially poignant in view of that artist's recent death. Jim Christy continues to be one of our best little-known writers; only Hugh Garner has captured skid-row life as well as Christy does in his story "New Living Quarters." Anyone who's come to love the Toronto Blue Jays despite all their inadequacies (as I have) will be delighted by Raymond Souster's "Wild Pitch." And I don't think anyone has captured the essence of E. J. Pratt and Irving Layton as effectively as T. D. MacLulich.

The greatest pleasure of all is being able to present the work of good new writers—poets like David Macfarlane and John Reibetanz. And some first-rate fiction writers. I'll never be able to think of mustard plasters in quite the same way again, having read Gloria Sawai's story "Mother's Day." Greg Hollingshead's "The

Sound" is a masterpiece of control. Guy Vanderhaeghe's "Man Descending" is the funniest new story I've read in a while. The conclusion of Darlene Madott's "Bottled Roses" moves me every time I read it. But enough: there isn't space to tell you why I like everything in this first volume of *Aurora*; it's time you took a look for yourself.

Morris Wolfe
May 1978

GUY VANDERHAEGHE

Man Descending

It is six-thirty; my wife returns home from work. I am shaving when I hear her key scratching at the lock. I keep the door of our apartment locked at all times. The building has been burgled twice since we moved in and I don't like surprises. My caution annoys my wife; she sees it as proof of a reluctance to approach life with the open-armed camaraderie she expected in a spouse. I can tell that this bit of faithlessness on my part has made her unhappy. Her heels click down our uncarpeted hallway with a lively resonance. So I lock the door of the bathroom to forestall her.

I do this because the state of the bathroom (and my state) will only make her unhappier. I note that my dead cigarette butt has left a liverish stain of nicotine on the edge of the sink and that it has deposited droppings of ash in the basin. The glass of scotch standing on the toilet tank is not empty. I have been oiling myself all afternoon with that glass in expectation of the New Year's party that I would rather not attend. Since scotch is regarded as a fine social lubricant, I have attempted, to the best of my ability, to get lubricated. Somehow I feel it hasn't worked.

My wife is rattling the door now. "Ed, are you in there?"

"None other," I reply, furiously slicing great swathes in the lather on my cheeks.

"Goddamn it, Ed," Victoria says angrily. "I asked you. I asked you *please* be done in there before I get home. I have to get ready for the party. I told Helen we'd be there by eight."

"I didn't realize it was so late," I explain lamely. I can imagine the stance she has assumed on the other side of the door. My wife is a social worker and has to deal with people like me every day. Irresponsible people. By now she has crossed her arms across her breasts and inclined her head with its shining helmet of dark hair ever so slightly to one side. Her mouth has puckered like a drawstring purse, and she has planted her legs defiantly and solidly apart, signifying she will not be moved.

"Ed, how long are you going to be in there?"

I know that tone of voice. Words can never mask its meaning. It is always interrogative, and it always implies that my grievous faults of character could be remedied. *So why don't I make the effort?*

"Five minutes," I call cheerfully.

Victoria goes away. Her heels are brisk on the hardwood.

My thoughts turn to the party and then naturally to civil servants, since almost all of Victoria's friends are people with whom she works. Civil servants inevitably lead me to think of mandarins, and then Asiatics in general. I settle on Mongols and begin to carefully carve the lather off my face, intent on leaving myself with a shaving-cream Fu Manchu. I do quite a handsome job. I slit my eyes.

"Mirror, mirror on the wall," I whisper. "Who's the fiercest of them all?"

From the back of my throat I produce a sepulchral tone of reply. "You Genghis Ed, Terror of the World! You who raise cenotaphs of skulls! You who banquet off the backs of your enemies!" I imagine myself sweeping out of Central Asia on a shaggy pony, hard-bitten from years in the saddle, turning almond eyes to fabulous cities that lie pliant under my pitiless gaze.

Victoria is back at the bathroom door. "Ed!"

"Yes, dear?" I answer meekly.

"Ed, explain something to me," she demands.

"Anything, lollipop," I reply. This assures her I have been alerted to danger. It is now a fair fight and she does not have to labor under the feeling that she has sprung upon her quarry from ambush.

"Don't get sarcastic. It's not called for."

I drain my glass of scotch, rinse it under the tap, and stick a toothbrush in it, rendering it innocuous. The butt is flicked into the toilet, and the nicotine stain scrubbed out with my thumb. "I apologize," I say, hunting madly in the medicine cabinet for mouthwash to disguise my alcoholic breath.

"Ed, you have nothing to do all day. Absolutely nothing. Why couldn't you be done in there before I got home?"

I rinse my mouth. Then I spot my full white Fu Manchu and begin scraping. "Well, dear, it's like this," I say. "You know how I sweat.

And I do get nervous about these little affairs. So I cut the time a little fine. I admit that. But one doesn't want to appear at these affairs too damp. I like to think that my deodorant's power is peaking at my entrance. I'm sure you see. . . ."

"Shut up and get out of there," Victoria says tiredly.

A last cursory inspection of the bathroom and I spring open the door and present my wife with my best I'm-a-harmless-idiot-don't-hit-me, smile. Since I've been unemployed I practice my smiles in the mirror whenever time hangs heavy on my hands. I have one for every occasion. This particular one is a faithful reproduction, Art imitating Life. The other day, while out taking a walk, I saw a large black Labrador taking a crap on somebody's doorstep. We established instant rapport. He grinned hugely at me while his body trembled with exertion. His smile was a perfect blend of physical relief, mischievousness, and apology for his indiscretion. A perfectly suitable smile for my present situation.

"Squeaky, pretty pink clean," I announce to my wife.

"Being married to an adolescent is a bore," Victoria says, pushing past me into the bathroom. "Make me a drink. I need it."

I hurry to comply and return in time to see my wife lowering her delightful bottom into a tub of scalding hot, soapy water and ascending wreaths of steam. She lies back and her breasts flatten; she toys with the tap with delicate ivory toes.

"Christ," she murmurs, stunned by the heat.

I sit down on the toilet seat and fondle my drink, rotating the transparent cylinder and its amber contents in my hand. Then I abruptly hand Victoria her glass, and as an opening gambit ask, "How's Howard?"

My wife does not flinch, but only sighs luxuriantly, steeping herself in the rich heat. I interpret this as hardness of heart. I read in her face the lineaments of a practiced and practicing adulteress. For some time now I've suspected that Howard, a grave and unctuously dignified psychologist who works for the provincial Department of Social Services, is her lover. My wife has taken to working late and several times when I have phoned her office, disguising my voice and playing the irate beneficiary of the government's largesse, Howard has answered. When we meet socially, Howard treats me with the barely concealed contempt that is due an unsuspecting cuckold.

"Howard? Oh, he's fine," Victoria answers blandly, sipping at her drink. Her body seems to elongate under the water, and for a moment I feel justified in describing her as statuesque.

"I like Howard," I say. "We should have him over for dinner some evening."

My wife laughs. "Howard doesn't like you," she says.

"Oh?" I feign surprise. "Why?"

"You know why. Because you're always pestering him to diagnose you. He's not stupid, you know. He knows you're laughing up your sleeve at him. You're transparent, Ed. When you don't like someone you belittle their work. I've seen you do it a thousand times."

"I refuse," I say, "to respond to innuendo."

This conversation troubles my wife. She begins to splash around in the tub. She cannot go too far in her defense of Howard.

"He's not a bad sort," she says. "A little stuffy I grant you, but sometimes stuffiness is preferable to complete irresponsibility. You, on the other hand, seem to have the greatest contempt for anyone whose behavior even remotely approaches sanity."

I know my wife is now angling the conversation toward the question of employment. There are two avenues open for examination. She may concentrate on the past, studded as it is with a series of unmitigated disasters, or the future. On the whole I feel the past is safer ground, at least from my point of view. She knows that I lied about why I was fired from my last job, and six months later still hasn't got the truth out of me.

Actually, I was shown the door because of "habitual uncooperativeness." I was employed in an adult extension program. For the life of me I couldn't master the terminology and this created a rather unfavorable impression. All that talk about "terminal learners," "life skills," etc. completely unnerved me. Whenever I was sure I understood what a word meant, someone decided it had become charged with nasty connotations and invented a new "value-free term." The place was a goddamn madhouse and I acted accordingly.

I have to admit though that there was one thing I liked about the job. That was answering the phone whenever the office was deserted, which it frequently was since everyone was always running out into the community "identifying needs." I greeted every caller with a breezy, "College of Knowledge. Mr. Know It All here!" Rather juvenile wit I admit, but very satisfying. And I was rather sorry I got the boot before I got to meet a real, live, flesh-and-blood terminal learner. Evidently there were thousands of them out in the community and they were a bad thing. At one meeting in which we were trying to decide what should be done about them, I suggested, using a bit of Pentagon jargon I had picked up on the late-night news, that if we ever laid hands on any of them or their ilk, that we should have them "terminated with extreme prejudice."

"By the way," my wife asks nonchalantly, "were you out looking today?"

"Harry Wells called," I lie. "He thinks he might have something for me in a couple of months."

My wife stirs uneasily in the tub and creates little swells that radiate from her body like a disquieting aura.

"That's funny," she ways tartly. "I called Harry today about finding work for you. He didn't foresee anything in the future."

"He must have meant the immediate future."

"He didn't mention talking to you."

"That's funny."

Victoria suddenly stands up. Venus rising from the bath. Captive water sluices between her breasts, slides down her thighs.

"Damn it, Ed! When are you going to begin to tell the truth? I'm sick of all this." She fumbles blindly for a towel as her eyes pin me. "Just remember," she adds, "behave yourself tonight. Lay off my friends."

I am rendered speechless by her fiery beauty, by this many times thwarted love that twists and turns in search of a worthy object. Meekly, I promise.

I drive to the party, my headlights rending the veil of thickly falling, shimmering snow. The city crews have not yet removed the Christmas decorations; strings of lights garland the street lamps, and rosy Santa Clauses salute with good cheer our wintry silence. My wife's stubborn profile makes her disappointment in me palpable. She does not understand that I am a man descending. I can't blame her because it took me years to realize that fact myself.

Revelation comes in so many guises. A couple of years ago I was paging through one of those gossipy newspapers that fill the news racks at supermarkets. They are designed to shock and titillate but, occasionally, they run a factual space filler. One of these was certainly designed to assure mothers that precocious children were no blessing, and since most women are the mothers of very ordinary children, it was a bit of comfort among gloomy predictions about San Francisco toppling into the sea or Martians making off with tots from parked baby carriages.

It seems that in eighteenth-century Germany there was an infant prodigy. At nine months he was constructing intelligible sentences; at a year and a half he was reading the Bible; at three he was teaching himself Greek and Latin. At four he was dead, likely crushed to death by expectations that he was destined to bear headier and more manifold fruits in the future.

This little news item terrified me. I admit it. It was not because this child's brief passage was in any way extraordinary. On the contrary, it was because it followed such a familiar pattern, a pattern I hadn't realized existed. Well, that's not entirely true. I had sensed the pattern, I knew it was there but I hadn't really *felt* it.

His life, like every other life, could be graphed: an ascent that rises to a peak, pauses at a particular node, and then descends. Only the gradient changes in any particular case; the child's steeper than most, his descent swifter. We all ripen. We are all bound by the same ineluctable law, the same mathematical certainty.

I was twenty-five then; I could put this out of my mind. I am thirty now, still young I admit, but I sense my feet are on the down slope. I know now that I have begun the inevitable descent, the leisurely glissade which will finally topple me at the bottom of my own graph. A man descending is propelled by inertia; the only initiative left him is whether or not he decides to enjoy the passing scene.

Now my wife is a hopeful woman. She looks forward to the future, but the same impulse that makes me lock our apartment door keeps me in fear of it. So we proceed in tandem, her shoulders tugging expectantly forward, my heels digging in, resisting. Victoria thinks I have ability, she expects me, like some arid desert plant that shows no promise, to suddenly blossom before her wondering eyes. She believes I can choose to be what she expects. I am intent only on maintaining my balance.

Helen and Everett's house is a blaze of light, their windows sturdy squares of brightness. I park the car. My wife evidently decides we shall make our entry as a couple, atoms resolutely linked. She takes

my arm. Our host and hostess greet us at the door. Helen and
Victoria kiss, and Everett, who distrusts me, clasps my hand
manfully and forgivingly in a holiday mood. We are led into the
living room. I'm surprised that it is already full. There are people
everywhere, sitting and drinking, even a few reclining on the carpet.
I know almost no one. The unfamiliar faces swim unsteadily for a
moment, and I begin to realize that I am quite drunk. Most of the
people are young, and, like my wife, public servants.

I spot Howard in a corner, propped against the wall. He sports a
thick, rich beard. Physically he is totally unlike me, tall and thin. For
this reason I cannot imagine Victoria in his arms. My powers of
invention are stretched to the breaking point by the attempt to
believe that she might be unfaithful to my body type. I think of
myself as bearish and cuddly. Sex with Howard, I surmise, would be
athletic and vigorous.

Someone, I don't know who, proffers a glass and I take it. This is a
mistake. It is Everett's party punch, a hot cider pungent with cloves.
However, I dutifully drink it. Victoria leaves my side and I am free to
hunt for some more acceptable libation. I find a bottle of scotch in the
kitchen and pour myself a stiff shot, which I sample. Appreciating its
honest taste (it is obviously liquor; I hate intoxicants that disguise
their purpose with palatability) I carry it back to the livingroom.

A very pretty, matronly young woman sidles up to me. She is one
of those kind people who move through parties like a wraith, intent
on making late arrivals comfortable. We talk desultorily about the
party, agreeing it is wonderful and expressing admiration for our
host and hostess. The young woman, who is called Ann, admits to
being a lawyer. I admit to being a naval architect. She asks me what I
am doing on the prairies if I am a naval architect. This is a difficult
question. I know nothing about naval architects and cannot even
guess what they might be doing on the prairies.

"Perspectives," I say darkly.

She looks at me curiously and then dips away, heading for an
errant husband. Several minutes later I am sure they are talking
about me so I duck back to the kitchen and pour myself another
scotch.

Helen finds me in her kitchen. She is hunting for olives.

"Ed," she asks, "have you seen a jar of olives?" She shows me
how big with her hands. Someone has turned on the stereo and I

sense a slight vibration in the floor, which means people are dancing in the livingroom.

"No," I reply. "I can't see anything. I'm loaded," I confess.

Helen looks at me doubtfully. Helen and Everett don't really approve of drinking, that's why they discourage consumption by serving hot cider at parties. She smiles weakly and gives up olives in favor of employment. "How's the job search?" she asks politely while she rummages in the fridge.

"Nothing yet."

"Everett and I have our ears cocked," she says. "If we hear of anything you'll be the first to know." Then she hurries out of the kitchen carrying a jar of gherkins.

"Hey, you silly bitch," I yell, "those aren't olives, those are *gherkins!*"

I wander unsteadily back to the livingroom. Someone has put a waltz on the stereo and my wife and Howard are revolving slowly and serenely in the limited available space. I notice that he has insinuated his thigh between my wife's. I take a good belt and appraise them. They make a handsome couple. I salute them with my glass but they do not see, and so my world-weary and cavalier gesture is lost on them.

A man and woman at my left shoulder are talking about Chile and Chilean refugees. It seems that she is in charge of some and is having problems with them. They're divided by old political enmities; they won't learn English; one of them insists on driving without a valid operator's license. Their voices, earnest and shrill, blend and separate, separate and blend. I watch my wife, skillfully led, glide and turn, turn and glide. Howard's face floats above her head, an impassive mask of content.

The wall clock above the sofa tells me it is only ten o'clock. One year is separated from the next by two hours. However, they pass quickly because I have the great good fortune to get involved in a political argument. I know nothing about politics, but then neither do any of the people I am arguing with. I've always found that a really lively argument depends on the ignorance of the combatants. The more ignorant the disputants, the more heated the debate. This one warms nicely. In no time several people have denounced me as a neo-fascist. Their lack of objectivity pleases me to no end. I stand beaming and swaying on my feet. Occasionally, I retreat to the kitchen to fill my glass and they follow, hurling statistics and analogies at my back.

It is only at twelve o'clock that I realize the extent of the animosity I have created by this performance. One woman genuinely hates me. She refuses a friendly New Year's buss. I plead that politics should not stand in the way of fraternity.

"You must have learned all this stupid, egotistical individualism from Ayn Rand," she blurts out.

"Who?"

"The writer. Ayn Rand."

"I thought you were referring to the corporation," I say.

She calls me an asshole and marches away. Even in my drunken stupor I perceive that her unfriendly judgment is shared by all people within hearing distance. I find myself talking loudly and violently, attempting to justify myself. Helen is wending her way across the livingroom toward me. She takes me by the elbow.

"Ed," she says, "you look a little the worse for wear. I have some coffee in the kitchen."

Obediently I allow myself to be led away. Helen pours me a cup of coffee and sits me down in the breakfast nook. I am genuinely contrite and embarrassed.

"Look, Helen," I say, "I apologize. I had too much to drink. I'd better go. Will you tell Victoria I'm ready to leave?"

"Victoria went out to get some ice," she says uneasily.

"How the hell can she get ice? She doesn't drive."

She went with Howard."

"Oh . . . okay. I'll wait."

Helen leaves me alone to ponder my sins. But I don't dwell on my sins; I dwell on Victoria's and Howard's. I feel my head, searching for the nascent bumps of cuckoldry. It is an unpleasant joke. Finally I get up, fortify myself with another drink, find my coat and boots, and go outside to wait for the young lovers. Snow is still falling in an unsettling blur. The New Year greets us with a storm.

I do not have long to wait. A car creeps cautiously up the street, its headlights gleaming. It stops at the far curb. I hear car doors slamming and then laughter. Howard and Victoria run lightly across the road. He seems to be chasing her, at least that is the impression I receive from her high-pitched squeals of delight. They start up the walk before they notice me. I stand, or imagine I stand, perfectly immobile and menacing.

"Hi, Howie," I say. "How's tricks?"

"Ed," Howard says pausing. He sends me a curt nod.

"We went for ice," Victoria explains. She holds up the bag for proof.

"Is that right, Howie?" I ask, turning my attention to the home-breaker. I am uncertain whether I am creating this scene merely to discomfit Howard, whom I don't like, or because I am jealous. Perhaps a bit of both.

"The name is Howard, Ed."

"The name is Edward, Howard."

Howard coughs and shuffles his feet. He is smiling faintly. "Well, Ed," he says, "what's the problem?"

"The problem, Howie, is my wife. The problem is cuckoldry. Likewise the incredible amount of hostility I feel toward you this minute. Now you're the psychologist, Howie, what's the answer to my hostility?"

Howard shrugs. The smile, which appears frozen on his face, is wrenched askew with anger.

"No answer? Well, here's my prescription. I'm sure I'd feel much better if I bopped your beanie, Bozo," I say. Then I begin to do something very stupid. In this kind of weather I'm taking off my coat.

"Stop this," Victoria says. "Ed, stop it right now!"

Under this threat of violence Howard puffs himself up. He seems to expand in the night; he becomes protective and paternal. Even his voice deepens; it plumbs the lower registers. "I'll take care of this, Victoria," he says gruffly.

"Quit acting like children," she storms. "Stop it!"

Poor Victoria. Two willful men, rutting stags in the stilly night.

Somehow my right arm seems to have got tangled in my coat sleeve. Being drunk, my attempt to extricate myself occupies all my attention. Suddenly the left side of my faces goes numb and I find myself flat on my back. Howie towers over me.

"You son of a bitch," I mumble, "*that* is not cricket." I try to kick him in the family jewels from where I lie. I am unsuccessful.

Howard is suddenly the perfect gentleman. He graciously allows me to get to my feet. Then he ungraciously knocks me down again. This time the force of his blow spins me around and I make a one-point landing on my nose. Howie is proving more than I bargained for. At this point I find myself wishing I had a pipe wrench in my pocket.

"Had enough?" Howie asks. The rooster crowing on the dung hill.

I hear Victoria. "Of course he's had enough. What's the matter with you? He's drunk. Do you want to kill him?"

"The thought had entered my mind."

"Just you let me get my arm loose, you son of a bitch," I say. "We'll see who kills who." I *have* had enough, but of course I can't admit it.

"Be my guest."

Somehow I tear off my coat. Howard is standing waiting, bouncing up on his toes, weaving his head. I feel slightly dizzy trying to focus on this frenetic motion. "Come on," Howard urges me. "Come on."

I lower my head and charge at his midriff. A punch on the back of the neck pops my tongue out of my mouth like a released spring. I pitch head first into the snow. A knee digs into my back, pinning me, and punches begin to rain down on the back of my head. The best I can hope for in a moment of lucidity is that Howard will break a hand on my skull.

My wife saves me. I hear her screaming and, resourceful girl that she is, she hauls Howie off my back by the hair. He curses her; she shouts; they argue. I lie on the snow and pant.

I hear the front door of Helen's and Everett's open, and I see my host silhouetted in the doorframe.

"Jesus Christ," he yells, "what's going on out here?"

I roll on my back in time to see Howard beating a retreat for his car. My tigress has put him on the run. He is definitely piqued. The car roars into life and swerves into the street. I get to my feet and yell insults at his taillights.

"Victoria, is that you?" Everett asks uncertainly.

She sobs a yes.

"Come on in. You're upset."

She shakes her head no.

"Do you want to talk to Helen?"

"No."

Everett goes back into the house nonplussed. It strikes me what a remarkable couple we are.

"Thank you," I say, trying to shake the snow off my sweater. "In five years of marriage you've never done anything nicer. I appreciate it."

"Shut up."

"Have you seen my coat?" I begin to stumble around searching for my traitorous garment.

"Here." She helps me into it. I check my pockets. "I suspect I've lost the car keys," I say.

"I'm not surprised." Victoria has calmed down and is drying her eyes on her coat sleeves. "A good thing too, you're too drunk to drive. We'll walk to Albert Street. They run buses late on New Year's Eve for drunks like you."

I fall into step with her. I'm shivering with cold but I know better than to complain. I light a cigarette and wince when the smoke sears a cut in the inside of my mouth. I gingerly test a loosened tooth with my tongue.

"You were very brave," I say. I am so touched by her act of loyalty I take her hand. She does not refuse it.

"It doesn't mean anything."

"It seems to me you made some kind of decision back there."

"A perfect stranger might have done the same."

I allow that this is true.

"I don't regret anything," Victoria says. "I don't regret what happened between Howard and me; I don't regret helping you."

"Tibetan women often have two husbands," I say.

"What is that supposed to mean?" she asks, stopping under a street light.

"I won't interfere anymore."

"I don't think you understand," she says, resuming walking. We enter a deserted street, silent and white. No cars have passed here in hours, the snow is untracked.

"It's New Years's Eve," I say hopefully, "a night for resolutions."

"You can't change, Ed." Her loss of faith in me shocks me.

I recover my balance. "I could," I maintain. "I feel ready now. I think I've learned something. Honestly."

"Ed," she says, shaking her head.

"I resolve," I say solemnly, "to find a job."

"Ed, no."

"I resolve to tell the truth."

Victoria actually reaches up and attempts to stifle my words with her mittened hands. I struggle. I realize that, unaccountably, I am crying. "I resolve to treat you differently," I manage to say. But as I say it, I know that I am not capable of any of this. I am a man descending and promises that I cannot keep should not be made to her—of all people.

"Ed," she says firmly, "I think that's enough. There's no point anymore."

She is right. We walk on silently. Injuries so old could likely not be healed. Not by me. The snow seems to fall faster and faster.

BRIAN DEDORA

That Signified

there was rose coloured wallpaper
in the corridor

he came in
just as i left

on the table in a glass vase
flowers stirred in the moving air

he had come
this time
to settle the matter

clouds
rather wisps
streaked the sky
blue

i thought you might come
she said
sliding the cup near the vase

the tea cup sliding across the table
caused the flowers to drop a fine dust
of pollen
that splashed yellow
on the table and cup

(the yellow splash
lost in the cup's rattle)

she came across the room
her arms outstretched

he came looking for rest

they met
and fell back into the room

the palm tree moved with the air

pieces of ash fell in the grate
leaving small grey clouds
caught for an instant in sunlight
to flash and settle

GEORGE WOODCOCK

Such Is My Beloved

Such is my beloved,
leaning towards me,
pallor marmoreal,
womb scraped clean of
another man's seed,
and risen
straight from that sickbed
of married commerce!
I look and think
how sharp
has become
your nose, how big
hands, feet,
how grey
lips, and
shuddering into
deeper love,
remembering
how scant my rights,
hence claims,
I am recaptured
by the intangible
domination
and forget
disgust, drown
jealousy
as those grey lips

close on to mine
and out of sepia
circles of pain
your eyes
in mine
seek anchorage.

Black Flag

When I die
let black rag fly,
raven falling
from the sky.

Let black flag lie
on bones and skin
that long last night
as I enter in.

For out of black
soul's night have stirred
dawn's cold gleam,
morning's singing bird.

Let bright day die,
let black flag fall,
let black rag fly,
let raven call,
let new day dawn
of black reborn.

SUSAN MUSGRAVE

Flying the Flag of Ourselves

because we have no country,
no place to return to other than
our own bodies

because we are alone
and have reached this place
together

because there is no one to
pray for us,
no one to worship.

It is the flag of innocence,
of joy and celebration.
When we look into each other's eyes
it is reflected there—
we see it is the flag of loneliness.

It is a beautiful flag,
it fills up the whole sky.

It is the flag we fly
because we are alive

the flag of our union
you, love, and I.

It Is the Night

I wake up blind.
I wake up with my heart beating.
I wake up looking for something familiar.
I wake up bleeding.

I wake up wishing I could
sleep forever.
I wake up beside a man who smiles and says
Good Morning.
I wake up deaf.
I wake up full of regret.
I wake up looking for someone to blame
for the fact that my life is
commonplace and solitary.

I wake up wanting to die.
I wake up waiting.

When it is time to dream
I wake up. It is the night,
the real night.

Break-Up

For David Arnason

All your life he has
lived in you, the
ice-fish. He has fed on
edges, on extremities.
All your life you have been an
ice-fisherman. Frozen and
hungry you are finally breaking.

You count the lonely minutes.
You count the hours.
Your heart beats against the breaking,
rages against the beating.

Your gentle hands are nets,
are knives. Your eyes remember a time
before the ice shifted.

Break a hole in the ice,
let the fish breathe.
Break a hole in your heart,
let the heart feed.

Wedding Song

She signs away the moon.
She signs away the wind and the stars.

She signs away cities,
she signs away men and women.

She builds a life out of the
ashes of children.
She signs away the fire.

The flowers go on opening.

She puts her signature to the
slippery black rocks,
to the winter earth,
to wild sage and peppermint.
She signs away darkness,
she signs away the sun.

The flowers go on opening.

By the ocean she sees
a graveyard filling up.
She puts her signature to the
unmarked graves,
to the ringing chapel,
the dead bell.

She signs away the earth,
she signs away water.

The flowers go on opening.

The beautiful flowers.

Sleeping Together

In my dream you have become
a fisherman. You are going fishing
in my sleep.
"Sharks come to light and blood,"
you whisper, as if you have always been
a fisherman. A shark surfaces beside me;
still I cannot stop dreaming.

In your dream I am a bird,
I am trapped inside your house.
I flap my wings, beat on the windows.
"My house has no roof," you say.
Still I cannot get out.

You touch me, very gently.
You want to make me happy.
You say so, over and over.
You want me to stop dreaming.

In your dream I am dead.
You have made sure of that.
Still I am stronger than you
and more confident.
My hand does not tremble as yours does
when you twist, again, the knife.

In my dream you have become an
undertaker. You are syphoning my blood
under a cold light.
"Sharks come to light and blood,"
you whisper, as if you have always been
an undertaker. Still I go on dreaming.

You touch me, very gently.
You want me to make you happy.
You want me to stop dreaming.
You say so, over and over.

A shark is swimming towards us;
still, we sleep.
"Stop dreaming," you whisper; he surfaces
beside me.
"Stop dreaming," you shiver; he nudges your
blind windows. The shark has become a bird,
like me. Trapped inside your house we are
flying, flying.

"My house has no roof," you cry,
but the shark, too, is dreaming.
Like me, he does not want to stop dreaming.
He does not want to stop dreaming.

I Did It to Attract Women

he said; there was no question
of an appeal. He had dressed them up
carefully and tried to conceal the blood.
After his initial disgust over their
badly decomposing bodies he took turns
telling them stories at night.

He had tried to make them eat but their
smell was sickening. They wouldn't co-operate,
they made him feel trapped. Their constant
quarrelling drove him to distraction. This was how
he came finally with their crushed heads to the
police station—calling God as his witness—
a good family man.

IRENA FRIEDMAN

Dimitri: An Unfinished Portrait

Dimitri is Greek. He lives in a village on the island of
Lesbos. He was meant—in his ancestors' dreams and in mine—to
be a fisherman or shepherd but he is a dentist. He is six years younger
than I but does not mind. I mind. I mind especially because we met at

a village wedding in which the bridegroom (Dimitri's ex-classmate) married a sixteen-year-old girl named Zoe. I am thirty two—twice her age. I have been halfway around the world and speak five languages. Zoe, whose name in Greek means *life*, will be a mother at seventeen. Right now, her face resembles Hogarth's Shrimp Girl. Mine, more often than not, is ironic as Mona Lisa's. Anyway, this is what Dimitri says, speaking of my smile. He knows nothing of art, however. He says it was my smile that first attracted him to me. He has never been anywhere out of Greece and my smile, he says, brought the world to him.

Dimitri's smile on the other hand is one of the few things in my life which are without ambiguity, though even that's not certain. For one thing, he has a wide gap between his two front teeth which, at least in the Middle Ages, would be a sure sign of a lecherous nature.

Dimitri is not lecherous. He is a splendid lover but lechery has nothing to do with it. He makes love like a man writing a poem, though the cards he and his friends use in the *taverna* have pornographic photos of winking blondes and redheads in black lace. He has told me—with absolute sincerity, I know—that sex in itself means nothing to him. Yet he has had many a one-night stand, with girls from Sweden or Australia, and speaks of them openly. It is not that he fails to see the contradiction—he is a thoughtful enough man—but that he is utterly unskilled in the art of rationalization. The contradictions remain. They complicate but never undermine the profundity of his sleep. Since we met last August, he has slept with no one else and does not quite believe when I tell him that he grinds his teeth like a madman. Sometimes I think it is sleeping beside me, the first foreigner he has ever lived with, that twists his mouth into a worm-like shape and makes the roots of his black hair glisten with perspiration.

We live, Dimitri and I, in a house which one of his aunts received as her dowry. It is a Balkan-style house, with a tile roof and orange shutters. Dimitri's family live in the village of Petra and his aunt's house had stood empty ever since her death ten years ago. Last year, when Dimitri began his practice, the house had no electricity and the floorboards had all been gnawed away by mice. It is still without indoor plumbing today and late at night we often hear the mice race across the roof and down through the hollow walls. Once a month or so, we spread out pellets of poison in every corner and thereby run the risk of getting our cat poisoned. Last month Dimitri tried using a cage trap for a change. after two days of waiting he did manage to trap a mouse, but then began to feed it through the metal bars.

We put up with the mice as we put up with slugs and ants. When all is said and done, this is an exquisite village, with narrow, cobblestoned streets and a medieval fortress overlooking the bay. Dimitri has always wished he could live here. "I am in love with the place," he says, as if speaking of a woman. He does not mind living away from his family. He is grateful that a congenital heart defect has kept him out of the army. Petra, where he was born, might have remained his home were it not for a twist of destiny which took him away when he was twelve. It is with some pride that he now tells me of the scholarship he had won to the American School in Salonika.

"There were seventy of us writing the tests," he says, "and only I got it."

"Seventy from Petra?"

"No, the island."

"And then?"

"Then I hated it. I hated singing the American anthem and hated my old friends laughing at my speech."

He stayed at the school for seven years before entering the university. He still hates America. Like most young Greeks with a university background, he thinks of himself as a Communist and is a little defensive about his vocational choice.

"I did not choose dentistry in order to be rich," he explains and, as often as not, lets the villagers get away without any payment. He is an excellent dentist, however, and says he loves his work.

"But how can anyone love this sort of thing?" I ask.

"I do," he insists. "I love the patience, the exactitude it requires. I never give up on a tooth unless it's thoroughly rotten."

This is true. He will spend hours over a gaping mouth rather than extract a tooth. His predecessor, Andreas Ducas, used to curse and pull them all out, he tells me. He is more than a little vain. He likes to be watched as he works and often I do watch and marvel at his probing, competent hands. Several times a day I go out into the courtyard to fill his earthen jug with water or empty the metal tray of recent saliva and blood. Dimitri is fair about household chores. He could not understand my wanting to take on this frankly odious task. Why did I choose to do it then? I don't know, but these days I carry out this ritual without so much as a grimace. My mother finds my life with a dentist characteristically ironic and cannot help but recall my lifelong abhorrence of dentists. "Do you remember," she writes, "how viciously you bit Dr. Salinger's thumb?"

Of course I remember. I was five and as yet had nothing against dentists or, for that matter, pain. It would not have occurred to me to doubt Dr. Salinger when he told me to open my mouth so he could have a look. "Just one little look," is what he said.

I opened my mouth. Sitting in a dentist's chair was a new experience and new experiences were rarer than they should have been at five. I opened my mouth. He pulled out a dangling milk tooth. Of course I bit his thumb. I bit it so hard the blood came oozing out from under the nail. After that—well, no one wearing white would ever be quite trustworthy again. No waiter or barber, and certainly no one bearing the title of Doctor.

And yet I trust Dimitri. I trust him with my love as well as my teeth. I have even learned to love the sharp dental smell which forever lingers on his skin and which I now associate with cleanliness and truth and a peculiar serenity which hovers over his waiting room. The room has no music and no magazines, but three or four patients are always to be found there, for they show up for treatment without appointment and think nothing of waiting for several hours. Sometimes one of them will arrive from a nearby village and wake us up at six or seven, then sit waiting outside until the two of us are ready. Some days it rains quite heavily and they must wait down in the *agora*. But they wait, patiently. Above all, they are patient.

November is an unpredictable month on the island. Some days are so warm the villagers refer to them as their "little summer." Others are a marvel of frenzied winds raging chaotically outside our windows. Getting Dimitri out of bed on such mornings is one of my unstated duties and I perform it with growing reluctance. On such days—and there are many of them ahead of us—we light the kerosene stove in the foyer and sit sipping our black Turkish coffee while the wind rattles the orange shutters and Sappho, our cat, whines for left-over fish heads.

The house warms up slowly. The kerosene burns fast. Twice a day we must refill the tank with oil, which we keep in a barrel outside our door. Twice a day Dimitri and I put on our coats and step out into the courtyard to pump oil into a plastic can. One of us holds down the can while the other pumps. Our hands get stiff and raw and we often get our clothes splashed with kerosene.

It is not an easy life. In the summer, the tourists flock to the village and saddle a mule, and eat fresh squid, and are charmed. They are happy to shower with a garden hose and happy to sleep out on the beach. They take snapshots of the little harbor, the alleys laced with wisteria. They do not wonder about winter; why should they? I did not wonder. I did not stop to imagine myself heating water for a weekly bath, or stumbling to the outhouse, or keeping food out of the reach of mice. I had not planned any of this, and I am a careful planner.

But what am I doing here, my friends want to know. What am I doing with a decaying house and trays overflowing with saliva and blood?

Well, I write back, I cook and write stories and read and make love. They are all things I like to do; it's not as bad as it sounds.

Yes, they say, but, but.

They don't understand and, I confess, neither do I. When they first heard I had fallen in love with a Greek, they all imagined some impetuous Zorba storming into my life to the sound of Santuri and crashing glass. Greeks were either fishermen or poets or both, weren't they? Well, Dimitri is neither. He is a man who walks like an adolescent, and laughs like one. but whose face is thoughtful and accomplished. He has an elegant way of smoking a cigarette. He is too reasonable to be a poet.

"But a dentist!" my friends write and I hear them laughing as they read my letter. They are thinking—they know me well—of what we had jokingly referred to as my Shopping List. I had not, let it be said, spent years looking for the right man empty-handed. Not me.

But my shopping list?

Well, all said and done, it was shamefully predictable and, for the most part, not even especially hard to fill. It was only the scribbling on the bottom—hasty, barely legible afterthoughts—that left me empty-handed every time.

But falling in love with Dimitri? I will tell you more about Dimitri. I will tell you the worst, for the best after all has left no raised eyebrows. Three things:

He does not read. The only book he ever mentioned was *The Old Man and the Sea*, which he remembers reading at the American School.

He likes Campbell soups and raspberry Jello.

He does not talk. He uses words — the tapestry my life is made of—to describe a fight between two village grocers or a woman caught by her husband sleeping with a soldier. He seems verbal only when amused or outraged.

He is seldom outraged, however. He is not really an old-fashioned man—not as old-fashioned as other Greeks at least. He asks no questions about my past and would not give a hoot if a hundred men had preceded him in my life. Yet he is brutally dogmatic about sexual fidelity and rages like a bull whenever I talk of a friend's open marriage or some people's need for sexual diversity.

"If you ever sleep with another man," he warns, "I will throw you out!"

He means it. He insists he is not jealous, however.

"What is it then?" I ask.

"I don't know. Not jealousy."

It does not really matter, I suppose. This is not anything like a problem just now, though we are certainly not without problems. We fight about homosexuals I befriend and some of the men Dimitri plays cards with. We fight about cards. About evenings spent playing cards, drinking ouzo, calling to the wives for ashtrays, for matches, for more olives, more ouzo.

I rebel. I will not wait hand and foot on your friends like Zoe or sit in the corner knitting like Sofia, I say.

"You don't have to," he answers. He is, as I said, a reasonable man. "Bring a book with you, a magazine, whatever."

"But why?" I demand. "Why can't I just stay home and do my thing?"

"Because." He hesitates. "I don't enjoy myself when you're not there."

I am disarmed. I forget to point out that card games are an inane activity for an intelligent man. I swell with the warmth of my discovery.

"I love you," I say.

"*Poh!*" he says, hugging me. "Love takes time."

We make love. We fall asleep in each other's arms. I am a poor sleeper and wake up often throughout the night. Whenever my breast rests against his arm or our legs entwine, I feel him swelling grandly, involuntarily, against my warm thigh. If I were to be honest, if I owed anyone an explanation, I would say it was my wonder keeping me here. Yes, as much as anything, my wonder.

So, each morning we open the shutters, light up the stove, eat bread and feta for our breakfast. The sea stretches beyond our windows. It is not the indigo sea of summer postcards but the amorphous, the utterly terrifying gray of Aegean winters. The days are getting colder, the house damper. Now and then, the roof leaks over our bedroom.

"When spring comes," says Dimitri, "we'll renovate it. It will be a good house then, you'll see."

Until then, he saves his money, depositing it in the mobile bank which arrives in the village every other week. Whatever it is other villagers use the bank for, it is not to save up for a new house, that's clear. A house is something you begin to build as soon as the money is there for a foundation. Six months, a year later, the first floor will be built, maybe a second. The doors will be installed, the shutters painted. Step by step. All over the village, houses in varying stages of construction stand awaiting completion. One or two have not progressed in over three years, I am told. The Greeks are not careful craftsmen. Sometimes the doors are too big for the frames, sometimes the floors slope. "Sigá, sigá" they say, and try again, undeterred by imperfections. One has much to learn from their tenacity, their faith.

And yet, what *am* I doing here? What am I doing with a man who chews mints and combs his mustache and rubs his genitals in public? A man who tells me that life is simple—that is only we, the foreigners, who like to complicate it. What, for that matter, is Dimitri doing with me, making plans with me, when a dozen dowried maidens sit home filling their hope chests with linen and lace? This is one question, I know, many a villager must be asking. In the waiting room, shy as schoolgirls, the women size me up but ask no questions. They are a shamelessly curious people, the Greeks, but they ask me nothing at all. I am the dentist's "fiancée" and I come from America. That's all they have a right to know—because Dimitri has a diploma from Salonika and is able to stop their toothaches. So they giggle, they tell Dimitri their problems, they spit blood. Once, I overheard a girl say she was not sure she wanted to have her tooth out after all. She was not afraid though, she insisted.

"Why then?" asked Dimitri. "You must have a terrible toothache by now."

"Well." The girl blushed, looking for the words. "It hurts, yes, but it's not a bad pain—I mean, I don't like it, yet I keep searching the tooth out with my tongue."

Did Dimitri understand her reluctance? I like to think so. *I* understood. I remembered my own dangling tooth at five or so. It may well be, I thought, that I bit Dr. Salinger as much for extracting the tooth as for breaking his promise. It is possible. I understand less and less about myself these days. I understand neither the woman nor the child I once was and see myself transformed into every now and then. I watch myself. I recognize the pig-tailed schoolgirl with that impossibly earnest face (it used be be earnest, it is ironic now). I see her raising her hand in the classroom, asking questions at bedtime—impatient, over-eager. So much desire, so little patience. Perfection to be found only in words, where else?

So I said to Dimitri one night: "Never trust a writer, they are all jerks, I tell you."

Hemingway had said that to his wife and I thought it was worth repeating, even after an hour of love. I wanted Dimitri to trust me as much as I trust him. I wanted to be worthy of that trust. Could he understand that?

"There you go again!" he said. He has learned to recognize my way of stirring up trouble. "What's eating you now?"

"I don't know."

"Why shouldn't I trust you?"

Sulking: "I don't know."

"You always complicate things," he said. His toes under the eiderdown were scratching at the sheet. "What is it you're after?" he asked after a while. It was the first time he had come out and said it.

"What am I after?"

"Yes."

"Well." I thought about this for a while. I don't know, I wanted to say, and what's more, I have not yet learned to live without knowing. This is what I should have said, but I didn't. "I want a daughter I can name Zoe," is what I said instead.

"What!"

"Yes." I smiled in the dark. It was such a splendid lie. At the very least, it justified my quoting Hemingway. It also got Dimitri to start stroking my back all over again. *Was* it a lie, however?

"Dimitri?"

"Hm."

"I want to tell you something."

"Tomorrow."

"No, it's important."

"Tomorrow. Go to sleep," he said, and I did—we both did—our bodies like two warm loaves of bread joined together through some graceful error.

GAIL FOX

The Coming

When you come, everything
changes, outlines become
flesh and glasses fill

I give up systems and
theories, religions, decorations
and indifference

And yield to open windows,
quarrels and reconciliations,
jokes of perfection

Dreams, innumerable fantasies,
the drunk, the need of the
beggar woman

The neighbor's petulence, the
welcome illness when we
do not work

But lie exposed to each
other's psyches and talk
rawly and with exclusion

While the world acts and
passes on, oblivious to its
civilizations

When you come, my credentials
evaporate, and you find me,
my true nature

Without name, country,
or significance, a pebble
to be thrown

Against the cliff where
the oceans smash the
world into a moment

So serious that outlines
become flesh and glasses
fill with wine

Raised over the broken steps
and protests of our
injustices, our

Histories, and those children,
caught in growth and
conquest of our hearts

When you come, something
dies which is not life,
but rage against our deaths

RONALD BATES

Un homme de quarante ans

But after forty it's all the same.
If you can get it up once a week,
you should be grateful.
SAUL BELLOW

having started out
with a puritanic doubt
concerning the place the flesh should hold,
the pleasure I find between your thighs
never ceases to surprise
now that I'm growing old.

KEITH GAREBIAN

Adam Meeting Eve
(parody of bpNichol)

```
mad        am
       i
mad        am
    madam
i'm        adam
```

sleeping with th grass
(parody of bill bissett)

i havnt made pomes fr years
what th hell my bodee is going
thru weird sensayshuns nd i
think i need a
downr or two to
pull me thru
th suns floor th
wind
i get grants
decisyun confirmed every year
my dumb tempr mints all th lettr writing nd
phone calls nd frends a lot fr shur
help nd more letters cum thru

6,000 dollars for th arts th grant
nd start to pay off luvrs nd dew sum
balling nd get redy to keep on trucking
with grass nd blew soap.
ium so relaxed sleeping with th grass
its easy to protect
th luck
ium still lucky
i havnt made pomes fr years.

ths lust ium in luv with

(parody of bill bissett)

whats lust
ium in luv with each whun
uv yr false parts with
yr rubbr nipplz yr powdr
milk yr face lift yr
ey lashes yr false nails
on th pillows
            i know yu
dont know it but yu probly
dont need ths lust or dew
yu

JOHN HIRSCH

Reminiscences

I have always loved the theatre. Everything I remember about my early childhood, and my schooldays in Hungary, pointed to what I am doing now. In fact I was interested in and loved all forms of art. At school I acted in plays; I painted, wrote, had my own puppet theatre, put on plays in our yard; studied piano; and every summer took dancing lessons from "Auntie Dancey," whose real name was Adorjáné-Mérö Frieda.

At the age of three I danced for Nijinsky, in Siofok, where my family lived. One day in July a friend of my mother's brought the peacefully insane man, with his wife Romola, to our house. In our salon sat the great, fat, bald, immobile Nijinsky, wearing a long, heavy overcoat despite the heat. With my mother's friend, Mrs. Mozart, at the piano, I danced, impromptu, in the middle of the room to the tune of "Who's Afraid of the Big Bad Wolf?" It was 1933.

This is my earliest memory of performing. From then on I can't recall that there was a time in my life when I wasn't involved with the theatre.

One of the most important events in my early life was my choice of a second country. Some immigrants feel the same way toward their adopted country as parents about their adopted children. They can say "I love you more because I chose you." This makes for an element of passion and determination in the relationship that is seldom present between ordinary parents and their children. (There are other immigrants who never learn to identify with their new

Based on notes for the Plaunt Lectures, given at Carleton University in 1975.

country. Their real home is forever "back there." They live in exile waiting for the day when they can go back and drive in a huge Cadillac through the streets of their birthplace. There'll be applause, admiration, and shouts of "Bravo! Look how well he's done!")

I did not choose to leave Hungary; I was an involuntary exile. When the Second World War ended I was sixteen years old and without a home. My mother and my young brother were killed at Auschwitz; my father was shot in Germany just before the war ended; my grandfather, with whom I managed to survive in the Budapest ghetto, died of starvation in 1945. There was nothing for me in Hungary but painful memories I wanted to forget.

For a while I wandered in Europe, from a camp for refugee orphans in Bavaria to Paris. I discovered I was too young to emigrate to Brazil; Argentina was interested only in lumberjacks; Mexico needed dental technicians; the United States rejected me because I was underweight. Then the Canadian Jewish Congress decided to take me. The Canadian Embassy in Paris took my blood three times within a week and judged it good.

So at the age of sixteen I came to Canada feeling like a growing plant plucked from its soil, roots in mid-air, desperately searching for a handful of earth—a home.

That home turned out to be Winnipeg. Out of my deep and urgent need for roots I became a "Winnipegger," a "North Ender," before I knew where I was, before I learned English, before I had any idea of the size of this huge country. I wanted to be part of something in a hurry.

Looking back on it, for me, a protected child of a well-to-do Central European bourgeois family, brought up with all the good and proper things in life—sent to school in Budapest at the age of eleven to be educated to enjoy the theatre, opera, galleries, and good restaurants—Winnipeg was a hard place to get used to, let alone love. But I was determined to do so.

I arrived in the fall, knowing nothing of the place, except the name—remembered from a childhood book *The Wolves of Winnipeg*, the story of a trapper who nearly starved to death when a pack of wolves surrounded his hut and would have eaten him but for the arrival of the Royal Canadian Mounted Police. That year the weather turned to 30 below in no time at all. The streets were suddenly full of women holding brooms but they weren't using them to clear away the knee-deep snow. It was only when I saw Mr. Shack leaving the house with *his* broom one morning that I learned about curling!

I had found a family—the Shacks—who lived at 148 Polson Avenue in the North End. Mr. Shack was a self-taught, intelligent man, born in Odessa, who was a supervisor with the Hydro's Steam Heating System. He spent most of his working days underground—a good place to be in Winnipeg. His daughter, Sybil, a born and bred prairie schoolteacher, was an active member of the CCF and a passionate patriot. Mrs. Shack, my new-found mother, turned out to be Tolstoy without the beard. She was an exceptional human being: an agnostic who kept a kosher house; a vegetarian who served great stuffed chicken; a socialist who, as soon as the New Democrats got into power, turned against them "because, no one, but no one in power can be trusted!" During the Depression her home was known by the men who rode the rails as a place they could always get a meal. Throughout the Second World War she held "open house" for "the boys" from overseas who trained as pilots in and around Winnipeg. All of them called her Ma, as I learned to. Her house to this day—she is now eighty-six—is full of plants, birds, good food, guppies in aquariums—and there is always a dog. Her sense of life, her contradictions within a perfectly balanced outlook, but above all her all-embracing love and kindness, gave me a new world and helped me immeasurably to grow in it.

The Canadian Jewish Congress, through an altruistic wholesaler on McDermot Avenue, outfitted me in a suit, and a winter coat that was not much thicker than a potato sack, and I went to work as an office boy every morning starting at seven o'clock at Aronowitch & Leipsic (an insurance and real estate firm). I changed the calendar, filled the water cooler with the block of ice left at the door, dusted the desk tops, went to the post office to pick up the mail, said "good morning"—practically my only English phrase—to all the bundled stenographers who arrived around eight. (I spoke no English when I arrived, but learned quickly at the office and night school at St. John's Tech.) Then I started my rounds through the bone-chilling streets, delivering letters to other insurance companies and banks.

Some people at the time told me that Winnipeg was "in the middle of nowhere." My new sister, Sybil, said it was the middle of the

"Bread Basket of the World." Ed Russenholt, who later on became our first TV weatherman, called it "The Heart of the Continent." But according to most university students (with their eyes on an outside world), Winnipeg was "the Asshole of the Continent!"

In retrospect, the city then was a remarkably lively place. In 1947 the university was full of war veterans. Everyone went to the famous Child's Restaurant—more like a European coffee house than a restaurant—at the corner of Portage and Main. Cavernous, with rows of square pillars, large mirrors, black and white tile floors, it looked like the warm waiting room of a railroad station. In winter the front windows were always frosted over; there was a city-block-long marble counter, and the North End waitresses, in black uniforms with white aprons and caps, scurried around with plates of thick pancakes, cinnamon toast, and innumerable, heavy china cups of coffee. It was *the* place in town—open until well after midnight. And it was where the local "intelligentsia" gathered.

To me Child's was very nineteenth-century Russia. Around the tables I found people like Adele Wiseman; she claimed to be working on a huge novel which, with the exception of her teacher and mentor, Peg Stobie, none of us had ever seen. But everyone talked about it. Years later that novel, *The Sacrifice*, won the Governor-General's Award, and it was only then I really believed it existed. There was Boris Margolese who was working on his Ph.D. thesis in history—I think it had to do with Napoleon's retreat from Moscow. I was told that he had been working on it for decades. And then there was James Reaney, a recent arrival from Stratford, Ontario, who'd come to Winnipeg to be an English lecturer at the University of Manitoba. He wore an ill-fitting blue serge suit (made to measure for him by a blind tailor in Stratford), a raincoat over it, and under his arm he carried a large alarm clock. He hated teaching so much that he wouldn't trust the university's bell system. So every time he walked into a lecture hall, he set his own alarm clock at exactly forty-five minutes and when *his* bell rang, he rushed out of the classroom.

It was at Child's that you could see Jamie writing his poems in a school exercise book in the middle of the night. It was there that you would find Ted Korol, the brilliant set designer of the Winnipeg Little Theatre, with Peg Green and her crew of thespians after an evening rehearsal. It was there I got to know Jack Woodbury and

Roman Kroiter . . . a lot of exciting people. The talk was of T. S. Eliot, of the Old Vic, of Virginia Woolf and her Bloomsbury Group, people who were aware of their own importance and who sensed, even at the beginning of their careers, that they would be part of history and that their lives around the tables in Bloomsbury were worth recording. I became quickly aware that for most of the people around the tables at Child's, "history" happened elsewhere. "Important" events occurred usually in England and not in Winnipeg, and certainly not in Canada.

At Child's Restaurant, in those days, most people were planning to go to London. I couldn't understand why no one wanted to stay put. They kept saying how dull, boring, and deadly Winnipeg was, and that everything worthwhile was elsewhere. They saved their pennies to leave, and there *I* was . . . newly arrived! I *had* to stay. This was the place that had chosen me and I, in turn, chose it. Here I'd found the Shacks, who took me in, and a lot of helpful, loving people. Here there was space; here there was room; here different nationalities lived together reasonably and in peace—a tremendous change for a Hungarian war orphan. In Winnipeg, Jews and Ukrainians were neighbours and didn't kill each other.

I had always wanted to be in the theatre; I had wanted to direct plays, tell stories. Now I lived in a city where there was no real professional theatre activity. When I spoke to people of my ambition, they laughed at me because clearly no such job existed; it was like wanting to be a theatre director on Mars. There was the amateur Little Theatre, which put on plays four times a year, for two nights, at the Playhouse Theatre; the plays were attended by the same faithful seven hundred souls. Most of the plays were by British authors—Shaw, Priestly, and Coward. Then there were the play readings by the Winnipeg Poetry Society in the basement of the Business and Professional Women's Club. The actors were English professors and graduate students. An audience of mostly ladies with feathered hats, furpieces, and gloves listened reverently to *Murder in the Cathedral* or *The White Devil*, after which tea was served with finger sandwiches and cookies dyed in pastel colours.

The theatrical climax of the year was the Dominion Drama Festival when the Little Theatres of Brandon, Dauphin, Flin Flon, and Winnipeg entered their productions of Shaw, Priestley, and

Coward to compete for awards for Best Play, Best Actor, Best Director, and so forth. These were grand occasions. The audience appeared in evening gowns and tuxedos and the lobby of the Playhouse almost resembled a garden party at Buckingham Palace. The adjudicators came from London, England, wore evening suits, and spoke like Gielgud or Olivier. The audience smiled at their wit, their theatrical in-jokes, and got gloriously drunk at the cast parties.

I realized that if I was going to stay and make a living by working in the theatre, I would have to start one myself. But I knew it would be an uphill battle. I was living in a society where artists were not accepted as useful, mainly because they did what they truly wanted to do, and enjoyed it. Work was considered punishment, and only suffering was rewarded with money. *I* wanted to earn a living at something that was fun. I was looked upon as a very strange and exotic bird, but a bird, I suspected, secretly admired by some.

I set out to discover if I was capable of achieving my lifelong dream, of doing what I had always wanted to do. First I had to find people who were interested in charity, good works, and education. I found them at the Junior League. "You are interested in children," I said. "you are concerned with this community and its cultural life. What about giving us three hundred dollars and we'll start a puppet theatre?" Kathleen Richardson, Marge Johnson, Beth Gourley and a few other women—bless their cashmere sweaters and pearls— thought it over and told me to go ahead. They took a chance on Tom Hendry, Mark Negin, Mac Price, and me. We formed the Muddywater Puppet Theatre and, driven by the "girls" through mud, rain, hail, and snow, we played every school, every community club, in the city. The children loved the shows, we had a marvellous time that first winter of nineteen forty-seven, *and* we got paid!

The next year the Junior League made it possible for us to start a Children's Theatre. People who during the day worked at the Buffalo Hat and Cap Factory, Arthur Murray's Dance Studio, and Chan's Chinese Restaurant could now spend at least a couple of hours every night doing what they really wanted to do. And so the Touring Children's Theatre was born. It was an exciting time for me because I realized exactly what pioneering was all about. I understood the incredible effort it took for people to settle in places like Winnipeg and make a home. Even for a rather anaemic Jewish orphan from Hungary, it was possible to start a new life and to build a future.

Next Jim Duncan and I fought the battle of the Rainbow Stage. The city had built a bandshell in Assiniboine Park with the intention of having Ukranian dancing, Hungarian pancake baking, and all kinds of ethnic activities all summer long. However, after a while they ran out of performers. The city tried everything, but the venture died. A couple of us went to City Hall and said, "What we need is an open-air musical comedy theatre. We need two thousand dollars to start it — money toward the employment of actors and musicians; to pay for costumes and scenery, etc." Douglas Chisholm, one of the aldermen, told us, "When you can prove that you can get as many people to a musical comedy in Assiniboine Park as I can get to a Yo-Yo contest, I will give you two thousand dollars." We didn't get the money, but somehow we managed to get a season going. By the end of the summer we had proved to Mr. Chisholm that we could get more people out to Rainbow Stage than the baseball club could get to their games. We revelled in our first big victory.

It was a wonderful feeling on a summer evening to be in that open-air theatre watching *Chu Chin Chow, The Wizard of Oz,* and finally one of our own musicals, *Do You Remember,* a show about Winnipeg. It was great to see three thousand people, some with their babies, going to the washroom every five minutes, running to get popcorn, sitting on their pillows, putting newspapers over their heads when the rain began ... It was a reward beyond anything monetary any one of us could have received. People came from all over the city. The waitresses from Child's were there, my sister and her schoolteacher friends, the "girls" from the Junior League, university professors — even Alderman Chisholm.

But for me that was still not quite enough. Next we started a guerrilla action within the Little Theatre. Through patient work, we converted it into what we wanted — a professional theatre. This happened despite the housewives who used to act once a year and who saw themselves as Sarah Bernhardts; it happened despite some of the professors of English at the university. We came along and said that we need a *professional* theatre; we have to work at theatre all day, full time. And we did. Tom Hendry and I, and a couple of other brave souls, got ourselves a burned-out golf school and started to work for the Little Theatre on a full-time, professional basis.

We used the people who were in Winnipeg—young people and old people who started to become professionals. Gordon Pinsent came from an Arthur Murray Dancing School because he'd decided he wanted to act and write. We used a lot of older people such as Jean Murray, "Spook" Sinclair, Ramona McBean, all of whom worked for CBC Radio Drama. Out of that nucleus we cast our season. Within a year the Little Theatre had turned into Theatre '77.

We worked at convincing the city that we were trying to create something that was their own. In rain, in snow, on icy roads, through mud and snowstorms, we delivered posters in a small Morris Minor, sold tickets, and created a Rube Goldberg of a theatre that eventually grew into the Manitoba Theatre Centre, the first of the regional theatre centres in Canada, and the first on the continent. In time people came up from New York and elsewhere to take a look at us. Even the Ford Foundation came. They examined this "thing" we had made and said it was "a model," something that "ought to be emulated."

We had a theatre that produced plays six times a year, for two-week runs; we had a studio theatre where small plays and original works were being performed; we had a children's theatre producing four plays a year, all original works by Tom Hendry, James Reaney, and myself. We had a touring company that went into high schools and elementary schools with programs related to the curriculum. We went around the province twice a year in a bus and did one-act plays. It was an ambitious program, considering our small human and financial resources.

During this period Tom Hendry and I spent an enormous amount of time talking to any group that was willing to listen to us. From United Church basements, where we talked to ten ladies, to Hadassah bazaars, where we talked to four hundred; from Rotaries to Kiwanis and Elks—we were everywhere. We talked and talked, telling them that they would like what we were going to give them, that they would acquire a taste for it, that it was educational and "good for the children," that it was HOME GROWN—it was OURS, and that one of those days they would be as proud of their theatre as they were of the Blue Bombers.

Slowly we were accepted. The Canada Council came along, represented by Peter Dwyer, an exceptionally cultivated, enthusiastic man who put his faith in people and not in institutions. To a great extent it was due to him that the Manitoba Theatre Centre was born.

In my wildest dreams in 1947 I would never have imagined that barely ten or fifteen years later Winnipeg, a "city in the middle of nowhere," would build a theatre for their own indigenous company. At that time it was the only regional company in Canada that had a theatre built just for it. This was before Centennial madness struck and buildings were erected in the hope that somehow companies would be found to inhabit them. In Winnipeg, in the 1950s, it happened the right way.

Having formed the Manitoba Theatre Company, the musical comedy theatre, and the children's theatre, I realized I had to leave. I had to grow. One of the dangers an artist is exposed to in Canada is that it's too easy. Now it must seem strange to you to read this, based on what I've already said, but it's true. One can become a very big boy in a very short time, if one has the necessary energy, imagination, and a fair amount of talent. There still remains a lot to be done here. But it can be damaging for a young man. For instance, I received the Order of Canada at the age of thirty-five, for which I was very grateful—but I felt slightly ridiculous.

My next move was to Stratford, to the Festival Theatre, where I became Associate Artistic Director. I did some interesting things there—I tried to Canadianize the place. I brought in young actors from the National Theatre School and the Manitoba Theatre Company. I tried to do Shakespeare with a Canadian sensibility, or at least a Winnipeg sensibility; I believed a Canadian production of a play by Shakespeare could be just as Canadian as a production of a modern play written by a Canadian. When I say "Canadian," I'm not speaking out of narrow nationalism; I'm talking about a sense of self-awareness—a joy of being oneself, a celebration of one's uniqueness in a homogenized world. It is only through being at times even arrogantly oneself that we can contribute to the world.

I produced one of the first successful Canadian plays at Stratford—James Reaney's *Colours in the Dark*; but I had to fight to get the play done. No one wanted to do it. They said it was too parochial, too local, too provincial. To me it was a beautiful piece *because* it was local and provincial, and written by a man who was writing his *own* mythology. The theatre was filled largely with people from Stratford and the little hamlets and villages around. They laughed and had the time of their lives. One Stratford designer complained, however, that they "were not the sort of people we wanted in the theatre."

I never felt at home in Stratford, partly because it was not like Winnipeg. For me, Canada still means Winnipeg. I felt like a stranger in Stratford. Tyrone Guthrie's genius consisted of planting a magnificent seed, leaving it, and hoping that it would grow into something unique. He wanted the theatre to become a Canadian theatre. It's a pity that in twenty-five years Stratford still has not quite become what the gardener intended.

Not long ago I spent a year travelling in Asia. On my way back from Tokyo, I disembarked at Vancouver at four in the morning and found myself in tears because I saw the space *we* have compared to that of Tokyo—it was incredible. That any group of people could be as fortunate as us—to have this air, this space . . . it was miraculous, and I kissed the Canadian soil in gratitude. From the airport I went to English Bay, left my bags at the Sylvia Hotel and walked the six miles around Stanley Park at seven in the morning, and I met only one person . . . one person! After Bombay, Calcutta, and Tokyo, to meet only one person in the heart of a city, even at seven in the morning, was a mystical experience and one which I will never forget. To this day, I do not understand why we cannot say more openly, more often, how much we love this place—how privileged we are to live here.

T.D. MacLULICH

Prologue: Columbus

out of a vaster silence
than our own
into a greater ignorance
he sailed west with only an idea
for wind, only his ambition driving him
to stem the mutinous tides
of an ocean reluctant to be known

the westward sea he mastered
like a foregone conclusion, storms he blunted
riding his faith over the ruinous waves
danger he prevented with his eyes
with a wag of his beard
dismissed
the rebellious tempers of men

his speeches charmed land
out of the hissing, desperate waters

four times he ventured blind
across that jealous gulf
returning once to astonished applause
while his name sang in his head
like a garland sweeter than power or gold
once with his name tuned to a lesser music
yet insistent, persuasive, hypnotic
& once in resentful chains, his name eclipsed
by the angry shame of a prisoner's weeds

the fourth time he crept back in tatters
with his name unpronounced, a burden of silence
unspoken, unheard in the Emperor's court

& you will say this is a sad end
for a hero, to expire disappointed
of his glory, exiled from the strangeness
he had discovered or made, not even allowed
his martyrdom, but rejected & released
a pathetic spectacle, an old man
numbering his illusions

yet who can say he did not expire
fulfilled, as men count their lives?

this was his fate—to die
with the Indies still a rich aroma
in his prospects, all the routes
finally charted and completion imminent
only a further easy voyage away

his purpose baffled, interrupted
but not annulled, to the last day
he never knew he had found
a place completely other, alien
his mind fading still caressed
the round world, which he knew
was pear-shaped, like a woman's breast
formed for love, at its apex paradise

knowing nothing of how history
would pronounce his name differently
knowing nothing of this new age
he had so devoutly blundered into being

Two Canadian Poets

i   E.J. Pratt

this smallest word
this *man*
this prof turned truant
escapes child-like
slides with a whoop
down the bumpy stairs
of evolution's ribs
he has gone on holiday
to peer into the guts of whales
& measure the appetite of dinosaurs
he has invented instruments to take
the pulse of lizard rocks
& discuss the taste of grass
on an ungulate's palate

but all this noise & scrutiny
is mere preliminary
invisibly impossibly
suddenly the final trick is done
whales oceans forests
plains & mountains all vanish
swallowed by voracious waves
of simile & metaphor
inside the professorial dome
appears an inverted globe
a macrocosmic landscape where
all the creatures space & time
& imagination can contain
creep fly jump run or swim
in singular conjunction
until the stars occlude an era

now he presides
only at celestial feasts

measuring angels with ethereal calipers
while his amphibious speech
fascinates the immortals
discoursing whales

ii   Irving Layton

a shambling bear
the shaggiest predator of all
his hairy growls
disturb even the wolves
alone he patrols his randy
territory marking the bushes
with his marvellous scent
& scratching his primate's back
on the brutal bark of trees

when he lopes ungainly
up the undressed beach
sunbathing ladies
mistake him for a satyr
& screech in salute
he includes them all
in an obscene greeting
distributes himself among them
like a salesman's free samples
he seduces with insults
& tales of other conquests
makes love like a tank
assaulting a stronghold
until they turn away
exhibiting a conspicuous boredom
he mistakes for subtle praise
of his own exquisite skills

when jealous night
pulls down the curtain
on this unruly king

he observes with philosophic eye
the ravenous gnats
come to dine on his flesh
his gaze intent as a boy's
pulling the wings off flies
he guesses the minutes
before they penetrate the bone
& muses on the putrid ballet
each good or evil life endures
leaving the chaste & silent bones
for its only epitaph

AL PURDY

Writer-in-Rez

I am watching from my window
          students on campus
          some with beards
          books broads etc
I count the ones without beards
               girls that is
hoping no males will knock on my door
               —at this moment
a blonde in tight green slacks
strolls among the pigeons
and I am about to call

out that I have some crumbs
for the pigeons
                        ask her
if she has crumbs for me
                        KNOCK KNOCK
All right come in I say resignedly
a little guy does and shakes my hand hard
(why do little guys always do that?)
He wants a list of 46 books from me
for students to read over Christmas
Migawd
        a Methodist minister
and the univ. prez will also
compile lists
                        I can't believe it
All right then I will compile you
a list of 46 salacious books
he doesn't know what salacious is
says okay and departs hence
                        By this time
the blonde is lamentably gone
replaced by a student with pimples
                        KNOCK KNOCK
Okay okay—and it's this Jewish kid
he says he doesn't know
whether to be a great writer
or work on a kibbutz in Israel
Why not do both?
It's the morality of it
                                    Huh?
If I'm a writer I'll be like evil Huysmanns
if I work in a kibbutz
I'll probably end as a saint
You got a problem I tell him
He fixes me with saintly eyes
and I tell him get the hell out
after we yak enjoyably an hour
By now the campus is quiet
blonde and pimples both gone

it's colder in here

KNOCK KNOCK

It's this children's poet with dimples
her name is Molly

I say Hello Molly

forbear telling her I hate smartass kids
Seems somebody sent back her poems
they need work they said
of course she wants me to do the work
Awright awright

let me read em

Of course they're shit
and now a problem
of morality does present itself
shall I say they're shit and advise
six months labour on a kibbutz
I give her my list finally
of 46 salacious books
extract the meat from Fanny Hill I say
the fat from 120 Days of Sodom
and send pemmican to publisher
and kick her ass out

The blonde is back
with pigeon crumbs
I am thrilled

lean out the window flapping my arms
like a pigeon mentioning
I am in need of provender
but do not convince
nor is she distracted or even attentive

KNOCK KNOCK

I sigh wearily

this goes on all day
Surprise

it's the blonde in green slacks
who is a pigeon fancier
her breast is heaving nicely
she wants an apology
I say Cluck Cluck

(pigeons don't talk)
I look outside my window
debating a course of action
for a man of action
the moment is not propitious
for pigeons
                    which is a pity
and her breast heaves nicely

FRED COGSWELL

A Respect: For a Poet

when he is dead at last
do not remember what he did
and say, In this he was good
or else, That sin in him was hid

deeds find a way to sink
down time's dissolving sea
that drowns both bad and good
all bodies and their memory

say rather, He carved poems
from the liquid hours that ran
and froze epiphanies
in words that all who read can scan

JOHN GLASSCO

Canadian Poet

I love all loveable things
I celebrate and adore them
The poor, the blind, the old,
Indians, Eskimos, winos,
The innocent deer, the baby seal
The lovely whale

I love sex too
I love my wife
And my kids
I write about them all the time.

I light candles too for murderers
Riels and Roses, lovely men.

There is in fact nothing I do not love
Except unlovely Americans
Expressway, skyscrapers
Big corporations, pollution, bureaucracy
And other things it is O.K. not to love.

But these are only addenda, interruptions
Of the old chartered song of Canada I sing:
Mother and dog, the farm, the street, the slum
And all the lovely regional quaintnesses
The verities of Gramps.

MIRIAM WADDINGTON

Lady Blue:
Homage to Montreal

Lady in the blue
dress with the
sideward smile
I see you at your
easel in the field
beside your house
painting the blur
of long-ago summer
in the night eyes
of children in the
dark mouths of
sleepwalkers in the
floating bodies
of rock throwers
and flame eaters.

In the soundless
streets of our
French bedlam city
with its old creaking
heart and venereal
stairways, its bridges,
spaghetti houses, railway
hotels and second-hand
monuments, there
Lady Blue of the

saint suburbs,
there, just there
you were lost; lost
under the mountain,
under the snows and
calèches, the steep cliffs
of Cote des Neiges,
there you were lost
under the fortress facades
of a thousand steel-
armoured apartments.

Under the slow blonde
sorrows of your tangled
hair we are all lost now,
lost in the distance of
endless streets in the
trackless wastes of our
vanished mother-city;
we are the ghost people,
uneasy night-walkers
locked up in Montreal,
and we can never leave
unless your tireless
brush moves us and draws
us into the blue-sleeved
avenues of your still
flowing rivery wonder.

HENRY BEISSEL

The Sniper

The storm has cooled things off a little. For about an hour
the rain came down in buckets. Maybe it's the same storm that gave
the prairies a dusting of snow last night. . . . No, that's impossible.
From here to Calgary is about twenty-five hundred miles. It would
have had to travel at over a hundred miles an hour. Most of the time
one forgets the enormous size of this country. It's all the pettiness
that surrounds us. It's you and your banalities. If instead you allowed
the distances and proportions of this land to structure your lives
you'd be thinking, and living, in astronomical dimensions. We, of all
people, should never be without a sense of the grandeur of time and
space. But you insist on measuring the universe in city blocks and
anniversaries. What small-fry souls you have! I guess that's why you
think yourselves so big. It's only petty people who regard themselves as the center of the world. Great minds realize their minikin
dimensions. Their insignificance in the cosmos. Their total
irrelevance to it. What I'm saying is not that he who thinks of himself
as small is really big, and vice versa, but that he who is really great is
really small. . . I know you've decided I must have an ego the size of
Jupiter. That's because you identify with me. But I'm a drop in the
ocean, a grain of sand, a microbe in the wind—take your choice. I
don't care. Your analogies have no meaning to me. I take nothing
seriously other than the fact that nothing can be taken seriously.
Remember, you're not listening. I mean, how absurd can you get?

There's a blustering wind that buffets my spirits into acute
awareness. Mercifully it also carries off all city noises, except the
swishing sing-song of tires on the wet pavement. About time we got

From *The Sniper*, a work in progress. The speaker is Roger, the protagonist of the
novel, who is tape-recording his reasons for deciding to take up a life as a sniper.

a break in the weather. This afternoon everybody was so irritable on the job that tempers crackled and exploded all over the place. Arnaud attacked Bill with a crowbar. He had to be restrained by two guys. Apparently Bill had given him shit for not wearing his hardhat. I wasn't there when it started. By the time I'd managed to get within earshot the fight had degenerated into a nationalist shouting match. I'd like to have seen Bill brained. That's what's going to happen to him one of these days. Most of these guys are Quebeckers. With a sprinkling of immigrants—Italians, Greeks—they're barely intelligible with their few, mangled words of English. They're hopeless in French. And they're damned if they're going to have it rammed down their throats. Bill speaks English to them, in spite of the new law that's made French the working language of the province. The rabid chauvinists among the Francophones hate him for that. Worse still, Bill has made it clear that he prefers English to French and that he's opposed to Quebec separatism. He's a Quebecker himself. Of mixed parentage. His father was English and his mother French Canadian. I know that because the militant separatists refer to him as a *vendu*, and one of them once said it wasn't surprising seeing that his mother had been a *vendue* marrying an Anglophone. What an issue to waste your emotions and energies on when you're dying. But these days you, my patriotic listeners, talk about nothing else. . . . No, no, no. You carry on. It doesn't matter. After all, chauvinism is the traditional bastion of blockheads and rowdies.

Oh, I understand why the nationalist issue stirs you all up. It brings a note of excitement into your lives. It provides a fresh topic of conversation on which everyone can gossip away without having to know or understand anything. The same as with the staples of human intercourse: the weather, the ballgame scores, and the rising cost of everything. Better still, it's almost, but not quite, as good as war in giving you the illusion that you're making history, that your paltry and vapid lives have a purpose, a cause, a commitment. Naturally without commiting you to anything. And without exposing you to any risk. On the contrary. It makes you feel that you are what you can never be: safe and important. Because political clashes like separatism polarize a nation. And that means they create two large herds, either of which offers safety and support to you. And the louder you bleat or bray, the safer and sounder you'll feel. Freedom, brotherhood, and equality—what more can you ask?

Nothing like a couple of political slogans to put the blinkers on you to conceal the abyss over which you walk a tightrope that the rats of consciousness are gnawing to shreds. But I am the pied piper of this holy land where every jelly bag cap covers a sainthood. St. Tite-des-Caps. Ste. Emilie-de-l'Energie. St. Polycarpe. If you believe in me you shall enter the kingdom of death in a state of enlightenment which is also the kingdom of life. St. Méthode. St. Zotique. St. Prosper-de-la-Lunacie.

Notice that there is not the slightest note of anger or impatience in my voice. I don't care what you believe or say or do. I'm indifferent to your so-called separatist crisis. I've held Quebec soil in one hand and in the other the soil of Ontario, and I couldn't tell the difference. And you, my divided listeners on both sides of the fence, the border, the ocean—you and I are in the same sinking boat with the same stinking epidemic aboard. We're in the same contaminated mother-ship Earth slowly going down to the bottom of time and space with a cargo of skeletons, and you want me to be drawn into an argument about whether the colour of my passport should be navy-blue or pea-green? You bet your life some of the guys on the construction job have tried to provoke me. They hate my guts. I'm an English Quebecker and therefore responsible for everything that's wretched and wrong with them. *Les maudits anglais! Les bons boucs émissaires!* Besides which I speak "French from Paris," and that's worse than not speaking any at all. Any hint of sophisticated speech reduces you to obscenity. Because you realize that your language is the measure of your humanity, and that you've got stuck somewhere between the horse and the monkey. If it's any consolation to you, the whole sagacious species hasn't developed beyond the ape. All language is meaningless. And no one can carry the burden of someone else's failures, much as the one may crave to unload and the other to shoulder it. So you are what you are and there's no getting away from it. You might as well decide to be what you are and accept responsibility for your miserable existence. Because if it doesn't start there it ends there. As you will find out in the last ten-thousandth of a second before the darkness explodes in your skull.

No, I didn't pick any of this up at university. Don't blame my education for everything. The fact is that my whole formal education, starting in kindergarten, led me up a garden path. It was designed to turn me into a Pavlovian dog in a consumer society. My father didn't realize that. He'd come over from the old country with a dream: his son must have a university education. To him that meant becoming part of the *crème de la crème*. I began to realize early in high school that the cream was thinner than skimmed milk, and even that turned sour before I got to university. That's what I owe the collection of prim amazons and proper buffoons who were my teachers. Except for one gym teacher all of them were women—faded spinsters, religious busybodies, disdainful culture-vultures. Oh I'm grateful to them. Their bigotry and obtuseness preserved me from walking straight into an elaborate trap they called "learning," designed to lobotomize me. By the time I got to university I was a confirmed skeptic, but I didn't have the heart to disappoint my father. He'd worked so hard to put aside enough money to see me through college. . . . Poor dad, you died before your dream came unstuck. It's just as well because it would've broken your heart to watch me degenerate into the drifter I've become instead of the doctor or lawyer you wanted me to be. I tried. Honestly. I finished my degree out of loyalty to you even after I'd stopped believing that loyalty or anything else mattered. That was as far as I could go. And I've spent almost ten years trying to undo the damage your hallowed education did to my mind. Sorry. The codes of duty and discipline and honour by which you were raised and by which you lived don't mean anything anymore. They belong to a world of illusions that were shattered in the laboratories of science, on the battlefields of two world wars and in the boardrooms of multinational corporations. For us the choice is between being a crook or a fool. Unless one opts out and becomes a bum. It's everybody for himself today, everybody ruthlessly grabbing all he or she can get of money, fun, pleasure, power. You heard the termites in the woodwork and predicted that the house would collapse. But you didn't want to know that it'd been built over an abyss. I remember your outrage at everybody's *egotistical frenzy as though death were at their throats*. It is, isn't it? Death, I mean. At their throats. A completely meaningless, a completely unpredictable, a completely merciless force of destruction. It was at your throat too.

I'll never forget the moment that cancer choked the last rattle of life out of you: the quick implosion of silence in the room that panicked my heart, the glassy stare as the last image froze forever in your blue eyes, your cheeks collapsed as though sucked in by a sudden internal vacuum, the waxen, grey-stubbled skin taut around your open mouth baring the edge of your teeth in a final, bitter animal grin of pain and protest. Pain and protest—that's what I felt too. My whole being became a scream of frustration and despair that acknowledged that you'd died even as I refused to believe it. Why did you have to die? Why does anyone have to die? Why don't we live forever? Yes, why does anyone have to live?... Did you hear my scream? Was that faint sweet smell a last flowering of your blood?... One moment you were there, a second later you were gone. I saw nothing depart from you, no spirit, no soul. And yet that rigid mound of flesh and skin and bones was alien to me already, from one second to the next, a single second that changed everything utterly, my father at one moment and an instant later the senseless body of a stranger I couldn't quite remember where I'd seen before, a corpse putrefying, a carcass that couldn't be loved. If God existed and if he'd been present in that small hospital room, I could've murdered him then and there, strangled him the way he strangled you, father.

Did you hear the thunder?... Don't worry. It's not god. It's round two of the storm. I guess the first one didn't get rid of all the atmospheric tensions.... I feel peculiar all of a sudden. Let me see if I can tell you exactly what the symptoms are. My ears are burning and there's a nagging ache in my belly, a bit like a throbbing wound. A sharp pain in the area of my heart now. Could be my lungs. I smoke too much. Lung cancer. You inherit a disposition to cancer. Would I like to die like my father, strangled by life itself? Because that's what cancer is—a cellular luxuriance.... Fear? Yes, fear is creeping inside me like an icy draft.... But fear of what? What am I afraid of? Death? That old scarecrow... No. Why should I fear the final reduction to absurdity of something that's always been absurd?... With you it's different. You think yourself immortal, my blessed listeners. That's how you act. You live your lives as though they'd go on forever. Which means that you never do any of the things you really want to do. Because you postpone them to the future. That's good, that's good. Because it's completely absurd. And you won't feel any pain. At 2,652 feet per second it will take the bullet less than one five-thousandth of a second from the moment it touches your forehead till it reaches the center of your brain. You'll feel nothing. Besides, you can't feel anything because you don't really exist. You are forever projecting yourself into the future and the future doesn't exist. But you don't understand that. You understand better if I tell you the future is full of SPS bullets. One for every one of you. And the last one for me. It'll be even faster than the one that'll hit you. It'll pass clean through my skull in the same infinitesimal fraction of time that it takes to reach your pituitary gland. Because the muzzle velocity of my Winchester rifle is 3,420 feet per second. If five thousand people put their heads together, in a straight line I mean, fronts and backs of heads touching, maybe in pairs looking deep into each other's eyes—picture it to yourselves: a row of heads three quarters of a mile long—the bullet would pass through them in a second. Quicker than snuffing out a candle.... Well, I guess it wouldn't work. Not for all five thousand of them. The hard shell of bone and the mush inside would slow down the bullet and stop it dead in its track long before it reached the end of the line. Too bad. It would've made such an efficient modern ritual for a mass sacrifice. Much nicer and cleaner than those gory slaughters with which the Aztecs propitiated their gods.

I should really leave you to your messy deaths. You don't deserve to be redeemed by one of these beautiful golden projectiles. Because you don't understand me. Every tick of this watch is a moment ticked off the calendar of your lives, a checkmark against futilities and frustrations. You don't understand that while you're listening to me some malignant virus is stalking you to your grave. Your brain is atrophying. Your arteries are hardening. Your bones are drying up. And all for nothing. A pool of tears for your pains, that's all. The epitome of consciousness is to know that the purpose of living is dying. Death is an excess of life. ... You see—nothing makes any sense. Anything you do or don't do makes as much sense as anything else you might do or not do. Put on your mask of comedy. You amount to precisely nothing. The mask is all that's left. Anything in this world makes as much nonsense as anything else.... That's exactly why I go on talking and scheming — because it makes no sense. Don't you understand that? Though I might of course just as well stop talking and scheming. In fact, I'll have to before too long. Because if I do what I do because it makes no sense to make sense in a world that makes no sense, then I'm making sense in making no sense and making sense I make no sense. ... But I guess it's easier to put a bullet in your brain than a genuine thought. Welcome, death! ... Now where is thy sting? And where is my fear? It's still shuddering faintly inside me. But fear of what?... No answer. There are no answers. No illuminations. I see only blood and thunder on a hot night.

O father, if you're anywhere about—which I know you're not... if in some way you can hear me— who knows into what dimensions these sound waves carry me?... I want you to know what you've always known but can no longer know, I mean I want to say what

I've always meant to say but never actually said, and I want to say it before all these invisible witnesses who don't know me...I want to tell you that I've always loved you...even when I hated you most, when your principles made you unjust and inhuman. I didn't know I always loved you till you died. When your last rasp broke I knew it. That scream that only you and I heard was a declaration of love. Inarticulate and therefore true. You understood that, didn't you?... Forgive me for not being what you wanted me to be as I've forgiven you for my being at all. My rebellion is my love. I'm a man of my time as you were a man of your time. Order is but a mask of chaos and the mask has come off. The world is showing us its bored, indifferent face. Or is that another mask? The old values are burnt out and an icy wind is blowing their ashes in our eyes. But I've cried my eyes clear-sighted and I can see there's nowhere for us to go. We're lost and pitiable but not lovable.... Forgive me, Father, also for what I will do in the future that may seem terrible and unforgivable to you—or would seem so if you knew.... If only you knew, if only you knew.... I don't ask you to believe in me because I cannot believe myself....I'm talking nonsense. I must do what must be done.... The truth is that there is no truth. Why did we never talk, Father, about dying?... Roger and over.

How to Build an Igloo Into History

Before blindness struck the Isle of Chios there was Baffin Island
and the tambour pulsebeat of a race of gods sterner than Olymp,
before Homer could drink to the sea with his eyes full of the dark
wine of his song the same sun was singing here
up north in the pinched eyes of men against the cold.
Bone rattle and lyre—two voices to the same heart, but the wind
is harsher here and sculpts the frozen plains for one season only.

DRAW A CIRCLE IN THE SNOW

This is Section 5 of a long unfinished epic poem about Canada with the working title, "North My Love North."

Who knows how often those whalers crossed the white desert
of winter, leaving no tracks, following no tracks but those the stars
burn into the circling sky or such as hares' paws might brush
across the crisp canvass of an October day at the pole. Goggle-eyed
they travelled by the scent and snort of blood against the icy sun
until night overwhelmed them and there at the centre of a dream
they built their homes into hives of light and endured the silence.

DRAW A CIRCLE IN THE SNOW AND CUT IT IN
SQUARES TO FIT A VAULT

When to the south and east of their imaginable world sunbaked
blocks of stone were heaved and fitted into Agamemnon's tomb
the men of Dorset mastered an architecture of the spheres so perfect
Pythagoras would've envied them. While the academies of Europe debated
truth, the eskimo curved his space from slabs of windbaked snowblown
marble so elementary it preserved the body's heat beyond Acropolis
and Coliseum, Chartres and Neuschwanstein, against the interstellar blast.

CUT A SNOW CIRCLE IN SQUARES WITH ANTLER BLADE
AND RAISE A GEOMETRIC SPIRAL TO HOLD
THE DARK AGAINST THE WIND

A simple form, always changing but never changed, rising
like a blister on the frostbitten face of this raw land,
or springing up like some arctic mushroom winter pushes
etiolated from the frozen ground, or conjured briskly as blizzards
flute upon the long night, an albino snake with monstrous scales
coiling about the fire in the stone, strangling the dark wind
closing in on the victim conjurer—the hunter and his knife.

RAISE SPIRALS OF SNOW GEOMETRICALLY AGAINST THE RIGID WIND
THAT IS YOUR ONLY SCAFFOLDING AND CARVE A DOME
OUT OF THE DARK THE SOAPSTONE HEAT
HEART HEARTH THE CENTRE

Nomads of the north moving from igloo to celebrate
their silver jubilee of centuries long ago and still their shadows
are cut down and cast in the snow by a sickle moon
from month to month—survival is both feat and feast:
eyes thin as the light a vernal equinox affords dawn
the hunter lures, softly scrapes the ice with whalebone paw
and waits hunched over the flame in his heart waits poised

STAND UP ON THE WIND'S SCAFFOLDING IN THE CENTRE OF THE FLAME
AND DRAW WHITE CIRCLES SQUARELY ON THE BLACK WALL OF THIS
NIGHT LIKE SHAMAN SPELLS TO CIRCUMSCRIBE EVIL
TILL UNDER THE DOME THE BLUBBER BURNS
AND LIGHTS THE EYE OF ICE

waits till through the ice-hole the sea comes up to snort,
then he buries his harpoon deep in a breath of blood—
death waits for its victim any victim at the edge of life's crater,
pounces as the air erupts into winter pure and absolute
and severs the jugular in a moment of utter peace. Thus survivors
survive—and they hauled their generations on sled and sleigh
across the tundra's northern lights home to a midnight sun.

CUT QUICKLY INTO WINTER'S BRIGHT FLESH AND SCOOP OUT A CIRCLE
OF DARKNESS TO BUILD UPON THE WIND'S SCAFFOLDING A VAULT
TO BEAR THIS ARCTIC SPAN OF NIGHT ARCHED ICEBLIND
OVER A HARD BUBBLE BENT LOW OVER
THE BLUBBER BURNING STONE
CARVING LIGHT

In kayak and in numiak they braved and battled seas and whales
more furious than a nightmare. They challenged icebergs with a paddle
when far away Ulysses set mighty sail for a more equal foe.
The men of Dorset gave way to those of Thule who defeated
Thorfinn when Europe's kings lay sodden in their castles.
Water is the wine of the north, and castles here are built
to a blueprint the soapstone lamp designs upon the air.
Where blood turns solid when the flame lacks food
life's defences are carved from bone—knife, bolas,
arrowhead, harpoon shaft, wolf bait and gorge. Epic
beyond any Homer, written firmly between the lines in the women's
faces frozen into the sky with their bite gone, their teeth
worn away chewing skins, chewing time against death by freezing.

SQUARE THE CIRCLE
IN THE SNOW

bpNICHOL

from The Martyrology: Book V

Brulé was the first recorded whiteman to see Ontario
1615
                    first cartographical sketch
the Molineux map of 1600
spoken of as the Lacke of Tadenac
"the bounds whereof are unknown"
Champlain's map of 1613
names it Lac St. Louis
or Brodhead's history
where Lake Ontario appears in 1615 as
Lac des Entouhonorons
or variously
Kanadario
Lac des Iroquois
Lake Catarackoui
Lake Cadaraki or
Lac de Frontenac
signifier tacking back & forth
because of the shifts in the signified
the white explorers' knowledge of reality

"the great earthquake of 1663
wrought havoc in many parts of Canada
and in the east
whole rivers disappeared and
others altered their courses"

an early map by Pouchot
shows a "crenated barrier of high mountains"
beyond Toronto
that "crumple down into hills on the lake shore"
west of La Riviere Aucredie
(the Credit as we now know it)
mountains that never seem to have existed
tho the watershed is there
possible traces of an earlier tradition
cloud range touching earth
birthed a story of such mountains
of the beings lived there
Pouchot drew what he heard

i write as i hear
often there is nothing there
beyond a rumour or a legend
sounded
                    the ground is
noise
            silence as it interrupts it
Bissett in '64
visited me on Brunswick
described a technique he used
sitting in a room
wrote down conversations as they occurred
focussing the ear at random
a writing of a listening
history
                    the white man's record
the indian's had their own legends
saw the whiteman as interloper
not explorer
rowed in with death
into their world
as the french viewed the englishers
intruders in the land they'd come to claim
white v.s. white
they took sides

French siding with the Hurons
English the Iroquois
H & I
the twisting round of speech
mirrored them
each in each
we talk of history honouring our claims
what we claimed without honour
set out to "tame" the New World
what was Old World
with its own legends
to another people
we name as fits our purpose
shape language to our own ends
all the lies, dishonour, death & treason such a use portends

RUDY WIEBE

In the Beaver Hills

In those days long ago when the Mountain and River Cree were never sick because there were always enough buffalo to keep them strong, they had a chief called *Mas-ke-pe-toon*, Broken Arm.

No one knows now where he got that name. Perhaps as some say it was from fighting a grizzly, or in battle, or perhaps from a vision he had on the Medicine Lodge Hills above the Blindman River when he was very young. At that time the Blackfeet already knew him as

The Young Chief, but even before that he was called The-One-With-Eyes-In-The-Back-Of-His-Head and he and his Young Men rode as far as they pleased from their country on the North Saskatchewan, south through the lands of their fierce enemies the Blackfeet and the Bloods and Piegans and the Crows, all the way to the Missouri River. There they met white soldiers whose guns ended in long bright knives. The soldiers took him with some other chiefs down that river for many days and up another and another and over mountains until finally they showed him what they said was their Big White Father in a place called Washington who hung a large silver medal around his neck. But when after three years he came back to the North Saskatchewan with all his Young Men still alive and more horses and rifles than the Mountain and River people had ever seen, he would not say one word about it.

"If I told you everything I saw by the Stinking Water," he said, "you would only call me a liar."

He stayed with his People then for eight years. His wives gave him sons and daughters, he hunted buffalo and killed Blackfeet as any man of the People must, and everyone might have forgotten his journey if he had not kept rubbing the silver medal which he had never taken from around his neck. It was worn so smooth now that the profile of the man on it, the man who gave it to him, could barely be seen even when it was held flat to the light. Once he told his wife Matono-wacap that while he was on the boat going down the river a white man had made a very exact likeness of his face with paint on a piece of leather, but she clapped her hand over her mouth in astonishment and quick terror that he had not killed such a devil immediately. After that he woke every morning to her bent over him, staring into his face, for she knew that just as he was wiping away that White Chief with his fingers, so that painter would one day destroy him; and paint on leather cannot last as long as silver. So he smiled at her every morning, his face more powerful and sharper than ever, and said nothing about the boat which had brought them back against the current of the river without either sail or paddle.

In those days when the Mountain and River Cree traded at Fort Edmonton or Rocky Mountain House they could only trade one at a time because the Hudson's Bay Company mounted cannon in the forts and locked the gates and would only open the small door with an armed man standing behind it. Maskepetoon traded hides and pemmican there sometimes for tobacco or tea, or a rifle if they let him, but during those eight years when he rode against the Blackfeet every spring what he had seen fasting as a youth on the Medicine Lodge Hills kept coming back to him. One day when his second wife, Susewik, enraged him, he drew his knife and with one swift, brutal motion scalped her. She did not, however, die of that. Gradually the top of her skull healed white and dry like a buffalo skull at the Thirst Dance and she protected it with a small cap she sewed of fur, but sometimes when she lay in his arms, laughing or crying with him, he again saw the Blindman River valley open below him, the high mountains at his back and Gull Lake a silver coin among the trees where the earth flattened away. And then the rainstorm would come up from the south again, from the Red Deer River canyons there and he would see his Mountain People riding south and the Blackfoot and Blood and Piegan warriors galloping to meet them with war cries shrilling high above the thunder and his People screaming in turn and his left arm would reach out between them, would grow huge until it split the prairies, a giant swelling log laid between his People and their endless enemies. "What does it mean?" he would whisper in Susewik's ear. And his left arm which could bend a bow or pull the largest horse to its knees in one easy, unstoppable motion, would cramp around her in agony and she would laugh at first, happily, and then recognise the pain in his face. "What is it?" she said then. "What is it?"

His father had told him something, though he really did not want to know what the old man had said. Every time he rode out against the Blackfeet his father, who could no longer walk and lay between robes all day long and thought, would say, "Is a man's true greatness to be sung in the scalp dance? What do your powerful eyes help if you see only what everyone sees, that war is glory, that killing is revenge? You have always seen different, why can't you see different about being a great man?"

But there were always so many mothers in camp wailing for sons and daughters lost forever to the Blackfeet, or fathers for sons and grandsons and brothers for brothers and nephews for uncles and young men for their blood friends and sweethearts and little boys growing slowly older on hate for their fathers' killers, that Maskepetoon could not listen. The Blackfeet had named him The Young Chief after his first raid when he killed three of them with two arrows and an axe, and often now they avoided his camp as if the very sight of his long shadow on the lodgehides were enough to terrify them; there were always so many Blackfeet that needed killing.

"There is truth and there is lie," his father continued to say. "Hate and love, war and peace, goodness and evil. What do you want? What do you see?"

Then seven years after he had come back from his first long journey, in the spring when the first grass is green and beautiful for horses, Maskepetoon and eight warriors rode south as usual out of the parkland to the prairies. They swam their horses across the Red Deer River and two days later as they came up between The Three Hills he heard birds chirping. At his signal the riders stopped, listened; it seemed the wide prairie about them was dancing with meadowlarks. "That is the enemy," he said and thrust his rifle, the only one they had, back into its scabbard. "We will ride slowly toward that low hill." They did that, and suddenly from the west a man appeared, coming toward them. The man rode very tall, blurred huge in the heat that shimmered over the plain. "Form a line behind me facing him," said Maskepetoon. "And no one touches a weapon unless I give the signal." So the warriors moved into line and Maskepetoon rode forward a little from them on the hill. He was peering into the mirage, the immense rider slowly, slowly floating closer and after a moment he said, "That's not a Blackfoot, that's a Blood." One of the eight Mountain People kicked his horse to run from the most magnificent and terrifying warriors of the plains, but Maskepetoon wheeled and seized the horse's bridle and hurled them both back into line. "Sit still," he said. "They are all around us."

The Blood on a beautiful bay stallion paced a wide half-circle about the base of their hill. The Mountain People sat motionless facing westward as he slowly rode up the hill behind them, then between them in the line. That horse carried that big Blood through them it seemed without so much as a thud of a hoof on stone, up behind Maskepetoon sitting rock-like on his horse and then past and a hand reached out, drew the rifle up from the scabbard against Maskepetoon's left knee as smoothly as if it were plucking a berry. Maskepetoon did not move. The Blood rode on, his back toward them all, then suddenly whirled his stallion and faced them. He held the rifle he had taken flat across his horse's withers.

You are a brave man, he signalled with one hand.

"All those birds sing so beautifully," Maskepetoon said in Blood.

"And you are very wise too," the Blood said after a moment. "Come."

He turned and raised his hand, and it seemed the earth all around them grew warriors like grass, none of them had ever seen so many Bloods, not even Maskepetoon on the Missouri. So they rode into that huge camp in the bend of Kneehill Creek and the buffalo started coming south then, so they helped the Bloods hunt and feast for sixteen days and then rode north again driving a herd of gift horses loaded down with presents, including meat and four better rifles than the Company had ever traded them, and they easily avoided a large circle of Blackfeet and galloped out of the trees into home camp beside Battle River Lake whooping their triumph. But there was no one to greet them. The bright green trees by the lake were black with funeral platforms. The Blackfeet had come and killed over half the camp, men, women, dogs, everything including Matono-wacap with all their children. And Maskepetoon's father under his robes.

"I cannot wail anymore," Susewik told him. "Your two oldest sons are alive. I think they will heal by fall."

She had been up early that morning, the two boys getting water with her from the lake. She had dragged the boys into the rushes but she had been unable to hold them back as long as it took the Blackfeet to destroy the camp and when they got loose the warriors were already so full of killing they casually cut down the two little boys charging them with hands full of gravel from the beach and left them for dead. Who needed to bother with children's scalps on such a morning?

Four of the men could find no one of their families alive to mourn with them and they came to Maskepetoon that same evening. "There are only fourteen warriors left now," they told him. "Come, we have to ride south again." But he would not go. Two days later seven of the thirteen came back and showed him their Blackfoot scalps. "We know who killed your father," they said, and before he could stop them they told him that name. "We left him for you." Not even that stirred his terrible rage; he could not fight but took the people north and east to the Beaver Hills beside the shallow lake where geese nested white as snow all year and there they healed that summer and fall and winter. The buffalo came very easily to their pounds and in the spring when so many birds came north they could barely see the water, the eighth spring since he had come back, he heard of a new white man in Fort Edmonton who spoke for The Great Spirit. The Cree who told him this said the Blackfeet were so impressed they were giving that God-man the hand nearest their heart to shake because they thought he had floated down from the sky in a small piece of paper which Factor Rowand at Fort Edmonton opened and he became big enough to step out of it.

Maskepetoon laughed aloud at that. When the man came to his camp shortly after he saw exactly what he had expected: one of those white men with a fringe of beard and white collar he had seen often on his first journey and to whom he had never spoken. But this man, whose white name, Rundle, as usual meant nothing, was very gentle; he carried a small cat on his arm so the camp dogs would not tear it apart and he prayed every morning and evening lying on his knees wtih his black book in his hands and so Maskepetoon let him touch Susewik's new son with water and give him his child's name, Jo-seph. A very strong name, Rundle said through the interpreter, a name to save his people.

For Maskepetoon now knew two things certainly: though the Young Men looked at him every day, he could not ride against the Blackfeet that spring, and he had not seen the Medicine Lodge Hills vision since his father was killed. And a third was fixed also: his left arm, which looked as thick and powerful as ever, sometimes hurt so much at night he had to talk to it. When he went outside then to look for the dawn it seemed the light was rising in the west, that the world had been turned inside out. And when he faced the sun there growing large above the Beaver Hills, praying as he always had with his eyes wide open, he saw the crimson light gradually darken into another colour through his tears.

That summer, eight since he had returned, Maskepetoon heard that Governor Simpson of the Hudson's Bay Company needed a guide through the mountains to the western ocean. Though he had never journeyed in that direction, he said he would take the Governor there, and he did. He left Susewik and her baby with his band and took his two oldest sons with him. The mountain passes with their terrible, roaring rivers frightened them and the smell of the bitter, undrinkable sea clenched between hills covered by trees as monstrous as the rivers and vines crawling everywhere alarmed

Maskepetoon in a way he could not remember of himself eight years before; though he knew now he was more and more aware of powers beyond things. The Governor went onto the boat waiting there for him. They called it Amisk, *The Beaver* and invited Maskepetoon aboard to sail around the harbour, so he went and the boat moved slowly without sails or paddles, shuddering deep within itself as it did so. This time he insisted they take him below deck into it. There he saw a stinking fire and machinery turning which they said made the ship go, but he could not see what made the machinery turn. So he had the Governor write on a piece of paper that he had been on such a ship and when he stood on land again beside his two sons he took the now featureless silver medal off from around his neck and threw it into that western ocean. When they got back to the Beaver Hills again, the paper with its incomprehensible markings was all he would show the People. And his two sons would tell them nothing either.

He would not kill their traditional enemies now. He told his people it was useless to fight, peace was the way people had to live and after a year he heard Rundle talk again. This time the white man spoke of a "Prince of Peace" and so Maskepetoon invited him to sleep two nights in his lodge. The story of Jesus who finally died hammered up high on a tree was worse than anything he had ever heard but the story of creation and fall stung him with happiness. He told Rundle the People were like young birds reaching up with their mouths open, waiting for food. And that summer for the first time Maskepetoon rode with his two sons into a Blackfoot camp carrying only a peace pipe and talked out a truce between the Blackfeet and the Mountain and River Cree that lasted all summer. The Company Factor at Rocky Mountain House was so happy for that he offered to teach Maskepetoon how to read his own language and in a few days the chief had learned the syllabics and could pronounce anything written in Cree, though it took a little longer for him to learn to write it. His sons learned the writing even more easily than he and a summer later Rundle touched them both with water and named them: Benjamin and Joshua. Benjamin went to Fort Edmonton and started to learn English from Rundle.

The next Easter Maskepetoon went with twenty men to trade hides at Fort Edmonton above the river bluffs. That evening they drank whiskey at Whitemud Creek and suddenly his terrible rage overcame him again and he took a man in his hands and very nearly killed him. He left then, south, without talking to Benjamin, and so met another white God-man called Father Thibault coming north who said Rundle did not really know the right way about Jesus, the Prince of Peace. For three years Maskepetoon thought about what these white men said again and again and again. He made another, longer truce between his People and the Blackfeet and one entire summer made another journey, guiding a fat English lord east past Fort Carlton to The Pas. There he met another white man named Reverend Hunter who said both Rundle and Thibault were wrong; he alone knew the way because he had a building with a bell which he rang when it was time to pray. Maskepetoon looked in his black book, which looked just like Rundle's, but he could read nothing there; it was all English. So he returned the two-month journey back to Fort Edmonton. Rundle said Hunter was of the Church of England and it did not matter what he said, no more than the Roman Catholic Thibault, but Maskepetoon told him Benjamin was coming back with him to the Beaver Hills.

"Each of you three," he said, "say you know the only way to heaven. Who can tell what you know? You should call a council among yourselves to agree on what you do not know. Then I would go with all of you."

Rundle gave him parts of the black book transcribed in Cree syllabics and Maskepetoon promised to read it, perhaps every day if he could, but said it was time for Benjamin to return now. That summer Joshua and a young man with six fingers stole Sarcee horses; the young man was killed doing it, so Joshua gave all the horses to his family. Later that summer Rundle went east with his cat down the river to return to his home over the Stinking Water. And that fall, eight years after Maskepetoon had first laughed to hear that Rundle had come from the sky in a folded piece of paper, the Blackfeet passed the camp of the People in the Beaver Hills on their way to Fort Edmonton. Maskepetoon with Benjamin and four other men rode to them to pledge a truce with them so they could trade for winter in peace. The Blackfeet gladly accepted these words from the man they still called The Young Chief and that evening their leading men came to eat meat with the People. As they rode into camp without paint or feathers, the women and children welcoming them with dancing and laughter, one of the warriors who had ridden with Maskepetoon when they faced the Bloods nine summers before came close to the chief and, pointing to a grey-haired man among the Blackfeet, shouted the name of Maskepetoon's father's killer. The happy shouts died. The chief stood motionless, a dreadful blackness hardening in his hard face. The Blackfeet looked about at the Cree warriors suddenly surrounding them bristling weapons; they could not deny either the name or the deed which had been sung long ago in so many of their dances.

"Bring him to my lodge," Maskepetoon said at last.

The Blackfoot stood alone in front of the lodge with the small group of his friends behind him and the People surrounding them, all waiting to see what weapon Maskepetoon would bring out. But the Chief emerged wtih nothing but his embroidered ceremonial suit in his hands, the old suit of beads and quills and scalps he had not worn for years. "Put it on," he said in Blackfoot, and very slowly the old warrior did that. "Bring my horse," Maskepetoon said then, and when it was brought he gestured, "Get on." The Blackfoot looked at his friends without hope, then mounted in one swift movement and waited, his face clenched to accept whatever hit him first. Maskepetoon looked up at him.

"Both my hands are empty," he said then. "You took my father from me, so now I ask you to be my father. Wear my clothes, ride my horse, and when your people ask you how it is you are still alive, tell them it is because The Young Chief has taken his revenge."

Slowly the old Blackfoot slid from the horse and faced Maskepetoon empty-handed. Then he took him in his arms and held him hard against his heart.

"My son," he said, "you have killed me."

That night Maskepetoon had a vision again. It was not a dream because he was not sleeping. He saw one of the Mountain and River People who had walked in the way of Jesus and been good, doing more than it was possible for a man to do. This man died and was taken up into the white heaven. There the man found everything beautiful, and numberless white men all happy and singing among their friends for there was everything that could be desired, and more. But for the man it was all strange. He knew no one, there was no welcome for him, he met none of the spirits of his ancestors, there was no riding or hunting and no feasts around the fire; and finally he grew very sad. At last God heard of it and called to him, "Come here," and he went. God asked, "Why are you sad in this place I made for your joy and happiness?" So the man told him. And God looked at him sadly. "I can't send you to the Indian heaven," he said. "You chose this one. But you were a very good man, so I will send you back to earth again. I will give you one more chance."

Maskepetoon lay under his buffalo robes staring into the pointed darkness of the lodge above him. He could hear his wives and sons and daughters breathing in sleep all around him. His left arm throbbed faintly, a drum beating perhaps or a bell ringing, he could not tell which. His long journeys spread like bright rivers, searching across the mountains and plains of his life. I will give you one more chance.

"What does it mean?" he said aloud. "What does it mean?" he whispered.

ELDON GARNET

i am red green colourblind

i am red green colourblind
i eat a green apple covered by red candy
the apple is yellow
the candy is purple
i bite & a pink worm sticks out his head
                     it had blue eyes
the apple is turquoise
the candy is burnt amber

my teeth are not white
i am black & white colourblind
i eat a white apple covered by black candy
the apple is red
the candy is green
i bite & the juice that rolls down my chin is brown
I can hardly see my fingers
                    my nails are unclipped
          the candy is fleshless
          the apple is peeled
i am perceptually handicapped
i eat a mud apple covered by mechanical worms
    the exhaust is choking
    the candy is metal
i bite & i'm hardly hungry
    the apple is magenta
    the candy is imago
    the worm is in the mirror & has albino eyes

a hill gently sloping down

a hill gently sloping down
                    to a pond
          surrounded by trees
                         leaves keeping time
                         with the wind
    you are swimming
          strong strokes
                    hands cupping cool water
          you cut through
                glide
                    turn over on your back
                float
          stare up through the leaves
                the sun blinks

she pulls your foot playfully
        from below
    like a fish at your toes
& you chase her underwater
        through weeds
                fans against your naked skin
out onto shore
    up the hill
by an ancient maple
            catch her
        her breath
    as you fall
            her laugh
            disappears thinner air
    she
        is grass
                a bee between your fingers
    you look up
        the tree bare
        snow against your thighs
    an owl swoops at your eyes

DARLENE MADOTT

Bottled Roses

"As if
The scene you play were mine."
Camillo, *The Winter's Tale, IV, iv*

Do I remember? It was here I folded your letter, and crushed it. For days it has lain subtly unfurling in the corner where I threw it, a swatted paper moth. You see, whatever answer I may have after a lifetime, hesitates to offer itself now. Do I remember? You don't ask about the London audiences these days, what the critics are saying to my Lady Macbeth, not about anything important to me now . . . but about *him*. Do I remember him? You want me to look back through the dark of some twenty-five years. If I risk it now, I do it for you.

Let's turn the glass then. Of the two women I am remembering, one knew the very secret of secrets, which is the art of keeping secret; the other knew how to use secrets, which meant at some time or other she let them loose. I don't know when I came to understand how confused their secrets were with mine. But I sense there is a pattern to it which the four of us complete — my grandmother, my mother, myself, and now you.

My grandmother was one of the women who had secrets. She was a formidable, Depression-made terror of a woman. I say it with respect; for whatever cause my mother and I both had to resent the old stinker, Nicolina Leone was more interesting than the whole pack of aunts and uncles put together. I know her differently than I knew her then, in a way which only the years could make clear to me. My grandmother and I shared an instinct for the theatre. That was what we saw in each other and it made a bond between us. Not that Nicolina ever went on the stage in any actual sense. But in a deeper reality, I don't know that she was ever off it.

The last time I went to visit she was still stubbornly entrenched in her own home (who could live with her?), still turning the earth of a garden she swore each summer would kill her, still covering her moustache and offering her cheek if you went to kiss her (that dark growth disturbing her vanity she'd wanted to have removed at seventy, when she first heard about electrolysis), and when I asked how it felt to be ninety-three, she said to me in broken English with her indomitable sense of humour, "I'ma ole. An' thisa house, she stink. *Ma,* I never be so sick I canna wash miself."

My great-grandfather begat Nicolina and seventeen others upon his first wife Francesca, and when she finally croaked (a horse having thrown her and the unborn twins twisted in her stomach), the old bugger married a widow named Vita. Vita had three sons of her own. Nicolina was sixteen when her father remarried and she fell in love with her stepmother's son Paolo. Although she was her father's favourite, or perhaps *because* she was, Nicolina was never allowed to marry her choice, and both she and her stepmother wept the day Nicolina was compelled to join lives with my Grandpa Rosario. For as long as I can remember, my grandmother spoke with pride of having refused to dance at her own wedding. When my grandfather came to her window at *Carnivale* with a lantern of candies and a troupe of hired musicians, he was trying to woo her heart now that he'd won her hand. She bolted her windows and corked her virgin ears. They were married anyway, after Lent. And yet she recalled these things to me with a kind of grim satisfaction, as if she believed she'd still won.

I remember the day she told me her story. We were sitting on the veranda peeling beans, because I hate to just sit, just as my grandmother hated to just sit, and it was fall, crisp and lovely. I was in love for the first time, which may have had something to do with it, for I was stirred by the sight of her harvesting her memories. She told me how my Grandpa had offered her a *bicchierino* of wine to celebrate their betrothal, and how her father had intercepted the glass as she reached for it. In the old country I suppose hands never touched. What must she have thought when all the wedding guests had left? My Granny blushed like a young bride at my implication. *"Che fare?* My Papa, he tella me marry. I marry." And she dramatized her legendary innocence, how that night after the song and banqueting were done, she got up to leave with her parents. Her stepmother Vita said, "No, Nicolina. You have to stay here now. Go to your husband." And this was when tears filled her eyes, as they always did with each retelling, right on cue, and when my own mother, hearing me repeat the story to my sisters, interrupted.

"She's full of shit and don't you believe a thing she says about your Grandpa. My father was an angel. And he loved her. Paolo was just an excuse, a might-have-been. It's easy to talk when there's no one around to say any different. I know what my mother was like. She just loved to make a scene. When we were kids she'd rage over nothing for days and my father would try to coax her out of it. 'Nicolina, Nicolina, aw c'mon.' She'd shrug him off, but you could tell she loved every minute of it. Then she'd threaten him right there with the loaf of bread she was slicing. They'd end up laughing. She didn't care who was around then. She's a bugger, your grandmother. Don't ever let her fool you."

A fascinating bugger though. Still, you can afford to be fascinated if it isn't your story she's rewriting. How many lives did she spoil, convinced that next to God, she of all his creatures was always right? Nicolina wasn't the least bit sentimental for all the tears she squeezed. If every now and then she plucked the dulcet string of feminine romance, you could be sure she had something else in mind.

When it came to her own children's marriages, she opposed all seven of them. Two of my aunts eloped with their unfortunate choices—one because she really loved him, the other because she'd rather die than marry anyone her mother loved. Granny's favourite, Vito, refused to breathe when he was three and so escaped the fate my Aunt Vitina undoubtedly inherited by coming after. (Vitina was the family's basket case.)

Granny's sacrificial lambs. All except my mother. Being the youngest, she must have had her eyes full. Although my grandmother cursed her marriage and its issue extravagantly, my mother's marriage was the only one that wasn't cursed.

Perhaps you'll understand then why I was nervous the day I introduced my grandmother to my fiancé. Because Paul, out of all the introductions to precede him, was the first Granny had ever smiled upon. And he took to her instantly.

On her eighty-fifth birthday, with all the aunts and uncles, all their children and their children's children assembled to pay homage, Nicolina looked down from her place of honour, scanned the crowd of related faces and thundered, *"Dov'è Paolo?"* Paul was painting his mother's house. I had to get on the phone and summon him because Granny refused to open one gift until he arrived. She had worn her best black dress and her wig for the occasion. My grandmother would never have dressed up for her own. After she bore her children she had little time or use for their private feelings. She was too busy looking after herself. Here was a woman who had clung stubbornly to life through two bouts of puerperal fever. To die in childbirth was just not her style. She had a sense of gesture. To have so many was sweeping but definitely not the way to go. The house was always full of *paesans* from Italy, and Granny wanted her praises sung in every letter, every photograph of her veranda and herself, posed grandly with her little tin-types clinging about her skirts, that went back home. During the Depression she even made over old clothes so that no one would suspect her family needed. They were thought rich while they starved. The guests ate meat while her own family filled up on bread. Undernourished, the whole lot of them. My grandmother was five-foot-eight. Not one of my aunts exceeded five-two. Yes, Granny was a clever chess player, interested not so much in the pieces as in her own control over their moves.

So I didn't like that "where's Paul," nor did I like what came with it, my blessed-among-women status and the *"sangue meo"* with which she claimed me as her own.

By the next year and only one week before the actual wedding I had called it all off. My reasons had something to do with his jealousy, which at first delighted and then exhausted me, being so impossible and unpredictable it required all my energy. I say his jealousy, meaning that intolerable, love-only-me part of love which won't recognize anything your mind can spin out singly, which says "I want no more than to see you happy," and means "I have to be your only happiness." I don't blame him. But I couldn't be expected to stick it out either, could I?

He thought to tempt me away from the world of theatres, insisting what I wanted to do most in life was superficial, not real, was making a spectacle of myself for an audience's amusement. Acting was not meaningful work. It was diversion, play. I knew of course that these were only words concealing the real reason for his resentment. I got tired of arguing; I told him *he* was the diversion.

An hour after I'd hung up the phone he was pounding on my door. I cried and cried on the other side but I wouldn't open. The wedding gown hung in the hallway. Nothing was disturbed. No one knew yet. But I wouldn't open. My stubbornness was stronger than my want, for at the time I still loved him.

How do you explain these things? He was so beautiful. Like a Roman statue. A cold, challenging beauty. I was nineteen when I met him. What did I know? I had never been in love before, never even lived yet. I only knew that I adored the fine arch of his nostrils, his strong jaw, the way his eyebrows met frowningly across his forehead, the feel of him holding me from behind in my favourite position, with my back nestled into his chest and his lips on my neck.

And then, he was so exotic, a lot older than my other friends, twenty-five when I met him. He worked as an engineer at an aerospace company, talked abstractly about the project he was then engaged with, part of a telescope France was building with Canada to fill the top of some dormant volcano in Hawaii. I thought it romantic that he should be a star-gazer, never realizing how full of coffee cups and broken pencils his world of circuit-boards must really have been.

At first it was comfortable to have him always there, knowing his eyes were seeking me somewhere in the darkness of the wings. I felt singled out, protected. He had a kind of sad charm with his briefcase and his ties and his trying not to get in the way when his mere orderliness amidst the props and dusty curtains was in the way. We were so unlike. But I loved him, made love to him at first through my lines. It was only afterward I understood how much this playfulness grieved him. He put up with it because he loved me.

"Why do you love me?" I asked him once. "What is it you love in me?"

I had taken longer than usual to change, and when I came through the door beside the stage, expecting to find him somewhere in the empty auditorium, I saw him on the stage, sitting at an upright piano with his back to it, legs outstretched, elbows leaning against the keys where old butts were stubbed between the cracks. He was smoking a cigarette, and in the darkness the slow burn of that single glowing point was very dreamlike, haunting. I was so moved by the sight of him waiting for me, I suddenly wanted to be forgiven. Why did he love me? He looked startled when I asked, as if to say, you mean you doubt me? But he never really answered. It often happened that his answers only silenced me, they didn't satisfy.

"If I could tell you, Jean, I wouldn't be in love with you."

This made me flinch. I didn't like the compulsiveness his words suggested, as if his own self were somehow suspended while another, taken by the experience, lacked the mindfulness to know what he was doing. Being able to say would be to somehow undo. But what if someday he should find himself needing to say, wondering? Paul troubled me the way a woman in the front row had once worried me by fixing her opera glasses on my face. I was flattered by Paul's attentiveness and frightened by it too. However guilty and uncomfortable it made me to acknowledge it, the truth was I did doubt him. I feared it wasn't me Paul loved, but some fixed idea of me, his own, which must alter if I were to remain my own, believing in my own changes. What then? When he found his image of me was out of focus he'd never forgive me. He'd believe I had deliberately deceived him. Whatever my doubts, I didn't want that to happen. I still wanted him to love me.

There was a dream I had about this time which I think holds some significance. I believe in dreams, if only because they stage the doubts I can't always face in the waking world. In my dream I was locked in a dark theatre. Something insidious was expecting me and I knew where it was but not what it was. I went to a costume cupboard and threw it open, unhangering every costume until I found it. It was an actor's mask, tied by ribbons to a nail and gaping with a drooped, evil grimace which seemed to mock me. I tore at it violently with a hanger, sticking my fingers through its lidless eyes and ripping them apart. Even when it lay in shreds I kept tearing at it, relentlessly, furiously, surprising a wildness in myself that was as sinister as the mask. Only when it was completely destroyed did I realize my fear hadn't left me. I had left me. I was moving like a grey shadow into the thing, becoming what I'd destroyed.

I told this dream to Paul after we'd had a bad argument. Weakened by tears and afraid of myself, afraid of the stubbornness in me that wouldn't let go even if it meant sacrificing my own happiness, afraid of losing me in the masking of me, afraid of never knowing how much to say and when to keep silent, I asked Paul to make me a promise.

"Promise me you'll never let me leave you." I was serious. I didn't trust myself to make the right decision. It was a moment of supreme fearfulness, childishness really, because I didn't want the responsibility. He behaved accordingly, his voice soothing and parental. "It's all right. Everything will be all right." My father had said this to me when I was four and I couldn't believe it then either. The words didn't take away the dark, the hands under my bed, nor the faces in my cupboard. Then why did I make Paul promise, my words sounding stagy and false? Why did he believe me?

It breaks my heart now to think just how seriously he took me. Paul gave me what I asked, tyrannously.

"But if she cannot love you, sir?"

"I *cannot* be so answer'd . . ."

But then, the Duke of Illyria didn't have Paul's mother. For I come to his mother.

His mother who had stood at the sink with her back turned to us, resolutely peeling beans and crying when he told her he was going to marry me; who sucked her teeth; who enjoyed misery because it broke the boredom of her days, because she liked to have her hand held and be coaxed back into smiles; who accused me of never looking her in the eye when it was her tongue whittling away at a back tooth I couldn't bear to watch; who accused her son of having forgotten her, her reproaches sounding not quite right, sounding too much the whine of a neglected lover—his fiercely jealous Mama, the only person I've ever truly despised.

It's useless even to talk about her, because she was pure cliché, Mater Dolorosa. The terrible thing about clichés is not just that they're wooden and fixed and horribly deficient, but that they're sometimes real. They exist, and in reality they're not at all funny.

It used to torment me that Paul didn't seem to recognize the game she was playing, that for every rose he bought me there had to be another on her kitchen table, that for every occasion she developed a sudden illness. In pulling him from her bedside I found myself playing an ugly tug of war where I lost with every gain because he was sullen when he came, because he passed his guilt from her to me like a plate of rancid meat.

Paul's mother was my rival. He belonged more to her than he ever could to me. He belonged to that silent apartment back in Italy where she locked him up as a little boy while she went to work at the factory. There was something dark and disturbing about him, something he must have carried with him from those distant rooms where he would play for hours at a time with the coloured buttons in her sewing box. Half his thoughts were in another language, forever foreign to me. Even the landscapes of his dreams, always secret and impenetrable, were doubly alien to me, who could never know how different the sound a cypress made from that of a pine.

Perhaps it was wrong of me to blame his mother. Perhaps Paul was never really deceived by her aches and pains. I can almost understand. For she was alone, more alone than ever my grandmother had been when she undertook the same journey a half-century before. My grandmother had more social sense, more inventiveness. She knew how to make her own fun and enjoyed her own company. Perhaps, too, I had never really understood the perplexities Paul faced, a boy of twelve with an immigrant memory, what bitterness he concealed when his mother embarrassed him, what guilt he felt, being embarrassed at all. I was a generation beyond having to undergo these humiliations. I sometimes think Paul couldn't forgive me for not having had to cross the boundaried world with him, for not having to waste so much energy struggling to forget.

Whatever the failure, there was something my father said to me when I went to him attempting to sort out my feelings, something I couldn't ignore or forget. "Acorns don't fall too far from the oak. He may think he doesn't like her now, but give him time. He'll want his wife to act just like her. You'll be peeling oranges the way she always did, making pasta every night, or you'll never hear the end of it. Salmon return home to spawn. Look at the mother."

Appalled, I never could look at those self-pitying eyes, nor think of the ignorance that dwelt in her walnut of a mind without fearing the primacy of blood. Could he, even in some hidden corner of his being, be like her? And I'd picture myself twenty years from then buying purple sweaters and Woolco purses, the same dark fringe above my lips, standing in fields of dandelions with hands pressed against my back to keep my stomach from toppling me. I was terrified of ever coming to resemble that, and yet I was filled with what I hated. And I hated her because she diminished life. *"La vita è dura"* was all she had ever had to say about this hugely engaging existence.

Paul couldn't have known what he did the day I was feeling depressed and happened to tell him I was. He made a curious slip. It was like a revelation. He grew impatient and irritable, and when he spoke his voice was oddly spiteful. "You remind me of my mother." Aghast, I could think of no answer.

It wasn't too long after we were playing out our scene on opposite sides of the door.

Had it not been for one terrible coincidence, that would probably have been that. I would have suffered for a time, but not been really damaged by it, the kind of mooning I overheard my father speak of one morning in the kitchen with my mother when I was thought to be sleeping late, like my sisters, but was in fact frozen in the hallway, convinced it was I they were discussing. "You can't keep flogging a dead horse," he said. And then I heard, "no wonder... can't sleep... walking the floors all night," which was what I had done the night before. When I laid my wounded righteousness on the table in front of him, my father looked up from his coffee and his only answer to me was, "You, Jean, could hear a butterfly fart." Later my mother assured me it was she he'd been talking about, but I suspect she just said this to take the pot off the burner. I do know we were then, and had been, conspirators.

The conspiracy I'm referring to is the one that made Granny our common enemy, and it was as much the outcome of coincidence as anything I've known. To me, it never can be funny.

My poor mother had to inform everyone that the wedding was off. I wanted it irrevocable as soon as possible but couldn't do it myself. I was afraid I'd crumble under the weight of a question. So after rehearsing her a few times I set my mother up at the telephone with a glass of rye, and by the time she finished going down the list she had polished off half a bottle and a box of Kleenex. The ordeal took her about four hours. I sat with her the whole time. She had made me write out on a piece of paper what to say and it went something like this:

"Corine? It's Fran here. How are you?... Not so good. I've got something I have to tell you. Jean isn't getting married this Saturday ...No, it's all for the best... *Well, I'd rather not talk about it.* (I had underlined this for her.) If you'll excuse me now I have a lot of calls to make...No, there's nothing you can do...Yes, I know they looked beautiful together, but looks aren't...Corine, I have to go now...."
And every time she hung up the receiver it took her ten minutes to recover. She'd tell me all over again everything she said and they said. And some said they had had a feeling all along, and others said what a shame it was, and so on and on, and it was awful, and people are awful, though some were wonderful.

It took the next few days to unmake all the arrangements and I spent them in terrible mental anguish. Cancelling it all wasn't the worst of it. There were the calls from Paul, the priest, Paul's friends, for Paul was busy begging everyone to intercede, and everyone felt they had a right to explanations.

I was terrified of everybody, didn't want to meet anyone I knew, ever again in my life. I couldn't bear the thought of the pain I was causing him. I couldn't marry him. I couldn't live. I couldn't die. Finally, when I couldn't take it any more, I pulled a new dress from my trousseau, did my hair, put on some make-up to cover the puffiness, made an appointment at the Gold Shoppe to have my ears pierced, and asked Mom to come downtown with me. We'd go to dinner, have a few drinks, book a trip somewhere, anywhere, it didn't matter, and maybe sleep that night for a change.

It was Friday, the twenty-first of June. I lived a month in that one day. When we got down to Bloor Street my mother and I were beginning to feel a little better. We were out and moving, though everything around us had a surreal stillness, as flat as those stagy train-window backdrops that move on rollers and return while the actors jiggle their bodies and get nowhere, undestined against their painted landscapes. It felt like high summer holding off a rain, for the sidewalks had that sewer and sweat smell, overbaked, dust-stuck like late July. The sun beat relentlessly through the rain-filled air, sucking in the pale tops of trees and over-exposing everything. Downtown the shoppers moved deliberately, so many flickering frames in a silent movie; over-worn images flecked and brittle with dryness. I watched as in a dark theatre, feeling very distant. And yet the day closed in on me. It comes back to haunt me whenever the air is white and steamy, whenever I wait for rain.

Before we entered the Gold Shoppe we paused, unaccountably, and looked at the window displays. With that brief hesitation I saw him, inside the shop. He was handing something over the counter. I dragged my mother to the nearest doorway and stood there in horror, panting as if I'd just run a mile.

"What's the matter?"

"I've just seen him."

"Who?"

"Him. *Him*, of course."

"Where?"

"In the Gold Shoppe."

My mother's expression changed. It sobered. She drew herself up as if preparing for a blow and looked at me. Her question drove the last spike into my indecisive heart.

"Why are you standing here, Jean?"

I don't know, Mom. I don't know." I was pleading with her.

"You know. In your heart of hearts you always know."

We were looking each other straight in the eye.

"We can go if you like." She was challenging me.

"But my appointment. What about my ears?"

"You can phone them from the next corner. Say you'll make it some other time." And then she said what we both knew.

"You want to go in there, don't you? You want to."

"We can walk quickly. Straight past him. He'll never even see us. It's at the back of the store anyway."

"Don't play games, Jean. Don't play games with your life."

But I was headed in and her warning struck upon deaf ears.

To this day I don't know what to make of this scene. It could be played any number of ways. At the time I thought it was *meant* to be, although I clearly had the option. It wasn't entirely a coincidence, definitely not the godsend for which my grandmother had been praying. For I had seen him. Can you know what that means? I could have turned away a thousand times if I had seen him in my imagination. But seeing him there, in reality, his handsome face distraught from so much suffering, intent now upon something in the counter, unaware that I was watching him, his elbows and forearms leaning on the glass so that his broad back appeared hunched and sadly beautiful, I wanted to hug him from behind. I was overcome by a strange excitement which kept turning over in the hollow between my ribs.

For there was the unknown. I *wanted* this experience.

There are moments in life when the truth comes to you like death. I don't think you ever recover.

The strange thing is, he didn't see us. Not until I'd had my ears pierced and came out of the back room into the shop again. Hearing my voice, Paul looked up startled, frozen in profile like a listening animal. I tried not to look at him. I had only glanced over to see if he was still there.

He came to me like a sleepwalker numb inside his dream. My mother sat stiffly on a Victorian chair not far from us. I don't think she could stand.

"How are you, Jean?" He said it very quietly, as if after days of telephone calls I wouldn't answer, he'd finally resigned himself to the fact it was over.

"I'll be all right."

"You had your ears pierced?"

"Yeah, it hurt too."

I tried to laugh but an unexpected tightness caught at my throat. I looked away and my eyes fixed on a pair of opera glasses inside the glass counter. He followed my stare. For a moment we were both looking at the opera glasses.

We talked, about such simple things, as if there wasn't that overwhelming knowledge between us, that coincidence too huge to speak of. The next day was to have been our wedding day.

I asked him what he was doing here, and he told me he was returning something he'd bought for me. He was careful not to sound accusing. He asked what I was going to do now, and I told him I wasn't sure, I hadn't planned on this.

I don't know when the months of bitterness heaved into my mouth — bitterness for expectations disappointed, beautiful dreams you won't ever believe in again after twenty-three. I think it happened when my mother lifted her face to kiss him and wish him good luck, when she left the shop. I wanted to say something then which would make him know why I'd done it, know that I'd suffered too, something which would avenge me for his being so good about it now, when it was impossibly too late, something he'd remember for the rest of his life. I said the cruellest thing I've ever uttered.

"Someday, Paul, maybe you'll be able to hate your mother honestly."

"My mother has nothing to do with this."

"Hasn't she?"

He was livid. His lips were like chalk, as if a fever he'd been suffering with for days had finally won and life was in retreat. His bloodless lips thinned to a hard line and I knew, I finally saw in his eyes the reason I had loved and hated him, drawn by fear to the person who most threatened me, running now to avoid becoming what he saw as me, escaping that final tyranny.

I turned, but his voice followed me.

"And you can tell *your* family to stop calling."

"Who's calling you?" Realization hit. "Granny!"

"How?...I never said..."

"It's Granny, isn't it? She would."

I was furious. I could read his broken promise to her all over his face. I left the store before he could deny it.

My mother was standing on the sidewalk, crying, oblivious to the parting wave of people that passed her. I put an arm around her shoulder. She felt so delicate, like a frightened little bird. My rage left me. Left me extraordinarily without bitterness or defence. Sad, that was all. Such immense sadness. What had I expected? To steal the show? I'd come off poorly. I'd convinced no one. Not even myself. And here was my mother, crying for me. For me!

I walked her towards the subway.

"Please Mom, it's hard enough."

"I'm sorry. It's such a shame."

"Mom, I don't regret it."

"Are you sure, Jean, are you really sure?"

"Yes. Please stop crying now."

Sobbing into one soaked Kleenex, she choked out her words.

"I'm sorry. It's just that love's such a precious thing. I'd be nothing without your father. Nothing. I can't stand to think of you without what we've got."

And I knew that for my mother, this was one of life's unstated truths. My father was the still point in her life, a man profoundly committed as husband and father to being what he was. He let us commit ourselves to what we were, even if it meant letting us make our own mistakes. I think my sisters and I learned to trust our parents' love in a way so deep the knowledge of it could be assumed. It had that quality of permanence which gives life its whole shape and meaning. As long as I knew them their tenderness never tired, never diminished, never grew old. I've probably always compared my loves to theirs, and as certainly as expectation haunts the reality, I've been disappointed. So my mother, at that moment on the sidewalk, was seeing things within her frame of reference and wanting the best for her children, she wanted love. Love such as she knew it, such as she defined for me with her simple words. Before her belief, I was overcome with nostalgia for something I'd never had.

"It's so important to love someone, to have someone you can share things with. What else is there? What does it mean? Without love it's all just selfishness."

I *had* to change the subject.

I told her about Granny. Her crying stopped instantly.

"She what?"

"She called him."

We had reached the entrance to the Bay Street subway station. Mom hiccupped, saw where we were through swollen eyes, and somewhat irrelevantly, reminded me of my promise to take her to dinner.

"How can we go, after this?" I said.

"Well, I'm not going home. That's for damn sure."

The minute we got to the Fifth Avenue Tavern my mother descended the stairs to the washrooms and got on the phone. She dialled with a fierceness I'd never seen in her before. Because it was her flesh she was defending.

"Ma. It's me, Fran. You know, your daughter. The one you're always kicking in the teeth. You called Paul, didn't you, Ma? . . . Don't give me that horseshit. I *know* . . . Never mind who told me. *I want to hear it from you* . . . Okay, Ma, question number two. Who did the dialling?" (My grandmother was illiterate. We knew she had to have an accomplice.) "Vitina! Why, Ma? Why did you make her do it? . . . You had to find out. Couldn't you have asked me? I'd have told you. Do you think Jean did it for nothing? Couldn't you have given my daughter the benefit of the doubt? . . . I don't care if he called you first. She's your flesh and blood . . . He wanted to find out how she was, did he? As if he cared. Don't you know bullshit when you hear it? Even if he did, what do you know about my daughter's feelings? You don't even know mine . . . Oh yeah, we've been having a picnic the last few days. Maybe I sounded all right, but I wasn't all right, Ma. Tell me, just one more thing, why are strangers always better in your books? Tell me, why do you always believe them first, over your own grandchild for Christ's sake . . . I'll swear if I like. I'm fifty-two, a grown woman with four grown daughters and I don't have to account to you any more. I'm not going to forget this one, Ma. I'll never forget it. I've had it."

I think my mother surprised even herself. Still holding the phone, as if trying to figure out how it got back up there on the hook, she blinked in disbelief.

"I shouldn't have done that. She sounded so upset."

"Good. You've got her worried for once."

"But she's an old woman."

"Old! She'll bury us all. And don't feel guilty. It'll do her good to sweat for a change."

"You think that's right?"

"Whether it is or isn't, you never let it sink in. Be smart for yourself, Mom. She's not worried about *you*."

"She's just an old woman."

"With a thick skull. C'mon, let's get a drink."

My mother had three Bloody Marys. I had three vodka martinis — straight up, and straight down. By the time I'd finished them nothing was at all straight, not the room, not the past, not the next moment.

With that one Kleenex drying out on the table between us, my mother and I grieved together. Since it was all over anyway, we claimed the memory, our right to resurrect the past after our own urgent needs. Had I said this, had I done that, it might have worked out, he might have loved me better. Who can say? What if I were not Jean, and he were not Paul? We lost our sense of the moment and what this implied.

What amazes me now is how incredibly innocent we must have been to look with such trusting eyes on this question of love, how it should somehow be possible to agree that the hug against the dark is worth infinitely more than proving who–hurt–who first. It seems to me now so obvious, I don't know how we missed it — that two people can fall in love without ever being able to tolerate each other's truths. I must have sensed this then, but not been convinced. My wings were only singed, not consumed, and as long as I could still see his face, burnt like a negative upon my mental plate, I had no will *not* to fly into that flame.

Three words to sever the silence. That's all it would take. I could even pronounce them proudly. Like me, he would be desperate for comfort. Three words ignoring everything that had happened, all that needed to be said, would have to be said if we were fools enough . . . Three words affirming what? That I still loved him.

I hadn't a doubt he would receive me. His siege had me convinced that if at any moment I lowered the drawbridge he would still be there. For this was love, this wretched devotion, this unwanted humiliation that happens to you, making you want despite yourself, despite what you want. What other force could have made me compromise all those beliefs for the sake of which I'd left him in the first place?

It was dark when we left. The subway was a press of bodies which shuffled at each stop without altering the terrible density. The air was thick, oppressive.

Darkness, flashing lights, closeness. My mother and I are disgorged into the upper air to wait for the bus that will carry us home.

A decision has grown in my mind to unbearable proportions. My desperate need to urinate lends it urgency. By the time the bus comes I have to go so bad I am almost nauseated. My head rolls on the back of the seat— my eyes closed, mouth an aching open hole. Even my mother's touch is painful.

"We'll be home soon," I hear her say distantly. She pats my hand.

I have become numb. The only two realities converge in my brain. Must call him. Must go. Insistent. Relentless.

The bus stops at Bathurst and Lawrence. I tell my mother I can't hold it any more. The Bay Company Department Store is open and somehow I make it to the women's section on the third floor where I know there's a washroom. My mother is right behind me.

What happens next must be a dream. I hear his voice. His hello hangs suspended in the telephone's clicking void. Thin echoes of unreal voices cross the wire connecting our silence. I am called upon to answer. Say it now for God's sake. Answer him. The words are out. I'm committed. There's a pause, and then, a torrent of unleashed anguish. He wants to see me. He wants tomorrow still to happen. It can happen without anybody, just us, alone. But a doubt insinuates. Jean, you won't do this to me again? Jean, say you won't leave me again. That persistent doubt. Someday, maybe nothing. Someday I may howl with the sudden discovery of final desertion. Say I'm not alone. I say it. I'd say anything to stop the pain I couldn't bear for one day, for one moment longer, not to save a lifetime of suffering. He's so relieved. I've given him back his happiness. It makes me feel almost light. I've done something merciful for a change.

"I've got to tell your father. Somehow. He's got to know." We walked the rest of the way home. I shivered the whole time. My mother was sick with dread. We walked slowly, as if trying to postpone it. It started to rain just as we got home. My father had waited up for us. I came into the warm room with mascara streaking my cheeks and blood running down my neck. Not used to earrings, I had partly ripped one earlobe with the phone. My father came up to me and said, "You've had your ears pierced?" And I left the room to wash myself, abandoning my mother to the task of telling him. When I came back into the room he looked ashen. I'd never seen him so miserable.

"What can I say? You don't know your own mind? My God, we all get it sooner or later. I can't stop you. But if you ever blame me or your mother for not stopping you . . . " He was crying, inside. I heard one whimper behind his tightened lips like a tap turned to a violent close.

"You're going into this with your eyes open. You can't say you didn't know. I wish you luck."

We were married three months later and parted a year after that. I spent some time in a home recovering from a nervous breakdown and when I got out I went to visit my grandmother.

I was twenty-four. I went because my mother asked me to go. "She's old, Jean, and she's sorry. What good can it do to hold a grudge?"

I was sipping tea. My grandmother got up and went over to the mantelpiece. She took a glass jar down from among the figurines and *bonbonnières* and lifetime's worth of dusty museum pieces. She wiped the glass clean with a corner of her black sweater. It was the kind of jar in which little round gift soaps are often wrapped.

She brought it over to me and I saw it held a dried corsage of faded roses.

She asked me if I knew where they came from. I told her I knew all right. *But she wanted to hear me say it.* So I said it, loud and clear. "Paul gave them to you to wear at our wedding."

"I'ma ole," she said. "I no understan' thisa worl' no more. *Tu lo ami. Lui ti ama.* You marry. Be happy. Ats all. Eh, whatsa use? Whatsa use? *Non capisco.*"

She told me to take my mother "fer sample." Did I think she'd always been so happy?

"Afore she marry your Papa, they have a fight. No see fer year. She tella him she no wanna see no more. But she get sick. Her hair alla fall out." And Granny waved her arthritic claw about her head as if tormented by some fly.

"*Ora,* you see *com'è.* They happy....Everybody fight. I know he good boy. *Lo so.* He good to me. Whatsa madder wi' you? *Testa dura* like your mother. *Ma,* Paolo no come back like your Papa. Paolo no come back."

A pattern was beginning to emerge, so claustrophobic I nearly choked on my ladyfinger when it occurred to me. For one brief instant I had a vision of the women in our family all giving birth to the same story, a tale which each successive generation must play out without anything ever being learned or redeemed. And if that weren't terrible enough, to witness it as well. Each player must pause in the wings for one last hovering instant, like the solstice sun before turning, and in that instant of outer darkness, to lose belief. For the play isn't done yet; another is taking up your script. While they pronounce, you must lip, powerless to utter or intervene.

My grandmother couldn't resurrect Paolo. Angered at her own impotence, she tried to take it out on me. She watched me, waiting for her revelation to sink in, while I sat with my finger locked in the tiny handle of her delicate teacup. How could I for one moment deny so extraordinary a thing as the human heart? How could I think all this stubbornness, this hunger, resilience, and dignity no more than a fixed pageant, without substance, without life?

I looked Granny calmly in the eye and smiled. She smouldered. I smiled. She glared at me with pinched lips and wore her fierce look of pouting, disappointed childishness. She'd met her match for stubbornness. There are times when the most practical thing to do is to sit down. Granny sank into her chair. Raising and dropping her hand on the doily she'd put across its worn upholstered arm, she looked for all the world like a wooden construction sign waving Rough Road Ahead. Together we listened to the clock. Her refrigerator trickled. I felt sorry for her. Because she had to listen to these endless silent sounds. Because of the boredom in this last waving gesture. Because her head trembled on the end of her liver-spotted neck and her throat wobbled like a chicken's wattles. Because everything about her was old and powerless—the room smelling of dust and bad breath and potted plants, and those God-awful snake plants you only see in Greasy Spoon windows; her greyed doilies, the matted wig she hatboxed every night, her chipped teacups, and her warped old ideas.

"Whatsa use. I'ma no good for thisa worl' no more. I'ma sick an' tire."

No, she wasn't. She'd had her wings pinned back is all. My grandmother never tired of life. She loved it up until the moment it finally had to shake her loose like a pair of knotted nylons — life, that fascinating puzzle over which she sometimes lost patience and loved losing it, because finding it engaged her.

No, Nicolina lived a long time after that, although at the time I thought she'd croak then and there just to spite me. I gave her bad gas. For me it wasn't that simple.

We are always limited by what we do not know. Granny thought she had my mother and me right where she wanted us. I had to protect my mother. From Granny, from myself. Because Granny had made me protector of the very secret that could hurt her daughter most, or, more precisely, had invited me to use it. Once I'd discovered one unknown, how could I ever be certain there weren't others? Granny had expected to rattle a whole chain of these questions. But instead of anger, I felt only awe — that I had lived twenty-four years with a woman whose capacity for mystery I'd never even suspected. I had underestimated my mother, and I felt immensely proud of her.

Granny may have been right about our hard heads. She was definitely wrong about our hearts. I never used my mother's secret against her, the way Granny tried to use it against me. I asked all right, and my mother told me everything. I told her it wouldn't have made any difference had I known. Knowing is not realizing. My mother had enough stubbornness to wait until she got what she wanted, by giving my father rope to realize what he wanted. My mother got her cake and ate it too. She was political. She was patient. Even if I had been these things I doubt if it would have made any real difference. For was there ever a time when I was certain of what I wanted? I've asked for much, and been reminded afterward that I asked for it. But the other — the knowing, really, what you want?

The church tower is telling me it's five o'clock as I look out my window for the first time today. If I'm ever to get this letter out to you, I have two things still to do. I must uncrumple that paper moth I thought I could avoid by ignoring, but find has been collecting my dust about itself these past three days; uncrumple it to find your address. And then I still have to answer.

So my sister disapproves of your marriage. I can't say I'm surprised. And you think it's because she's had her eyes full of me.

And you think you can find a friend in me, that I'll understand because I was once wild and unreasonable. If you only knew how easy it would be for me to become your friend you would distrust me. I have only to tell you what you want to hear. But you'd better know I'm not committing myself to you the way my sister committed herself to you — from her womb through all your tears and smiles to that second spilling of her blood wherever it was you and he made your first bed. I've less to lose if you lose.

And when you ask, can I bring him to you . . . will you have us in your home if we stop over in England on our way to France? I want with all my heart to say, "yes, yes, bring him with you." Because I see two young lovers walking arm in arm, eating ice cream in some January park just to be different; I see the Toronto of my youth; I see the darkly fascinating man to whom I gave so many hours; I see you, in love, with that effulgence love spreads across a woman's skin. How charming your hopefulness seems to me. And yes, I want to be in love all over again. Because love, in spite of all it has made me suffer, is still so beautiful.

I was jealous of your mother when you were born. I wanted that experience too. But I must have known I wasn't cut out to bear my sister's pain. I can take most things that happen to me. I don't know that I can stand watching. The way mothers are forced to watch. Blamed if they do. Blamed if they don't. I must be in the play, not the audience.

So I've rounded my life out in many roles, and I have enjoyed playing many people. Make no mistake of it, I have enjoyed. But what do you really know of my life? The one story my sister told you about me, told her way, trying perhaps to use it against you. We all use each other's stories. This story is one of the brown moths blown and stuck by chance to the night bush of your imagination. You can do what you want with it, pluck it and bottle it, because its wings are closed with the day.

You think you see yourself in me. I'm flattered. I'm jealous too. Don't interpret me, goddamn it. And I'd like to bitch at your mother too. What right do you think you have to play upon this one story? There are others, you know. You haven't heard the whole of me. But I'll save my breath until you come.

Because I'm alone now as I look out onto this London. Because it's five o'clock and raining. Because I want to taste youth again, feel I still have a part to play in life. Because you are my blood, *sangue meo*.

Ah, I finally recognize my grandmother smiling to me from the wings. As the curtain comes down, tossing me up on applause and voices, I feel the pain again, an unexpected rapture catching in my throat, there in the circular magic of the lights, revealing me as I bow to the nameless faces, there, a revelation astonishes me. I know what it was I wanted all along. The way I knew standing outside the Gold Shoppe when I said I didn't and it took my mother to know I did. She had that extraordinary gift of knowing almost by instinct. The way you know now what it is you want and aren't sure you're happy with the knowledge, because it's dangerous to say for even one day at a time.

But your question. Weren't you really asking me if I'd have written the script another way? Not whether I remember the lines, but what it does to me to remember? Whether I now believe it harder to live with one loud, unretractable word than with all the walking shadows of might-have-beens? My dear, without knowing you, I'd say you have my grandmother's taste for bottled roses.

JOHN REIBETANZ

Melba Sheppard in Her Garden

"I would give you some violets, but they withered all when my father died."

Well you had to stun them with a mallet first,
A thing about so long; then came the sticking,

These poems are part of *Ashbourn Changes,* a sequence of dramatic monologues now nearing completion.

Just the right touch with a pointed blade, to burst
The vein so the meat bled slowly. Such bungling
I've seen: either they'd miss the pig entirely
Or drive the blade through its eye or what have you—
Is it the pain makes one recall so clearly?—
That steel screech, like train brakes, even when a true
Expert like Bill Bowers—it sent me running
Back to the garden, here by the hedgerow, tight
My hands over my ears until the evening
Grew quiet again. (Why Bill stuck pigs at night
Was on account he thatched by day: you can see
How they fitted together, both called for skill
With the knife, his jobs I mean.) Papa found me
Here and wove daisy chains to make me laugh while
The light lasted and made his round face rosy
As a big harvest moon. Do people still weave
Daisy chains? Our dresses cried out for lacy
Trimmings—frills, ribbons, flounces—whether of live
Flowers or cloth ones, every well-dressed young girl
A walking garden; that got us into trouble
On rainy days, the mud would squirt up and spoil
Your skirts—made them filthy. I remember Bill
Lifting me over puddles to no avail
When courting—yes, that just a few years later
Than when I ran from the man who'd come to kill
My plump beloved pig. Papa's big Daimler—
The first motorcar in these parts: Papa loved
Intricate machines—that was ours only on
Special occasions, mostly we walked and braved
The sloppy roads, even at spring fair time when
Bill made me a regular May Queen, throwing
At Aunt Sallies until my breast could hold no
More of brooches or neckbands; and every spring
He'd spoil *his* clothes shinning up the greased pole to
Try for the prized leg of mutton. Of course we
Also walked to the travelling-theatre plays:
Sweeney Todd, Charley's Aunt, all delights to see—
Probably considered rubbish nowadays,
But without this everlasting sex problem

Stuck in them; and the piano played such fine
Classical tunes, Rossini, Lehar, the theme
From *Traviata* — that one a favourite of mine
From Sunday afternoons at home when Papa
Gave his rendition; he had a wonderful
Touch, and a silver voice. Mind you don't step on
Those irises! I've pinched the spent flowers, but still
They're not as neat as clipped tulips, and they droop
Over the flags. That's sweet william beside them,
Just come into its own, and I like to keep
A primrose border here, like the flowered hem
On an old-fashioned dress. I used to grow sweet
Violets instead, but they wouldn't thrive; apart
From the phlox they've been my dearest loss. The sight
Of phlox can still bring tears: I put all my heart
Into those flowers ("We Sheppards must always tend
Our phlox" — Papa's little joke), but after years
Of care, two seasons ruined them. First it rained
Too much in May, then not a drop fell; flowers
Get stunned by such changes, let alone phlox which
Want a constant moist soil, but what did them in
Was the eelworm: it burrowed clear through the patch
And killed all the leaves. That's the grandfather: when
It strikes the hour, you can hear the chimes back here.
Papa made that and it still keeps perfect time,
Except for the movement that used to figure
The changes of the moon: the works stopped, and I'm
Left with it stuck forever at the plump, full
Face. Well I think of what Bill said when he saw
The clock for the first time — (you see, if you kill
A pig when the moon is growing, you get more
Meat, because pigs killed in a waning moon will
Shrink down in cooking; so a pig-sticker's trade
Was tied to the moon) — Bill said he didn't need
Any clock to tell *him* when the moon was full.

Will Travis, Blacksmith

This fire will drive away the night's
Chill—come sit awhile. In my father's day
When songs rose over the blowpipes' roar
This forge was like a sounding board,
And laughter rang the anvil between hammer strokes;
But now I keep a quieter fire.

My father and his father stood
Here where the hand shapes what the flames have softened,
And swung their hammers to the same rhythm
You feel shiver through that bench.
I have their hands: faces change, but a village
Sees the same hands age upon age.

They hammered out necessities:
Harrows, ploughshares, shoes for the horses, scythes
So light and true a man could mow
All day, and have an arm to swing
A squealing child high as the evening sky.
Their hands fed the whole village.

These days, my neighbour picks up his
Briefcase—no scythe for him—and runs to the station:
Hello 8:40, goodbye fields!
He buys his bread in town, but expects
Me to get mine by standing here forever
Planted in the old ways like a tree.

He comes to the forge and wants my hands
To make what hands made here when hands made all.
If I oblige with a firescreen
Or grate some blacksmith in my past
Might have contrived for a patron in his past,
I feed his hunger. And my own:

Something inside me lives for this work,
Making, doing—this is the highest thing—

When the hammer speaks, and imperfections
Fall away flaking fire,
And quenched steel stammers to express a shape
The mind held in a storm of flame,

My fire reclaims what the old ones lost
To the earth that covered them with their bolts and horseshoes,
And fuses it in blood-red heat
With the forgings of my hand
Into a solid frame tempered to last
Long after time beats mine to dust.

When I was ten or twelve, I watched
Men dig an ancient ship out of the earth,
And heard their shovels click against
Iron clench-nails an old one forged:
The nails gave back the sunlight, though their timbers
Had spoiled and seeped into the sand.

These are light-holders for our church:
Children will pick them out through the sweet smoke
And trace the patterns figured in
Their scrolls of hammered leaves and flowers.
The leaves turn red now, but they'll never wither;
My hand's in every one of them.

Andrew Whittaker, Local Preacher

Before I start, would some of you young fellows
Throw open the windows? It wouldn't do
To hibernate when all the rest of the world
Opens its eyes at the tender urging
Of spring sunshine: even our slow old ash—
My brother!—is sporting little green buds this morning.

Now you can smell the sweetness of new life
Burst from the earth; and did you see
Those daisies set a gold crown on the hill
Across the road? So many gifts!
But I'm going to talk about one we overlook,
Not great like trees or glorious like flowers: grass.

Grass is always with us, it never fails us:
Grass feeds the beasts, and they feed us;
It clothes the meadows, and in the early morning chill
Its breath mingles with ours as we work.
Its green colour rests the eye, and after
A long day the feel of it rests the body.

Perhaps it's time to root this grass in a text.
Here's my text: just "the grass of the field."
In the Book of Kings these words tell us how little
Man's power amounts to; but Christ lets them show
How much God gives us, dibbling the grass with flowers
That pass, but sowing man with the seed of love.

And our Lord's "much" sorts well with Kings' "little":
We and the grass are of small power,
Both green in the morning, as the Psalm says, and wrinkled
By evening—I'm proof of that—yet God
Has covered the earth with us, out of his skies fall
Showers of rain for the grass and mercy for man.

How little the grass is, measured against our much!
Moving but never leaving its place,
Grass wears the beauty of youth but never feels
Its passion; that's why nature-worship
Never answers our needs: how could we give
Our hearts to a god not free to love and suffer?

I think Christ must have found the grass a comfort,
Lightening his walk and his sufferings,
And maybe he cocked an ear to catch the music
That spent stalks make with the wind

When they wither standing; or watched an autumn's red
Sunset reflected on millions of shining dry bents.

That's a sight you still may look for at harvest-time,
When the earth has rendered up its tithes
And the sun's rays come level with the ground; I saw it
Every night of the week when my boy
Was carried home from the war to die—a man's
Senses be sharp when his blessings be slipping away.

But it's spring, and the Bible calls spring grass "tender," not sharp—
Tender to the jaws of the young calves
In their first pasture, tender to an old man's mind.
It grows out of our deepest sorrows
And spreads fresh green, even over mounds
Of black earth turned by the spade in a stone's shadow.

It's time we picked up that "much" and "little" again.
Christ, who made much of the little of Kings,
Comes to us now, and makes our much seem little:
New-risen grass brings much comfort,
But Christ new-risen brings life the August sun
Can't wrinkle, and the fall's frost will never chill—

Eternal life, God's dearest gift to man,
Bought with the blood of his only son;
A crown that Kings would trade their riches for,
But one that's ours just for the asking:
So let the tender grass open your senses
To spring, and let spring open your hearts to Christ.

GREG HOLLINGSHEAD

The Sound

I still wasn't used to living in the house when I disappeared. It happened the night I heard the sound, which didn't come from the house itself but from somewhere in the larger neighbourhood. It was all the same to me. I had settled as yet into too few habits to be either very curious or very discriminating: the sound was one more aspect of the 360-degree strangeness of my new surroundings. I had spent the early part of that evening sitting in my car on the old city pier watching the birds and debating whether or not I should drive off the end of it. If I didn't, it was only because Anne took my will along with everything else.

My new place was twenty minutes from the docks. I had driven up the dirt and cracked-concrete lane that runs behind the houses in that block and turned in at my garage when I first heard the sound, but only after I'd got out of the car and fully straightened up. I couldn't hear it inside the car with the engine idling and the doors closed, and I couldn't hear it once I'd opened the car door and not yet got out, struggling to undo my seat belt, which jams. When I did stand up, I heard it, even above the idling engine. It came from a direction on the other side of the car, beyond a clump of lilac trees. Through those trees I could see the lights from the back of a house two lots down and across the lane. I associated the sound with that house. Absently (all of this absently) I thought of a tape deck set up on a back porch or by an open window, playing not music but a tampered-with recording of a party of women, standing around in dozens, talking and drinking, or perhaps a recording, made from some distance, of the squeals and cries of birds or rodents. The reason I thought the sound recorded was its thinness, its vulnerability. I noticed this as I stepped forward to open the garage door and the sound faded almost to nothing. It seemed to emanate down particular narrow radii. From where I hesitated in front of the garage, the lights from the house across and down the lane were as clear as when I stood beside the car and yet the sound was faint, almost inaudible. I put the car away and locked the door. By the time I was crossing the back lawn, marvelling at the emptiness inside me, I'd forgotten the sound, but as I reached the top stairs to the summer deck at the back of the house, I heard it again, louder that ever: a clamorous gathering of shrillness.

I went inside and forgot about it. I ate a meal from cans and did my evening's deskwork. I couldn't hear the sound inside the house. Even at my desk, with the ventilation holes in the storm window frames uncovered, I could hear nothing except the furnace below me and the refrigerator on the other side of the wall. At midnight I went onto the deck for fresh air, and the sound was out there, reinforced by distant traffic- and street-noise, by the manic commotion of Saturday night. Self-conscious now, I went to get my jacket, telling myself that in the early morning, before the day has begun, and late at night, when the day is finished, there is time for anything, whether or not it is possible.

I followed the lane in the direction of the house I assumed to be the source of the sound. Before I reached it, a white bungalow, dark-windowed and harsh in the glare of a bare two-hundred-watt bulb mounted on a dead young elm, it was obvious that the sound originated some distance beyond, and yet near enough (or perhaps now intense enough) not to splinter into fragile radii. I imagined a small park, the branches of the trees alive with congregations of small creatures.

I continued down the lane, considering the houses on either side of me. All of them, whether dark or brightly lit, were silent and still. What did the people inside know or think about this din? Could they, like me at my desk, not hear it? Or was it so familiar that only someone of my particular degree of strangeness to the neighbourhood could notice it? Was there some local name or explanation that had spread like an epidemic to kill curiosity? Or if I knocked on a door, would I find the people inside as grim as characters in a bad play, and yet as willing to recount for me, the stranger, every detail of their fight against those forces responsible for this threat to their happiness, the petitions they had circulated, the fight with city council . . . and, of course, The Child Who'd Ventured Too Close, propped up in his curtained crib, ten years old. . . normal once, if not brilliant, but now. . . .

I reached the street laughing to myself, and turned right, down the middle of it, toward the source of the sound. The moon was gibbous and huge, half-obscured behind dark, fast-moving clouds. In the blue fluorescence of the streetlights its beauty seemed fatuous and soft, irrelevant. It was the senseless, hard reality of the street that came through, of the city night, of the streetlights that buzzed and flickered at frequencies like nothing in-nature, of creatures as frantic and clamant as technology itself. A block ahead, the street ended in the darkness of trees. I was staring into that darkness thinking that those trees should have been the source of the sound and why didn't I think so? when out of a lane on my left appeared a boy and a dog, not a German shepherd, at least not a pure-bred, but a similar powerful kind of animal, straining against its leash. As we passed perhaps twenty feet from each other, I was about to ask the boy (although he didn't look very articulate) about the sound, when he made a noise in his throat, the kind of nervous, habitual throat-clearing noise an old man will make, but I, in my hesitation to speak to him, must have been assuming that he would either be silent, anticipating my question, or else say something to me in greeting, the way people do in England (where Anne and I have lived, off and on) when out walking at night, and so I thought that the sound came from the dog, and started. The dog noticed and barked at me. The boy gave an immediate yank on the leash, strangling the dog's next bark in its throat, and they were past. I could hear the click of the dog's nails on the asphalt and the steady heavy heels of the boy crossing the street to the far sidewalk. I was shaking.

To the left of the trees was an open field and beyond it the glare of the outside lights of warehouses or factories. I decided the sound came from there. I couldn't see them clearly because of the white substance that curds on the insides of my contact lenses when I'm up past my bedtime. In the darkness I couldn't risk removing and rinsing the lenses with my saliva, so the buildings I could see across the field were smeared, and the powerful lights that burned on their outside walls to discourage trespassers had jerking, sliding white coronas.

The field was long grass and weeds, deadened and flattened by August heat and the uncommonly heavy rains of a cold September. At its far side was a ditch and beyond the ditch, railway tracks. I jumped the ditch and scrambled, scraping my hand, up the bank toward the larger white stones on top where twenty-five years collapsed to nothing and I balanced, a boy again, on one rail, until I could feel the train rumbling up through the soles of my shoes. I could hear it too, a lower and altogether more substantial sound than the one in the air around me. I could see the engine's headlight in the distance, yellow, like the heart of a flower, its petals an aureole of whiteness. As usual in such situations, I was tempted not to move. I waited a few seconds, for as long as the thrill of fear remained delicious, and then, with plenty of time, I stepped off the tracks, wondering what Anne's response to suicide would really be, whether under any circumstances she'd consider the gesture justified, that is, innocent of self-consciousness. I hardly thought so. I moved away from the tracks in the direction of the nearest warehouse, not wanting to be right up next to the noise of the train. As I crossed two more sets of tracks I noticed a freight car sitting on a third set of tracks that ran along the back wall of the warehouse. I turned and watched the train pass, uncomfortable in the racket. As it faded I expected the creatures making the sound to be cowed for a moment to silence by the roar and clatter, but the sound was still there, louder than ever. *Birds,* I said out loud, *thousands of them.*

I was standing near one of the receiving doors of the warehouse, an enormous flat-roofed building of concrete blocks painted white. Over the edge of the roof I could see the tops of three green neon letters, R (or perhaps P) A M, backwards, part of the company's name, mounted along the front of the roof. I decided that some clerical error had resulted in a warehouse floor entirely covered by chicks, squealing and squalling their chick-style outrage at being detained until Monday morning. But the sound was no louder when I walked closer to the receiving doors. I walked on toward the front of the building. It must, I thought, be coming from my right; from a building about two hundred yards away, not as deep as the warehouse and set back farther from the road. I could see the front of it then. A school. I thought of the noise of children at recess, played loud on a poor sound system in an empty classroom, and then I thought of an echo, the sound originating indeed at the warehouse but bouncing back from the wall of the school. I looked back up at the warehouse and saw them: two gulls, sitting on the roof watching me. I thought of all the rain recently, a pond up there, a thousand gulls gathered, two look-outs. By that time I was standing in the glow of the company's name. A magpie sat under the E, saying nothing. I walked closer; a third gull appeared. It stepped off the roof and glided in a tight loop over my head, far enough away for me to understand it had an eye on me. I was tempted to shout. I wanted to see the whole flock, magpie attendant and all, lift off. As it was, I made no sound. Part of me didn't want to disturb them, and besides, I wasn't sure that any sound I could make would be heard above their noise. Also of course, I was, I supposed, trespassing, and didn't want to draw the attention of the watchman who would probably be somewhere inside. I paced around in front of the warehouse. A second magpie appeared at the edge of the roof. He made a circle over my head and returned immediately to his perch. He watched me silently for a moment and walked away out of sight.

I knew I had to find out what was happening up there. I returned to the freight car at the back of the warehouse. It was easy climbing to the top of it, up a steel ladder bolted to its side, but I'd have needed a chair or a stool to be able to see anything on the roof of the building, and a ladder to get me onto it. I climbed down and walked back to the receiving doors of the warehouse. In front of the third was an industrial skip filled to overflowing with broken-up packing crates. A metal roof supported by chains bolted to the upper wall of the building extended the length of the receiving area. I climbed into the skip and by making a wobbly pile of broken crates was able to pull myself onto the metal roof. From there, by throwing one leg over the chain and just about dislocating my back, I hauled myself onto the main roof of the building. I thought the screeching would deafen me.

There were no birds on the roof, and none in the air. The screeching was, as I say, deafening, but there were no birds. The roof was asphalt and crushed granite, a quarter covered with rainwater, an enormous shallow puddle that reflected the moonlight. I thought of invisible water creatures from outer space, screaming. I thought again of birds inside the warehouse, under my feet, the sound coming from ventilation ducts high in the walls. I thought of a loudspeaker mounted on the roof to attract, the way duck calls are supposed to attract, flocks of birds. I thought I was dreaming.

At the other end of the roof was a right-angled triangle, in silhouette, about eight feet at its vertex. I walked toward it, around the water. The intensity of the sound did not diminish or alter. I knew I could go anywhere on that roof and still remain at the center of the sound. The triangle turned out to have three dimensions, to be a metal structure enclosing stairs that led down from the roof. The door was heavy, wood-framed, covered in metal casing painted beige. It was unlocked, and when with difficulty, because of the difference in air pressure, I got it open, the air around me whooshed and whistled. The bird sound was only slightly louder inside, but much clearer. A weak bulb burned somewhere farther down the stairs, which were sloppily covered with carpeting that looked like grimy black felt. The carpeting didn't observe the geometry of the stairs but sloped and bagged and folded back on itself and at the iron lips of many of the stairs was worn right through. The stairway smelled like oil and metal; it smelled like a gun. I thought of the hard, fantasy worlds of night watchmen. I thought of guard dogs and of being shot for trespassing. I tried to remember whether or not private security staff in this country carry weapons. As the door closed behind me, the sound became even clearer. When the door clicked, I tried the knob in a panic; it turned and the door opened, the wind whistling as before.

I let the door close and started down the stairs. They circled an iron pole and ended at a metal floor like a landing on a fire escape. A forty-watt bulb protected by a bubble of iron mesh lit a circle of concrete wall behind me. The gouts on the wall made sharp black cones and circles of shadow. Cupping my hands at my temples, I walked to an iron railing and faced out into the darkness. Nothing, and then the machinery was there, massive, darkness mostly itself, rising out of that other darkness, not with eerie majesty or any lesser kind of menace but a dull and stubborn assertiveness, as if to say, And then there is this, and this too is ordinary and undeniable. Within its outlines of black on deeper black, the surfaces of five or six glass circles reflected the bulb behind me—dials, I supposed, sewn like buttons onto the darkness, out of which narrow clusters of bluish tubing, like slender organ pipes, rose and curved to return parallel to themselves, and to plunge back into the darkness. Beyond that, nothing, except the sound, directly, it seemed then, below me.

Along the railing to my right was an elevator shaft. I pressed the button, a bubble of plastic glowed red on my hand, and the cables I could see between the crossed diagonal brass slats of the door whispered and slapped against each other while the cage, travelling upward from a long way below me, from what must have been, in fact, some distance below the ground, made a whirring sound as it rose. If the night watchman hasn't noticed me yet, I thought, he is deaf and blind.

When the whirring stopped, I pulled the door aside and fell onto the floor of the cage. It had stopped a foot short of floor level. Sweating with anger and with the shock of the fall, I got to my feet and pushed one of the lower pair of six buttons, but the cage did not begin its slow descent until I had closed and fastened the door. Descending, I tried to see out through the network of moving metal, but there was even less light down here than above, and I could see nothing. I could smell machinery, I could hear the elevator and the bird sound coming from below, and I could feel pain beginning to assert itself in the muscles in my right ankle, but I saw nothing. The button I pressed to descend didn't glow. It seemed minutes before the cage came to a stop and I was stepping into a corridor with concrete block walls painted pink. The ceiling was white acoustic foam, the floor anonymous large-sectioned tiling. The corridor itself was unlit, but light came from another that met it twenty feet to my right. That second corridor was about thirty yards long. It was pink too and lit by bare fluorescent tubing. I limped down the corridor to swinging doors like those leading into cafeteria kitchens.

I don't know what room I entered. It could have been a kitchen. It was lit like the kitchen of an institution, brightly. The patches of wall I could see were green. The air smelled like the sea, or like seaweed boiling in an open pot. There were no burners, no pots. In the far wall, an empty black hole the height and length of a small car. I imagined the sea below it, a moonless night, flocks of gulls on the rocks. Not possible, of course; I stayed where I was. Some of the counters had sinks, double and triple ones, with high spouts. The ceiling was jammed with fat, writhing aluminum ducts. Occasionally one hung down over a counter for sucking up odours and other inpurities, or so I decided. I also decided that the three large metal cabinets at my left hand, their surfaces reflecting the fluorescence, were refrigerators. I opened the first. It was warm inside, and something moved, seemed to scrabble against glass. As I'd done on the platform at the top of the elevator, I cupped my hands at my eyes and stared into the darkness. I could see a cylinder. I pulled it toward me, gingerly. It was filled with a clear liquid, and something in the liquid was moving, violently. I cupped my hands at my temples. Lidless eyes like yellow beads for stringing, tiny claws against the glass. I carried the cylinder to the nearest counter. It had a plastic-stopper lid. The creature was elegant, perhaps three inches long, green in colour, in shape like some variety of lizard. It seemed to be drowning. Lizards don't have gills, do they? When its mouth opened, tiny bubbles escaped, and then it thrashed again, and stopped, as if transfixed. By me or by death? I considered taking the lid off but the creature frightened me; I didn't want it loose, and I reasoned that if it hadn't drowned yet it never would, and besides, I'd be meddling with someone's experiment. I tapped the glass by its eye, which didn't move though its head turned fractionally away. A few seconds later, when it started thrashing again, I put the cylinder back into the metal cabinet. Even after I had closed the door, I could hear it scrabbling against the glass. The other two cabinets were cool and empty.

I crossed to the knocked-out hole of blackness in the far wall. I wanted to see the sea, and gulls on the rocks below. And that was what I saw, the moon swollen with itself, the sea silent, though not calm, its great black swells rising and falling among the rocks below, now swallowing, now sucking back to reveal, now swallowing, now sucking back. The gulls were there too, with their constant racket, though their number was disappointing, no more than four or five dozen of them scattered among the rocks, flapping up into the air with wild cries when the sea buried their perches, settling down still squalling as it bared them again. When I leaned out and looked left I could see an iron conduit, perhaps six feet in diameter, dribbling rusty effluent onto the rocks below. When I looked again at the gulls, they were fewer, because there were fewer places for them to perch. Each time the sea drew back it exposed less rock. But the noise of the gulls remained as intense as ever because the battles for purchase were all the more raucously bitter. The ones who left circled a few times before flying toward the roof. I could hear no new chorus from up there, but perhaps all sound from the roof was obscured by the noise of the birds who remained below to do battle for diminishing territory.

So the sea was rising. Along the base of the wall was a kind of ditch into which the effluent from the pipe trickled when it ran off the rocks. The ditch was scattered with litter, bits of clothing, the top of a two-piece bathing suit, odd shoes, milkshake cartons, cardboard and plastic containers for French fries and coleslaw, a pair of broken sunglasses, all the detritus of humanity-by-the-sea, as well as with cases of empty beer bottles, bottles and cans of all kinds, crushed

cans and smashed bottles. Some of the gulls were foraging along
there, strutting in their absurd, stately way through the garbage,
jabbing suddenly and ferociously into the slop, swallowing down
cold French fries and bloated hamburger bun, the rusty liquid
squirting down their necks. As I watched, one of them flew up,
squawking, surprised by the first small splash of sea that trickled
through the barrier of rocks. Within minutes the sea was pouring
into the ditch, slapping silently against the wall of the building itself,
lifting the garbage from its trough to be carried outward and away.
A dozen gulls were scattered among the highest of the rocks. And at
last the sound was gone, separated into the single cries of twelve,
eleven, ten, tenacious, outraged creatures.

When the last five gulls rose into the air, the sea returned none
of them a perch. They circled awhile, exasperated, screaming
remonstrance. Four of them flew upward to the roof. The fifth
landed a foot from my left hand. It stood there making a kind of
kneading movement with its feet, gripping and ungripping its claws
on the ragged concrete. There was no sound, except its claws
scratching. The sea itself, climbing the outside wall, was utterly
silent, unless the conch-roar in my ears belonged rightly to it. I will
not, I told myself, take the corridor to the elevator and climb the
stairs to meet the gulls on the roof. They will only fly away. Whereas
this is for me. Like the pain in my ankle, like the stares of these
creatures, like the loss of my wife, this drowning is mine.

When the first splash of sea water came over the ragged sill, the
gull flew up into the night and I stepped back deeper into the room.
The water spread across the floor as calmly as if it came from an
overflowing sink. The gull was back on the ledge, watching me. He
lifted again and that time a good foot of water came over the sill. I
was almost to the doors, backing up, not knowing how to do this.
The water splashed against my ankles, soothing the strained one. I
backed through the swining doors into the corridor. The next swell
burst them open and caught me at knee level. I turned and waded
with the flow. The next one almost knocked me over, and the next
would have, but I was running down the unlit corridor that ran at
right angles past the elevator into darkness. I have never run into
pitch darkness before. It's madness, but I couldn't think of anything
else.

The watchman was there in the darkness, oblivious to me, like an image in a dream. Keys hung on a chain around his neck, an old man's turkey-gobbler neck, but the face was young, my grandfather's face, a boy's, sticking out of his uniform. And Anne was there, though I couldn't see her, alive without me, what was left of me. The pain had risen from my ankle, my right leg consumed by it, I was floundering. It wasn't a gun the watchman held out to me but a set of keys he'd drawn from his pocket while already turning away, my car keys, which I couldn't see but knew by the feel of the plastic cube (with the red swan inside) were mine. The watchman was gone, Anne was gone. I looked up. A slat of grey. I must, I remember thinking, be at the bottom of a canal. Were the iron doors of the lock ahead of me, or behind? My ankle gave out. I got to my knees in a field of mud that stank like sewage and hung above itself in patches of grey-black mist. The air was murky, the silence a great pressure. I thought my eardrums would burst. I thought I must have been my grandfather in the trenches. Hell at low tide, he used to say. The iron doors of the lock were closing behind me. I could see them, towering fifty feet over my head. I could see whatever I wanted to see. I could see piles of jagged blocks and slabs of concrete rising out of the mud-mist, and the tires, where the mist cleared, more than I could count; I could see seaweed, green and slippery, combed flat against the pocks and bumps in the mud; I could see fish flopping and gasping, some of them tangled in the weeds, some lying still, mouths going, in shallow puddles; I could see crayfish, hundreds of crayfish scattering before me; I could see boats, one enormous one like an iron bathtub two thirds under mud, and smaller ones, the wood rotted sharp like tines of an old pitchfork, like ribs exposed, like something human, and fibreglass and even aluminum boats, their motors half collapsed, all scummy and sadly draped in weeds; and I could see from where I knelt, my head and shoulders alone above the mist, the rest of my body invisible, even to me, more than twenty cars, hulks now, shells, driven off the pier for how many years? Even mine was there, just arrived, past the axels in mud, facing me. I unlocked it and crawled in. The seat was dry. I fastened the seat belt, which jams. I would not be out of it so soon. I wound down all four windows. I turned on the radio. The seagulls were broadcasting, in their wisdom, in their savagery, a hundred feet above. I leaned out my window and looked straight up. Nothing. Murk. I started the engine and roared away in neutral. I put it in gear and spun the tires. I turned off the radio and waited for the sea to emerge from behind its iron doors. When they parted, the water seemed to hesitate for a moment and then come sliding out from under itself. At first it rushed past the windows of my car as if it had other things to do, but finally it got around to me. And I was so relieved, because I couldn't have done it myself.

JOYCE CAROL OATES

Small Miracles

After the first death there is a shrinking.
Miracles to fit in a spoon.
The sun rolling free and crazy as the wheel of a baby buggy
        decades old.
The patchwork macaw in the children's zoo dipping
            its oversized beak up and down, up and down,
            merely to amuse.
The God of Trash flinging himself broken to the sidewalk.
The minutes that drain away noisily as we sleep.

Death?—but it was only a piercing, the fleeing
            thread through a needle's eye,
or the shy escape of steam that coalesces
on the first cold surface.

After the first death there is stillness.
The gaps of night between street lamps.

Hard-packed earth that turns to mud, and
      then to earth again, baked by the sun.
After the first death there is a pause.
And then the second death: a pause,
and the third.
This is what we have always known, but forget.

Is each subsequent death easier, one yearns to ask.

ROBERT BRINGHURST

Six Epitaphs

Malmsbury, 881 A.D.,
Erigena, aged about seventy,
stabbed with a pen
in finibus mundi, "for heresy."

Ephesos, 475 B.C.,
Herakleitos, called atrabilious, called
the obscure, sweating out his last fever
on the barnfloor, lathered to the ears in new manure.

Hunan, 289 B.C.,
Ch'ü Yüan, finding air insufficient
for certain syllables, taking
the springwater into his lungs.

Shensi, 90 B.C.,
Ssu-ma Ch'ien, his left hand hovering
where his balls had been and his beard going, still pushing
the brush, bringing the record to its end.

Weimar, 1832 A.D., not
stared down, staring back, nor even
staring, gütburgerlich Goethe simply
peering in at it, muttering
for more light, more light, more light, another angle.

Sicily, 456 B.C.,
a stone in the wheat stubble speaking
for Aeschylus, charging in summary: only
seacoast trees and surviving
enemies be permitted to praise him.

KENNETH SHERMAN

Lepers

Note how each face rots identical:
cartilage goes first
the nose caves in
the ears wither.

The skin about the skull
shrinks

pulling the mouth back
into a forced grin.

Leprosy
I am told
is the least contagious
of all the diseases.

Leprosy
is a live glimpse
of that stinking sameness
we all break down to.

PONDICHERRY, INDIA

JOYCE MARSHALL

The Escape

She had always felt that if she could just get herself out and the door closed, it would be over. And it was. It even seemed to her, as she gave the knob the sharp up and sideways thrust it needed, that Rolfe and the boys were all in the house together, she was shutting them in and away with the furniture, most of her clothes and the key ring she'd placed at the last moment on the table with her note. Which, any way you looked at it, was nonsense. Rolfe and John were out with their own lives. And Peter—surely she didn't have to remind herself that Peter was lost, had never even lived in this house on the barren street.

She felt no relief, just surprised at having moved at last after so much delay. And why today of all days should have become her time to leave she couldn't say. Except that quite suddenly, right after lunch on this early summer afternoon, she'd been able for the first time to *see* herself going, getting into the taxi with her little bag, unnoticed by neighbours she'd never troubled to know.

She'd always found it hard to see the future, had wondered whether others too had this difficulty, felt as firmly fastened to the present as if something grew down from their feet to the centre of the earth. But now that she'd broken free, the plan she'd made with such care and examined again and again would carry her, she felt sure. There was a flight leaving for Toronto in an hour; with any luck she'd get a seat. As she did. True, she hadn't had time to go to the bank, but there was enough of the month's housekeeping money left to tide her over till she got a job. No problem there. She'd never had trouble finding work in unknown cities. She'd kept her shape, which was trim enough though skimpy, her swiftness of movement — important when you could no longer claim to be really young — and her looks such as they were, a matter chiefly of small simple features and good eyes. And her skills — typing, shorthand, office practice — she'd kept those too. Except when the boys were little she'd always worked. Until these last two years in Sudbury, of course, when she hadn't wanted to work or even go out of the house, had formed the habit of returning to bed and sleep as soon as she was alone. Rolfe had never suspected. Or had he? It hadn't seemed important. . . . "Tired?" he used to ask sometimes, struck probably by her heavy eyes and hair too quickly combed. And she would reply that she was or wasn't tired, whichever occurred to her first. . . . Sleep had held her longer and longer, till three o'clock, till four. Then deserted her a few weeks ago, leaving her to lie all day in her darkened room, listening, feeling, trying to make that first tiny movement that would take her away. . . .

The plane was not large and they were rather rapidly airborne. But she did not look down, did not want a farewell view or anything else of Sudbury.

"I don't think I'd have liked it under any circumstances," she told the man beside her. "All that rock bursting up everywhere. And the ground that should be solid, cut under you with passages, rooms. And all those miners down there, hacking away with picks, tunnelling, deepening..."

She stopped, astonished that she should have said such a thing to this stranger (dull—salesman?—absorbed in papers from briefcase). But before he could answer, if he meant to, the stewardess was at their side wtih coffee and soon a blare of sound was telling them that seatbelts, scarcely unfastened, must be fastened again. Such a tiny flight, she thought, a mere polevault from life to life.

She'd never lived in Toronto, which was one of her reasons, apart from its closeness, for choosing it now. But even so she had found a job and an apartment in a week. Rolfe used to chide her in the days before they almost stopped talking to one another: "My God, Inez, why don't you get something for once you can put your teeth into?" And she'd answer with one of the little formulae she'd used to cover doubt, that home was her real job, she didn't want anything to take her attention from that. (How fraudulent I've been, she thought. When have I spoken as myself? What is my self?) Now that she was going to be alone with no one to please or try to copy, she must find work that would call out more of her. But first she'd have to discover what there was in her to call. Meanwhile the summer replacement job in the typing pool of the insurance company would do very well. The apartment on the downtown street would also do. Tacky with chrome and vinyl, it could be rented by the week without a lease. It would take time to learn what her tastes were. Learn or perhaps find them.

She discovered that she thought very seldom of Rolfe and John, almost as if they'd been rubbed out behind her. That was what always happened to past people and places with her. They went somewhere out of her reach. Perhaps because she'd had to move so often in her marriage with Rolfe. And going back, the few times she'd tried to, a mistake. Bulldozers had been at work; friends had new vocabularies and interests, told stories about strangers. It had begun to seem better just to walk away. But she'd have to think quite soon of Rolfe and John. Arrangements must be made, her clothes sent for. Her note had said simply that she knew what she was doing, they weren't to worry, she'd be in touch when the time came. She tried sometimes because she knew she should, to imagine Rolfe reading those scrawled lines, discussing them wtih John, who was old enough now, eighteen, to be included. (John his iron father's son, as Peter had seemed hers.) She even made words for them to say to each other but, rather as if this were a book she was writing not very skillfully, the words rang false.

The three days between her hiring and having to present herself at the typing pool she used getting in a telephone, arranging for the transfer of her bank account, buying sheets and things for the kitchen. Because it had always been her way to make lists and hurry, she forced herself simply to wander about, buying things as she thought of them. She knew two or three people in Toronto — people met on the zig-zagging journey Rolfe's work had taken her across Canada — but she didn't intend to look them up. Here there were strangers to know, she saw them walking the streets, tied to this single act as strangers always seem to be. She could not be alone forever. But if she felt no eagerness yet about not being alone, this didn't trouble her; eagerness was for later when she'd found whatever there was in her to find.

It was sticky-hot so there was no temptation to slip into her old habit of sleeping, even on these nothing days. She slept very little, in fact, lying for hours listening to the unknown sounds of the unfamiliar street, as enclosed and safe in the single moment as in her small high-windowed ground-floor room. After the last night, the hottest, she was up with the sun at five, with the sense that she hadn't slept or even moved. She felt stiff but a bath loosened and softened her. She seemed not to have thought either, recalled, could almost feel, the long interval of lying while time moved over her . . . and underneath the tunnels ran, connected, edged apart, the earth was porous with them, evil honeycomb . . . But that's what I came away from, she thought and sprang out of the tub, dried herself, dressed quickly, She was calm again as she did her hair. It was early still, she'd walk to the office, eat nearby, to enjoy the cool before the tarry heat took hold. Not to avoid having to take the subway. The violence of the denial shocked her and she said to herself (said it aloud even): Why not be honest? I'm free now to think anything, admit anything. She didn't like the subway, didn't like the sense of being drawn headlong through a tunnel, nothing to breathe but the powdery stench of perfumed deodorant over sweat. And she feared it. Feared going underground. Admit that. Admit everything. No one was watching now. No one could hear her thoughts.

The first day, as she'd expected, was very slow. She and the others hired for the summer were assigned lunch hours and coffee breaks, given desks with typewriters, left to sit. Then, with some apology, she was asked whether she'd mind going with five or six others to the filing room. Just for a few days. She didn't mind. She was the oldest there, much the oldest, and felt suddenly terribly visible, surrounded on every side by streaming hair plunging to shoulders, waists, submerging faces. Peter's girls, she thought, unnerved by them as she used to be when she was till Peter's mother in Saskatoon. Peter. His face flicked before her — that fair, seemingly open face and little smile. Then it withdrew. It was not her fault he had turned as he had turned. Rolfe was wrong, she hadn't pampered and babied the boy. Failed finally, of course, but that was an entirely different thing. She thrust the thought away — or perhaps it was the thought that relinquished her — and after a minute or two she picked up a bundle of folders and began to file them. Finalized accident claims, she was told. Some were very bulky, Without curiosity she filed — for the rest of the morning and all the afternoon, It was too soon to think about Peter or about anything.

"It's still too soon." She repeated the words two evenings later when her new phone rang for the first time, splitting the little room.

"But Rolfe's frantic, Inez. And John — don't you even care about John? — he's frantic too. They're afraid you're — ill."

"Don't you mean crazy?" Inez laughed. She'd been washing her hair, it hung forward, wetting the phone, her chest, the table. She might have realized Rolfe would be able to track her down. People knew people in Sudbury, she'd transferred her bank account, Rolfe had found out where, had rung through to Ruth, who'd been his secretary the first year, used to come to the house. What had the girl looked like? A lot of hair? One of the young submerged?

"I *will* get in touch," she said. "I told him that. I told him in my note."

"Then do it right away, Inez. Please. It's been hard on him too, haven't you realized — ?" She paused. Inez mopped her head with the towel, still trying to fit some kind of face, even submerged, to this voice that called itself Ruth. "Hasn't it occurred to you that he also cares about — Peter, not even knowing where he — ? My God, what kind of woman are you anyway, Inez?"

I don't know, Inez almost said and: How come you know so much about Peter? It's not like Rolfe to talk — talk to a secretary. Then it came to her. "You two were sleeping together," she said and when there was only silence, "Weren't you? Weren't you?"

"Yes," Ruth said rather faintly, "we were. My God, he needed me. Someone. Haven't you any idea how badly he needed someone?"

"Yes," Inez said, "I suppose he did. Yes, I suppose so. But Ruth, don't call again. I don't think you belong in this. I don't think you belong in it anywhere," and still no further at remembering what the girl looked like, which was odd when you thought of it, repeated that she would write to Rolfe, she would do it when the time came.

The discovery wasn't a shock to her. It wasn't anything really, just one more thing tunnelling underground, making the crust of earth thinner. Had Rolfe had many affairs? At once she knew he had. He'd always been a very sexual creature. She'd accepted this as she'd accepted the iron in him. the firmness, sureness. And once she'd found that sex wasn't really a joining, not for her, she'd done what she must, in this as in everything. Always till the loss of Peter, done what she must.

She went into the bathroom, combed her hair, decided not to roll it, just let it dry out loose. Next day she went into the filing department wearing jeans and a bra-less shirt. None of the submerged little creatures smiled or seemed even to notice. She felt less conspicuous, which was what she wanted. To disappear in a sense, while she thought her own thoughts about the remnant of her forty-six-year-old life. The next morning she came in without makeup, slipped off her sandals and went barefoot about the room. She had always thought it important to be neat, buy what was in fashion, turn her head over to a hairdresser. Now she discovered that what the young said was true; clothes did change you. She began to move more lazily and freely, not so conscious of her firmness of outline, and to speak less sharply. It seemed to her that the little creatures no longer circled around her, visible adult lump.

After a week or so, because the grey in her greeny-brown hair stood out so when it was loose, she bleached it, was startled by the sharp lemony colour when she took off the towel, the way the tan she had gathered walking to and from the office sprang up ruddy. What am I doing? she asked the strange dark face with the pale lips within the straight-combed lines of lemony hair. What madness to think, even fugitively, that she should become one of those little creatures. Or that she could. She didn't even like them. They frightened her. All so muted and, in some way she couldn't catch hold of, knowing. Like those murmuring veiled little beings Peter used to bring to the house in Saskatoon. And Inez would try to draw some words from behind the screen of hair. Feeling so timorous, unreal.

Nothing new about that. When had she ever felt real? It seemed to her that all her life she had felt like an imposter and that at any moment someone was going to tell her she didn't belong, didn't belong anywhere in life, she should leave all this to someone who could handle it. She used to wonder as a child whether anyone else felt that way. would try to imagine a time when she might know someone well enough to ask. When she met Rolfe, she'd actually thought of asking him. No use. It was clear he felt no such thing. Still she'd have liked to tell him, tell someone. But she'd always been good at making motions, finding grooves for herself, appearing happy, She wondered now whether her own mother, who'd always seemed as firm and definite as Rolfe, had been just as timorous in secret, as afraid of her own children as Inez had always been of hers. From the beginning. Peter, laid in her arms for the first time, had looked at her briefly, looked away, as if he were thinking: Who are you? Where is my real mother? She'd continued to feel this about both boys as she urged them, dutiful, to do their homework, wash before supper, that someday they were going to turn to her and say: But who on earth are you?

No wonder she'd always missed the signals. Hadn't understood about Ruth. And all the others there must have been. Hadn't realized what was beginning to go wrong with Peter — Peter who'd always seemed so open even though quiet, smiling his little smile. Not because she'd pampered the boy. She'd merely tried to look after and understand him, John too, give them both what boys should have from mothers, without ever quite knowing what that was. She'd loved them, no one could say she hadn't loved them, their smooth bodies and faces, shadowy beginnings of beards, loved to look at them and, as long as they would permit it, hold them. She just hadn't known what she was supposed to do with them. So Peter could become a pusher, quite a considerable one, right in their house and under her nose. And if Rolfe had blamed her for any of the right things in those first terrible moments when they sat alone after the boy's arrest, she might have confessed what had been wrong with her from the beginning — not being too indulgent, too meticulous in mothering and housekeeping but simply a person who seemed to have been born with certain lacks. He might not have forgiven her but he'd have realized that she would have done more and better if she could. Because though she'd been aware of dangers, no one could have been more aware, she'd missed the one essential clue — all those people coming to see Peter, that parade of feet down to the basement room. Anyone else would have known what that meant.

The boy understood, of course . . . "I don't want you," he'd said when she visited him in the training school . . . "I know you don't," she almost said. "You saw through me, didn't you. From the very first." . . . But Peter was looking past her, saying he didn't want the old man either. And he was still smiling. He was smiling when she left him. (Who is this boy, she'd asked herself, who was able to be deceitful for so long? She no longer knew what she'd thought him.) . . . So Rolfe had arranged a transfer and they moved to Sudbury. Which they shouldn't have done, she felt . . . "He'll come to us," Rolfe kept saying. "When he wants us he'll come to us." . . . But he hadn't. They'd only known of his release when her last letter was returned. They should have stayed closer. She could have gone through the motions of trying to visit. People might say they didn't want you but that didn't mean they wanted you to forsake them. Or did it? She didn't know and, because she didn't, couldn't find words for why they ought to stay. When she wrote the letter that still had to be written to Rolfe, she must get right down to the nub of it: "I'm sorry. I've never been able to be open or spontaneous because I've never quite known how to be a person. People like me do great damage. You and John will be better without me."

At intervals during the hot, monotonous but oddly safe summer she tried to imagine what they were doing. Rolfe used to reach home at half past five; John's summer playground job kept him out till six. She tried to picture them in the house together or walk them out of it, fit Rolfe into his car, turn John to the right, then down the street to the bus. She couldn't. Their shapes, remembered as shapes but only shapes, were stiff and heavy. Even their names turned strange at times, hung flapping in her mind, empty letters.

She grew more and more careless about her appearance, bought cheaper and flimsier T-shirts, left her toenails jagged. She did not plan any of this. It happened. And perhaps because of this sloppiness, she was left all summer in the filing room. She was one of the best filers, she was told, it would be a pity to shift her. And she *was* good, speaking in her new lazy voice only when spoken to, strict about lunches and coffee breaks. She liked routine. She always had. And though some of the little creatures looked inside the folders, discussed various accidents rather learnedly with one another in their low flat voices, she never did.

They saw her, she came to feel, as a more or less silent older sister. It was good to have a place she didn't have to work for. She usually lunched now with a group of them in the sunny square at City Hall, buying cokes and chips as they did, learning things that surprised but did not shock her, perhaps because she never managed to believe in their lives away from the filing room. Most of them had well-off parents — fathers like Rolfe, she supposed, mothers like the mother she'd tried to be. There was a Mary, a Sharon, two Cindies, a Victoria, but in spite of their different names and various sizes, they were, she felt, interchangeable. But they were unhappy, many of them, or puzzled, and when they confided, in her or in her presence, she listened. Listened, looked at what she'd heard, then forgot it. That one of the Cindies had had two abortions, the Sharon had hitch-hiked through Morocco with what Inez could only think of as very unsuitable companions. And still had an infant smile. It was remarkable how little people expected of others. That they listen without interrupting. Not much else. Or did she mean that it was remarkable how little people could get away with giving to others? Now that she no longer tried very hard, it was strange that no one found her indifferent. And yet she was, alarmingly so, she sometimes felt. And then would make the sort of effort she used to make, to care about something one of the Cindies or the Mary was saying, imagine her as a real self who walked away from the filing room at night to— She could never follow. Never. But because she made so few efforts nowadays, it frightened her to try and fail. And it was always after such attempts that she would lie in her bed or her bath and try to move those straw shapes of Rolfe and John down the walk of the Sudbury house. And she would think again about the letter that must explain everything and that she still wasn't ready to write.

But on the whole the summer was safe. The ground was as solid, probably, as it would ever be for her. All the motions required of her were easy. She was surrounded. Didn't stand out. For the first time in her life she didn't stand out. By August she was thinking less and less frequently of the old life, though she did sometimes wonder what the autumn would bring and why she didn't think more actively about the autumn. One by one, as September approached, the little creatures left, the Mary to spend the last of the holidays lazing at the family summer cottage, the Victoria just to goof about the house. It seemed to her that she was saying goodbye to the same half-hidden face again and again. (Yet they had told different stories, which she ought to remember.) They said in turn that they'd liked knowing her and hoped they'd see her again. In these last minutes, she realized, they were certainly not seeing her as one of their own a little older. Perhaps they'd never seen her as this for as they said finally "Have a good winter," they were all wearing that little smile of good but withholding children. (The smile she'd grown so used to seeing on Peter's face. Had she been wrong about the summer? Deliberately been quiet, unobtrusive hoping to discover something? Understand something for the first time in her life? Well, too late now. She'd missed the clues. If there'd been clues.) And now there would have to be winter. After the safe summer would come wind and rain, snow, freezing, slop. The ground would turn treacherous. She would have to find other more stimulating work. Make a life that had some sense to it.

She was asked to stay on in the filing department.

"Granted it's not much of a job, Inez. It might lead to more but honestly I can't make any promises. But you know the ropes and there's a vacancy. So. Unless you have other plans?"

"I have no plans," Inez said.

"Fine then, we're glad to have you. Oh and Inez . . ." The woman clearly didn't like saying this, was trying to make light of it. "We're a bit freer summers because of the student help. But really, don't you think women of her age . . . ?" And her eyes took in Inez's hair, loose figure, unkept fingernails.

She might as well stay. Take it easy for a little longer. Weak of her perhaps but she found that she couldn't feel very alarmed about being weak. Or particularly stung by the supervisor's words and look. Whatever she was supposed to feel, she couldn't feel it. Perhaps she was simply through with feeling. Or feeling was through with her. Perhaps this was the sort of nothing future that had always lain ahead of her—an efficient filer of other people's accident claims.

She felt cold on the walk home. She hadn't brought a coat from Sudbury or even a warm sweater. She must send for her clothes, explain herself finally to Rolfe. If she could. She seemed no closer to finding words than she'd ever been. . . . My failure . . . my inability . . . never able to be quite, do what others . . . forget me . . . just forget me . . .

And in the hall outside her door she found two great cartons—her clothes, her parents' photographs, the things that had stood on her dresser. Rolfe and John must have scoured the house for everything that belonged to her—bits of cream in jars, run-down slippers, a finger painting of Peter's she'd hoarded in the back of her cupboard.

No note. Just a letter in her box from a firm of lawyers. Only lawyers could have such names, she thought, turning it over in her hand—McTavish, Narkowski, Simpson, and Bolduc. She didn't open it at once; she could guess what it would say. She would have to search out lawyers of her own to send an answer, names to match these. It was all out of her hands now, she was safe. She wouldn't have to write to Rolfe, try to dig right down to the heart of her failure, find some sort of explanation that first would satisfy herself.

DOUGLAS BARBOUR

a waiting

always so goddamnd awkward   look
it shd flow

cant even hug
others right   awk

ward   move to
ward them

off   should be

touching   close
holding
on   always

so goddamnd   awkward

i cd cry .

for phyllis webb, 12.5.74

long beach   walk
walk into the mind
's misty questions

a haze of   possible

logs   sand   rock

/dont worry dont
question
anything
                now

Jack Chambers —'Nude' 74-76

it is an empty room .   it is
the artist's studio .   it is not
empty   the presence of the young woman fills it
the artist present too   &   perhaps
we are present in the aery spaces of the empty room .

there is a radiator along the left side wall   a
radiator along the back wall   they are very
straight   &   the edges of the floor are clear .
the windows high to the young woman's right
almost glow   they are white   they are the light
floating into the room .   the back wall is there
you can see the wall sockets   the paint that's been
swathed on in testing for colour   a paper stuck onto
the wall .   it is not there .   it is there .   it's not there
he has painted the air .   solid & fleeting like the time
of the woman who stands there to stare out at   us .

the wall fades   the linoleum shifts beneath her feet
in/substantial .   the lunar landing site   bright in
                space/
the earth parent & waiting for rain .   & again
there is presence .   & light .   & delight in the forms .
she is there .   she is body bodying forth
all the life he can see   he can paint
what he sees   what he sees
is much more than at first   we would
know of a young woman naked
alone in a large sunlit room where the walls
open out to the cosmos .

& she stands with her body
a system of brush strokes   a series of planes
& curve of muscle   of flesh

the painting refuses to
hold all in place

yet it places each element
all four held together
all contraries gatherd
into one   that light
in the body

             that body
in the light

as the room   & the artist   &
the woman   within
hustle thru space to
the time of the stars
to the time of the eye
which has seen   & expresst
in the colours & patterns
of oil on canvas
that all this once was

& it opens   it
opens   the wall
is so solid & yet   where the corner
would be   is   a   light
& the mind of the painter
his sight   his delight
is   all there
with the woman
who stands & is solid
is present   as human
in   a space   that is only
a room   full of space   those
boundless bounds opening   we all know
in our hearts   to be there .

14.4.77 — 24.5.77

the poem & the policeman:

for hans jewinski

the poem as outlaw:
poets & fool saints
following the words through
the wall   maybe?
getting away
                    with what?

copping a plea:
please officer,   the poems say,
if youd only listen
this time to the sung words perhaps
youd understand

            and perhaps you do.

so where are you
now   o policeman

high,   & gone
en paroles/

but language is not
a prison   is it

and their words
shall make them free

in the shade of
the poetry

the subtle reverberations
of dark & light,
shift   continuous
of meaning .

on parole
where the cop & the poet
meet on the beat
& exchange
                    words .

HANS JEWINSKI

!:—;; My Theme

the chase is real
even if my theme
music doesn/t cut
in as the engine
makes the car jump

the chase is real
even if the dispatcher
repeats 'use caution 5107'
'keep up your location 5107'
in most un-hollywood fashion

the needle climbs
and the tires squeal
through long blind curves
and quick stops

i can only see the
tail-lights 'give us
a licence number 5107'
'keep up your location 5107'

westbound on queen st
in rush-hour traffic
the mustang is running
all the lights — then
the wrong way on a one way
through a busy parking lot
over a curb   grass   through
a hedge   and a pedestrian
nearly stays in the way

'let him go 5107'   yeah
follow policy 5107 'disregard
5107' 'your location 5107'
don/t get any bystanders hurt

'your location 5107'
i turn off my red light
i lower my highbeams
and tell the dispatcher
i/m discontinuing the chase
'last direction of travel 5107'
last direction of travel 5107

don/t let it get personal
forget it — just another chase
'your location . . . '

my guts tied in a knot
i pull to the side of the road
and turn off the blaring radio
just another chase   and the theme
music in my veins boils over
and i vomit all over the dash

JIM CHRISTY

New Living Quarters

There is a traffic island where Parliament Street meets Gerrard and when people with money began moving to this area of the city which historically is an area where people have no money, or very little, the powers that be decided the traffic island should be fixed up. A fountain was built in the middle of the triangle and it was surrounded by geraniums, sod was laid, trees planted, and benches installed. It looked very nice but, of course, the people with money do not use the park as a meeting place. The bums, drunks, derelicts, and the old people with no money do.

That's what McGarrity, Ossie, and Barney Bay, among others, were doing one cold Saturday evening in late October. They were sitting close together on a bench facing Parliament Street and sharing a bottle of Napoleon Port. Ossie coughed from time to time and wiped his nose on the cuff of his overcoat, which was very old and very dirty and much too big for him. When he reached for the bag containing the bottle you couldn't see his hand, it was as if a handless sleeve was holding the bottle. McGarrity noticed this and made a joke of it; "Say, Ossie, why don't you put your collar over your head and you'll look like a ghost. A ghost in a Goodwill overcoat."

"Hell," said Barney Bay, "it's so cold even a ghost needs a coat on."

"Yeah," agreed McGarrity. "It's colder than a witch's left tit, ain't it?"

Little Ossie hacked and coughed from deep down in his gray old overcoat.

Barney Bay said, "If he looks so much like a ghost, maybe he could go over there to the fucking Chateau Gai and scare somebody into giving him a bottle."

McGarrity grunted and took the bottle from him. He didn't know his drinking buddy's name. No one else seemed to either. They just knew he came from a little fishing village in Newfoundland called Barney's Bay. It didn't matter anyway.

"Anybody got a butt?" Ossie asked in a raspy voice punctuated by a sniff.

"Nah."

McGarrity saw that there were two guys waiting for the streetcar at the corner and he got up and walked over to them. McGarrity wasn't all that far gone and he still maintained a bit of what it takes to get along, or rather a remembrance of the things it takes. He knew people here and there and he had certain capabilities. Nevertheless his hair was dirty and his clothes were dirty and his face was probably dirty too, but he had spent so much time of his life out of doors and thus his face was so dark you could not tell whether it was really dirty or not. He had not eaten this day, and the day before his only food was an order of French fries, which he had bought, and a sandwich, which was given to him at a church on Jarvis Street.

He checked the men out; one wore an overcoat and carried an umbrella. McGarrity didn't bother with him but approached the other who was in work boots and a macinaw and had a face like he had lived his whole life in the east end. The guy leaned his face away from McGarrity's breath but fished two cigarettes from out of a pack he took from his shirt pocket. McGarrity thanked him profusely as he backed away.

McGarrity gave one to Ossie and lit both with a wooden match he ignited with a thumbnail. McGarrity was dressed in the pants from one suit and the coat from another and he had a Paisley scarf around his neck. Barney Bay handed him the bottle, which was almost dead, and sang out, "I'se the bye . . . " and then he quit and giggled to himself.

Ossie coughed and spat and there were specks of red in the phlegm.

"He caught cold in his new living quarters," Barney Bay told McGarrity.

"His new living quarters? What are they like?"

"Are they ever nice. Ossie got green broadloom all around and a garden and a good view of the property."

"You don't say? And what would the name of this place be where he's living?"

"It's called Allan Gardens."

They laughed and Barney Bay hooted and sang, "I'se the bye. . ."

"It ain't so fuckin' funny," Ossie muttered and wiped his nose. His eyes were bloodshot. "I slept out three nights in a row and it rained the other night. I think I caught the fuckin' pneumonia."

"You oughta go to the clinic."

"It's closed," said McGarrity and he looked over to the Chateau Gai store and nodded toward it. "And it's closed too. Six o'clock. Stupid. I'm gonna move to Vancouver where a man can get a drink. You ever been to Vancouver?"

"Sure, I been to Vancouver," answered Barney Bay and he thought of a song. "I been everywhere, man. Cross the. . . cross the desert fair, man. . . I been everywhere."

Barney finished off the bottle and tossed it into the wire basket flanking the bench. "Fuck it. Whatta we do now? Wanna go try the Gerrard?"

"I don't think we could get served."

"We can try."

"What about him?" McGarrity indicated Ossie, who responded with a fit of coughing that flushed his face red and caused a vein to stand out on his forehead.

"Let's take him. Maybe he can stand in the hallway if we can get in for a drink and that way he'll stay warm."

They each grabbed hold of one of Ossie's arms and helped him up. He struggled his arms free. "I can make it on my own."

In back of them, lying on some faded orange geraniums, was a fat Indian woman in stretch pants and a nylon windbreaker who definitely could not make it on her own. She would struggle to a position on her hands and knees and hold the pose for a moment before collapsing again into the flowers.

An old man sat on another bench with his dog. It was a brown and white mutt and it was feebly supporting its considerable aged weight on bandy little legs. The old man patted the dog and held its leash, a length of rope, in a trembling hand.

The rag-tag trio of McGarrity, Ossie, and Barney Bay made their way toward the Gerrard House Tavern. McGarrity the leader, Ossie the sickly one, and Barney Bay, good for a laugh. They were a sorry sight in their stinking clothes but they weren't the sorriest sight.

McGarrity and Barney Bay went through their pockets and went through Ossie's pockets and discovered they had enough for a couple of drafts. As they approached the tavern two middle-aged women came out in their curlers, overcoats open to reveal the bulge of stomach over their crotches. They'd probably been going to the Gerrard House since just after the war when they were Cabbagetown beauties competing for the returning soldiers. They crossed Gerrard Street to Regent Park.

Ossie spied a beer bottle near the door, bent down, and took aim on it. He swayed back and forth and moved his hand around in the vicinity of the bottle like one of those mechanical hands you try to grab prizes with in the carnival. Finally he latched on to it and rose in a spasm of coughing. Barney Bay pounded him on the back, which just made him cough more. They waited for him to finish and when he did he raised the bottle for a drink. It was half full and there was a cigarette butt floating on top of the beer. They made Ossie put the bottle in his coat pocket and they went in.

They were greeted by the usual noise. It was too early for the band but looking down the narrow hallway past the washrooms you could see the place was packed and hear the shouts, the arguing, the laughter, and the sound of bottles and glasses meeting Formica. To the right of the entrance a young lady, barely twenty, was screaming into the phone at somebody she considered to be an "asshole."

The bouncer hove into view and positioned himself at the end of the hallway and the entrance to the beverage room. Ossie and McGarrity decided they would have to hide Ossie in the men's washroom before trying to get into the room. They waited for the bouncer to make his circuit and then they hustled Ossie down the hall and into the washroom.

The floor was wet with urine and covered with toilet paper. The toilets needed flushing and men had pissed on the seats. They set Ossie on one of the seats and he didn't complain. He fumbled in his pocket for his bottle and coughed into his sleeve.

McGarrity ran the water at one of the sinks and threw some on his face. Barney Bay wet his hands and ran them through his thinning and tangled hair. They tried to make themselves respectable enough for the Gerrard Tavern.

Two young men flung open the door and one was saying, "Next time I'm gonna put the boots to that cocksucker."

His buddy approached the sinks to check his hair in the mirror and said, "Out of the way, you fucking rubbies."

Barney Bay bowed his head and edged away and McGarrity

moved but said, "You don't have to talk to us like that. We're not bothering you."

"What was that? What did you say, you fucking wino bastard?"

McGarrity didn't reply, he turned and followed Barney Bay out the door and heard the guys laughing.

The bouncer wasn't looking so they hustled into the beverage room and took the first vacant table, which was near the stage and separated from the dance floor by a railing. The waiter, in black pants and white shirt sleeves rolled up to show beefy forearms, passed them by without a glance. McGarrity and Barney sat there quitely. When the waiter made his next circuit and was passing them again McGarrity called to him as humbly as possible and asked for two drafts. The waiter looked them over and grimaced as he decided on his move. They were filthy all right and smelled pretty badly but they didn't seem all that drunk. "You got any money?"

McGarrity and Barney Bay nodded like supplicant children.

"Well, look, see that table over there? Go sit over there in the corner."

McGarrity and Barney Bay got up dutifully and walked to the table the waiter had indicated. They seemed to glide around the edges of the room as if keeping in the shadows and took their seats at a place no one wanted behind a post.

They removed the coins from their pockets and held them in their palms while they counted. The coins looked tiny and insignificant in their dirty hands, yet precious too. Then they placed the nickels together and the dimes together and the one quarter off to a side on the wet Formica table top.

Still, the waiter didn't come with their drafts. They waited ten, fifteen more minutes. Barney Bay cursed under his breath but McGarrity, who was older and used to the treatment, said nothing. Finally they stood and walked out of the room.

"That son of a bitch, who the hell does he think he is? Thinks he's a big shot cause he has a crummy job as a waiter in the Gerrard House. He works there because he's too dumb to get hired in the Royal Oak."

Barney Bay laughed in spite of himself because he thought he had said something pretty damned funny.

They found Ossie sitting in a corner near the urinals, the beer bottle smashed and scattered into pieces about the wet floor. He was hacking and spitting. "Jesus, boys, I'm sick awful bad."

"You want to go to hospital?"

"No, no. I got to have a drink."

"Yeah, me too," said Barney Bay who turned to McGarrity.

"How 'bout that kid you know at the Shopper's Drug Mart. We could get us some Aqua Velva. It's better than rub and he'll give it free, eh?

"Yeah. You wanna do that?"

"Sure fuckin thing, man."

"Okay, let's get him moving."

They got Ossie to his feet and he was able to stumble along and out the door with a little help. He could walk after a fashion but he had to keep stopping to hack and cough, so McGarrity and Barney Bay took him under the arms and led him back to Parliament and around the corner. They walked north and the citizens passed them either looking straight ahead or smirking at them. The Greeks and the Jamaicans had come in the last few years but the Scots and Irish women had always been there. They used to have men at one time or another and now they had four baby bonus checks every month.

They came to the drugstore and McGarrity said to Barney Bay, "Take him into the doorway of the shoestore and wait there. I got to find the kid."

Parliament Street was dark except for the light from the Shopper's Drug Mart and McGarrity stood in that light looking through the windows past the signs for lottery tickets and vitamins. He knew the kid that worked in there. He had no idea how he knew him except that he did and the kid knew his name. McGarrity had probably stopped him on the street one night when the kid was coming home from striking out with his girlfriend and told him his life story. Sometimes McGarrity was given to asking young guys like that whether or not he had met them in Alaska or Australia. He had been to neither. Anyway, at some point or another this particular kid, nineteen or twenty, a nice kid, had taken to saying hello to him on the street and even inquiring as to his health and laying coins on him now and again. Maybe the kid liked to cultivate characters or "neat old guys," as a teen-aged girl had referred to him not too long ago.

McGarrity went into the store and came out a few minutes later with the young man behind him pretending to be throwing him out. When they were on the pavement the kid said, "Gee, McGarrity, don't put me on the spot like that. I could lose my job."

"Sorry, kid. Really appreciate it. It's for my sick friend over there.

He's got the shakes something awful. See you around, buddy."

McGarrity joined Ossie and Barney Bay in the doorway of the shoestore and took one of the four bottles of Aqua Velva out of his jacket pocket. Ossie poured some down his throat and Barney Bay took his drink. McGarrity sucked on the bottle and gave it back to Ossie. He took another bottle out and handed it to Barney Bay.

He had seen guys smash the short neck of the bottle to get at the blue-green liquid, to make it come faster. They would swallow the bits of glass and not give a damn. It wasn't bad, Aqua Velva. Didn't taste any worse than that stuff he had in Japan when he was in the Navy. Sake.

"Let's go down to the park," said Barney Bay.

They crossed Parliament and walked west on Carlton. Barney Bay wiped his mouth. "Ah, this stuff'll knock you out. S'better than rub any day."

They discussed the merits of rub and after shave and other things.

"I saw this Indian this one time. This was down in Delhi, eh? I was picking tobacco. He couldn't get a drink nowheres and he went into this drugstore and tried to buy some after shave but they wouldn't sell it to him and he says, why not? And they told him it was the law. They couldn't sell no after shave to Indians. That's the truth too. It's a law in this province and this Indian he was so goddamned mad he went off the deep end and started wrecking that drugstore. They came and took him away."

Barney Bay contemplated the story he had just related, grunted, and took another swig.

There was a drizzle now and McGarrity thought the street lamps glowed like stars. They walked past a couple of fancy new restaurants and crossed Berkeley and Ontario and down by Bleecker Street he could see the girls hustling outside the greasy spoon on the corner. Cars were parked at the intersection and the girls were working them. On the other side of Carlton Street cars were parked with their lights on and the men inside them watched the scene. There was always at least one man in the cars pulling himself off.

The pimps came and went from the restaurant and the transvestites offered some competition. Behind the steamed and dirty windows, old men sat at the counters surrounding coffee cups and punks commandeered the booths talking tough.

A car going east stopped and a girl came over and opened the door and got in. They watched her, saw a bit of thigh as she got in. They knew she was probably a junkie, dirty as them, and probably queer too but the leg flashed and they had their secret thoughts.

"Hey, McGarrity? When was the last time you had any?"

"Too long ago. And I don't hardly like to think about it."

"What about him?"

They were supporting Ossie who, it seemed, hadn't stopped coughing since they left the Gerrard.

"I can imagine him doing it in the past but I can't see it happening in the future."

"Yeah. Shit, I ain't had nothing in three years except I plugged a faggot in the Hideaway Hotel last Christmas. Near made me sick but I got a couple of bucks out of it, enough for a bottle. And, it was, it was a *person*. And I closed my eyes. You know what I mean?"

McGarrity didn't answer. He looked over at the restaurant. "I would get cleaned up and get a fuckin job and work a whole year without a drink for just one two-minute piece of ass."

"Why don't you?"

"Why don't *you*?"

They both laughed and Barney Bay asked another question. "How old are you?"

"Forty-seven."

"Well, that ain't so bad. But what about me, eh? I'm only thirty-four years old."

As they were passing the church at the corner Ossie seemed to get heavier and then he went limp. He moaned and his eyes rolled back in his head.

"Let's get him over there," McGarrity said and they grunted and dragged him over to the church steps. Ossie lay sprawled on the damp stone and his breath came in shallow wheezing gasps. "This man is sick bad," McGarrity said.

"Shit, what should we do? Give him some more of this stuff?"

"Put some up his nose. Maybe it'll make him come to."

Barney Bay shook some Aqua Velva onto Ossie's upturned nose. Ossie gasped and uttered a sharp cry.

"Maybe we should take him over to the park and lay him down on some newspapers or something and think of what to do."

"Yeah, yeah. Let's do that."

They lifted him and dragged him to Sherbourne Street and across to the park, his shoes scraping along the ground. They dropped him on a bench and Barney Bay collapsed on the ground while McGarrity grabbed papers from a trash basket.

Barney Bay raised himself to his knees and then to his feet and cursed the after shave and the world in general before dutifully taking Ossie under the arm.

"Let's bring him over near the greenhouse."

They dragged Ossie along and no one paid them any attention. Winos passed them, homosexuals, some young toughs wearing their boredom on their faces. They finally got him to a spot away from the street and dropped him by a tree near the greenhouse. They sat down themselves and had another drink and Barney Bay lay on his back repeating, "Jesus . . . oh, Jesus . . . Oh, by Jesus."

McGarrity spread the newspapers out on the ground and they pulled Ossie on to them and rested his head against the tree. They sat down on either side of him and didn't say anything for a few minutes while they caught their breath. Ossie's breath came in short wheezing gasps. Finally Barney Bay said, "You didn't mean that, did you? What you said about getting a job?"

"It doesn't matter whether I want to or not. I couldn't. Even if I was able to get a job I couldn't. Not me. Know what I mean?"

"Yeah. You know what I want to do?"

"No, what?"

"I want to go back to Newfoundland."

"There's no jobs there."

"It don't matter. You can be drunk anywhere, eh? That way I'll be among my own."

"You think you'll do it?"

"No."

They were quiet then for a moment and they took a drink and noticed that the man between them was also quiet. "He's not moving at all."

Barney Bay put his head on Ossie's chest.

"Can you hear his heart?"

"Can't tell."

McGarrity took Ossie's wrist, "Yeah, there's a little bit of pulse. Maybe we should call the ambulance."

"Yeah. You go call. I'm pretty smashed."

"Rub his chest or something."

"Yeah."

Barney Bay started hitting Ossie lightly on the chest and talking to him and McGarrity walked across the park to a pay phone. He came back in a few minutes and Barney Bay held out the bottle of after shave to him, "Here, take a pull."

McGarrity threw his head back and sucked out the blue-green liquid, which no longer stung him going down. He wiped his lips. "How is he?"

"He shit himself."

"Must be dead."

McGarrity went on his knees and put his face close to Ossie's and saw the little man's eyes were open and staring straight ahead.

"Yeah, he's had it."

"I found this in his pockets."

Barney Bay held up a little gold-plated cross."

"He must of been a Catholic," McGarrity said, "Are you a Catholic?"

"Yeah."

"You?"

"Uh-huh. My old man in Sudbury, he wanted me to be a priest."

McGarrity took Ossie's head from the tree and moved his body away from it and laid him flat out on the ground. Then he stood up and they both looked down at Ossie. Barney Bay reached down to close Ossie's eyes but they didn't stay closed and he didn't try again. Instead he folded Ossie's hands across his chest and placed the little gold-plated cross between them. Then he straightened up and crossed himself. McGarrity got the last bottle of Aqua Velva from his pocket, took off the top, and passed it over Ossie's body sprinkling the liquid on him. Then he backed away and Barney Bay crossed himself again.

They heard the wail of the ambulance behind them and turned and saw it coming up Sherbourne with the lights flashing. "Let's get out of here," McGarrity said.

They walked around Ossie's body and started across the park toward Carlton Street.

"He's better off that way," said Barney Bay, looking back.

"Yeah," said McGarrity. "Maybe we can still get a drink."

RAYMOND SOUSTER

Wild Pitch

again for Cid

In that Blue Jays
Red Sox game
one beautiful
one hysterical moment
to stop all cameras —

batter set in the box,
big bat swinging,
sweat of concentration
beading his face;

the catcher crouched,
signal just given
and the big glove ready,
body taut spring
ready to uncoil anywhere;

umpire bent low,
set squarely behind him,
chest mask moved up
underneath his chin,
his attention focused
on that white projectile
soon to hurtle in;

then all three frozen
in one glorious second

when the ball's released
from the pitcher's fingers;

comes bulleting in
to sail high high
higher
over batter
catcher
umpire
six feet above their heads;

with no motion made
so great their disbelief,

all eyes
refusing to look up
to catch
winging high and wide and far

the screwball
that came unscrewed.

DON BAILEY

Offhand Comments

Rushing through the black
Spring night, stones

rattling against
the car's body as if
they resent speed, then
the tires sliding with
protest on to the smooth highway
and beside me, quietly sweating,
a young man filled with
years, his own secrets.

I am returning him
to the prison where he's spent
the last ten years
for killing a policeman.
He hardly remembers the event
and tends to smile awkwardly
when asked about it.
He admits to being drunk,
stupid and young,
perhaps in that order.
He's sorry it happened.
He talks of trying to make up for it,
of starting a new life.
Perhaps ten years from now
he'll get the chance.

Today he was
released by special permission
to attend his father's funeral.
I was chosen from the guards
because I have a reputation for being
tough-minded.
I don't con easily,
but I'm not a mean bastard.
I took the cuffs off him
before we reached the graveyard.

It's been a good day.
The sun shone, but not too hot.
The birds sang as if it had just rained

and the clouds made themselves into sky animals
that reminded me of when I was a kid.
We only had the one bad moment.

The young man became angry
when the undertaker wouldn't open
the coffin. The father
had refused to visit
him and he'd brought a camera
so at least he could have
a picture to remember the old man.
I had to grab his arm
and squeeze it, not hard,
enough to remind him.
Then he was quiet.
His mother was there too,
but she never said a word
and the young man avoided her.
They didn't want to embarrass
each other, at least
that's how it seemed.

He sits beside me in the dark
smoking nervously, the cuffs
rattling like loose change.
Actually he has nothing to worry about.
I'm the one who's late.
In the restaurant
he refused a second cup of coffee
while I drank those extra two beers.
I'll get into shit for being late,
not him. I can't help it,
I hate funerals.

Already the prison lights
shine on the horizon.
They loom up out of the countryside
like a sudden carnival that's been set up
on the edge of town. Sometimes

on the night shift I almost
expect to find the place gone.

Less than five miles to go.
I push harder on the gas,
feel the young man shift as if
he's bracing himself for the return.
If I thought about it, I suppose I could
feel sorry for him,
but his situation really
has nothing to do with me.
He won't get it in the neck
for being late.

Something's moving in front of me,
an animal. I see him
in the headlights for a second,
swerve to miss him but
he moves forward, toward me instead of away.
I feel the car butt at his body,
hear the shattered scream.
I brake suddenly and the young man
bangs his head against the dash
and then begins to laugh as if the
whole thing were a joke.
I slam into reverse and then
there's the animal in my rear lights
up on his haunches, shaking
and screaming like a crazy woman
given herself over to a primitive dance.

I hold my flashlight on him,
and an ear and a piece
of his skull are missing.
But still there is enough left to recognize
a raccoon,
and his masked eyes remind me of
comic book villains,
the raccoon always playing the part

of a robber with an automatic
clutched in his hand
who in the end is always captured and led off
to prison, if he isn't
killed in the shoot-out.

No rock handy, so I hit him
with the flashlight. I hit him
several times and the lens is covered with blood, still
he moves away from me and his
constant, throat tearing scream,
popped angry eyes
make me think of the security control panel
that goes wild
when a prisoner tries to escape.
I'm tempted to kick him, I've got boots on
but I'm frightened of the long clicking teeth.
The young man is moving behind me.
I see his shadow bend towards the ground
and when I turn real fear clogs my throat.
He's carrying a heavy stick and I stare
as it arcs in the air, comes down on
the creature's head.
Three times and then the animal is quiet.
The young man hurls the stick into the night
as I roll the body into the ditch.
"We had to put him out of his misery," I call out.
"Yes," the young man replies, back in the car.
"Yes, we did, didn't we."

A friend was working the gate, so there's no
worry about a late report.
I said goodnight
to the young man
who politely thanked me.
I headed home, contented and pleased to know
my efforts were appreciated.
When I passed the spot where the raccoon lay
I felt suddenly uneasy

and I haven't stopped in the next village to call
the wife who always worries when I take
a prisoner on a pass.
She says one day one of 'em
will take me hostage.
I always laugh it off.

There's only one phone booth
in the village, the light
flickers as the door swings
precariously open and closed.
I listen as the operator makes the
right connection and then
as the phone begins to ring
I notice a large dog limping toward me.
One of his legs has been twisted away
and a piece of bone shows at the first joint.
There's blood at his mouth
and he seems to be having trouble breathing.
Perhaps some tourist
high-tailing it to his cottage has side-swiped
the dog, he
might have had a bad fall.
Anything could have happened.
The dog rears up on his legs,
leans against the door until
his face is level with mine.
He snarls and bares his teeth
as my wife answers.
She bears the fierce barking, asks
if everything is all right.
I laugh like a kid when
something horrible had happened to someone
that I didn't understand.
There's blood on the door from the dog's mouth
and he pounds his head against
the glass with some great, unknown intent.
I feel foolish, trapped and angry.
None of this is my doing.

I've lived as decently as anyone.
I've never consciously harmed anyone.

My wife's asking
am I all right?
I've stopped the laugh and I'm about to explain
when the dog drops to the ground
and moves away slowly with a whimper
that's long and somehow sad
like a survivor in a flock of ducks
who openly mourns the loss of his mate
and friends to the hunters.
I reassure my wife, tell her
I'll be home soon.
She says she'll chill beer
and we both kiss the recievers
and hang up.

I do intend to search in the dark
for the wounded dog,
but for a second I'm almost afraid to leave
the safe booth.
I think of the young man
back in his cell,
of his dead father being lowered
into the wet soil, and then
the broken body of the raccoon.
I run to the door and drive away quickly.
There are shadows in the darkness.
I can't see them
but I know they're waiting there.
I drive away remembering that
once I was a young man, and thought
I understood everything.

STEPHEN SCOBIE

Deputy Bell

When he was first brought in, he couldn't stand the sunlight—asked Bob and me to close the windows, close the windows and shutter them up. Bob wouldn't do it, of course. Bob made him sit beside the window where he could look out into the street. Billy just closed his eyes instead.

He was sitting like that one day—Bob was out for lunch—and I closed the shutters for him. He seemed to relax, opened his eyes slowly, ungumming them like they were stuck with sleep. "Much obliged," he said, "Deputy Bell."

"Why d'you want 'em that way?" I asked. Having closed the shutters, I figured I had the right to ask him.

He looked at me with his narrow cat's eyes—I never could see past his eyes—"If you had only three weeks' sunlight left," he asked me, "how would you feel about it?"

"I guess I'd want to see as much of it as I could," I said, not really thinking too much about it.

"Well," he smiled. "Yes. Exactly." But I couldn't at all see what he was agreeing to.

When Bob came back he bawled me out for closing the shutters. But he never could get Billy to open his eyes.

I remember another time I was sitting cleaning my gun. Slowly, one piece at a time. It had been my father's gun, he fought with it in the war—a beauty, a real old beauty. A fellow in Lincoln County once offered me five hundred dollars for it, no kidding, but I said no. Anyway, suddenly I looked up and there he was watching me—closely, intently, cat's eyes all narrowed.

Bob Olinger was over in the chair by the door, watching a corner of sky through the unshuttered window. Across his knees, though, the shotgun was pointing at Billy.

And Billy smiled, his whole face smiled. He didn't say a word, not to attract Bob's attention, I guess. He just looked at my gun and smiled.

Maybe he was just admiring its beauty, I don't know. I sure hoped so. Nothing in the world can give you the shivers like a condemned man smiling at your gun.

It's true, like they always said, that Olinger was a bastard. He knew all the little ways of rubbing salt into wounds. He would count off the days each morning ("fourteen more to go, Billy!") and again at night ("thirteen nights of dreaming, lucky number, who can we get for you tonight, Bonney?") He would comment on the building of the scaffold ("Good strong wood, Billy. Good strong rope") and taunt him about making his will ("Half of my no worldly goods I give to Deputy Olinger, the other half to Deputy Bell. Only people you got left to give to now, Billy"). Oh, and dozens more.

Billy never paid attention. Just sat there for hours and hours with his eyes closed. You could never tell whether or not he was sleeping.

My mother never did like playing-cards. I guess that's why I became so good with them. Hours that other kids spent getting sick on chewing tobacco, I'd be out on my own somewhere flipping cards around. The Devil's picture book. Every fancy shuffle in the business, I could do it. Deal aces from top, bottom or middle. Cut the Jack of Diamonds every time.

None of it did any good. When I sat down to poker I was always too scared to cheat. Not honest, just scared. I used to deal so thumping slow you'd have thought my hands were paralysed, and I always got bad cards. I was the kind of player, every time I managed to put together a straight, the other guy was flushing.

The only person I ever won anything off was Billy. And that was my own money I'd lent him to start the game.

He wouldn't play at first, wouldn't do anything, just sitting with his eyes closed. Bob swore at him all the time, and it was beginning to get on my nerves too. I'm an easygoing person, but there's something goddam disturbing in watching a fellow sit so long, awake, with his eyes closed. You get to wondering what he's seeing.

So I snapped the cards, did a few fancy shuffles, and offered to lend him ten bucks to play with. First dozen times I said it he didn't answer—that was okay, nothing unusual. Then at last he turned, opened his eyes, and held out his manacled hands. Bob in the corner cocked his gun. I gave him the money and won it all back in half an hour.

It wasn't that Billy wasn't trying, and it wasn't, I swear, whatever Bob Olinger says, it wasn't that I was cheating. I just kept on dealing myself these aces, straight, honest, and above the board.

"Show you a little trick," said Billy at last, after I'd cleaned him out. He picked up the deck and started to build a card-house, very precarious, the cards all leaning up against each other like shanties on the poor side of town. When it was three stories high, he pointed to one of the cards at the bottom. "Take that one away," he said.

"It'll all fall down," I protested.

"No it won't," he said.

I pulled the card away, slowly. The whole structure just shivered slightly, like a leaf in the wind, but it stood there, Damned if I knew how he did it.

Bob had come over to watch. "Do that again," he demanded.

But Billy had closed his eyes.

Being a deputy isn't exactly a well-paid job, but sometimes it does have its compensations. Being jailer to Billy the Kid attracted me a fair amount of attention. I didn't have to buy myself too many drinks out of my own money these weeks.

There were all kinds of newspapermen in town, from all over. Some came from back East, some from out in California, one even came all the way from Canada. Bob Olinger wouldn't talk to them at all, so they came to me.

I got to telling them pretty much what they wanted to hear. I told them Billy ground his teeth and drooled a lot; they liked that. I told them he used to beat his head against the wall and grip the window bars tight with his hands. I told them he started moaning along about sunset. They wrote it all down in little notebooks.

But I never did tell them the truth, that he was just sitting there day after day with his eyes closed.

I made up stories about myself as well. I told one fellow that I came from New Orleans and that my uncle was personal aide to Robert E. Lee. Told another that my mother kept a fancy boardinghouse in Boston. Told the fellow from Canada that I'd been up there on a hunting trip once, fishing the St. Lawrence all through the Rockies.

Well, it sort of passed the time. In fact, of course, both my parents are buried right here in Lincoln, God rest their souls, and aside from the war the farthest I've ever been was a cattle drive through to Dodge City. But nobody would want to hear that.

Anyway, I didn't figure these newspapermen were really all that interested in me. Sooner or later they all got round to two questions, the only ones they were really keen on. One was "Can I get an interview with Billy?" And the other was "Where in hell is Pat Garrett?"

Actually, the answer to that second one was easy enough. Garrett was upstairs in the hotel, locked in his room, drinking. He'd been drinking ever since the trial, steady. I've heard it said by some people (that Canadian reporter was one) that Pat could hold any amount of liquor, that he never got drunk. Well, all I can say is, he sure as hell was drunk the afternoon he finally got up the nerve to come and see Billy. I know, I was there.

Me and Bob Olinger. Garrett had us standing just inside the door, stiff as sentries, you'd have thought we were back in the goddam army. Staring straight in front of us, pretending not to see or hear.

Pat came rolling in, drunk as a polecat, pulled up a chair beside Billy, and belched. Billy's eyes flicked open, just for the smallest second, I'm not sure Pat even saw it; then he lapsed back into his usual pose, gave no more sign of hearing than if he'd been struck stone deaf in a thunderstorm.

"We-e-ll, Billy," Garrett began, drawing the first word out like an old door creaking on its hinges, slamming it shut on the name. Billy said nothing.

"It's come to this then," Pat observed, for all the world as if he'd said something new. "Can't say it's exactly the way I wanted it, but I guess it'll have to do." He took a bottle from his side pocket, drank a swig, and waved it vaguely under Billy's nose. But that didn't work either.

"Remember the first time I seen you, Billy," Pat declared. Olinger shifted wearily on his feet; Garrett told this story on average about twice a night. "Back in old Beaver Smith's saloon. Fort Sumner. Real rough town. I was tending the bar there—kind of down on my luck, you understand"—this was a confidential aside, and since Billy didn't seem to be listening, Garrett half-turned in his chair and tried addressing it to Bob—"so there I was, pouring cheap whiskey, rot-gut piss, and trying to keep some kind of accounting, when one day Charlie Bowdre walks in and announces, 'Billy's coming.' Like you was a king, Billy, with a man out in front of you blowing a big gold trumpet. And everyone in that bar just quieted down, like pet birds when you drop a cloth on their cages." Pat was especially fond of that line. He repeated it. "Like a bunch of birds, with the night-cloth draped on their cages. Night-cloth like a hangman's hood. Now of course I'd heard of you, Billy, I mean, who hadn't? The bloodiest hired gun in the Lincoln County War, who hadn't heard of you, Billy? But when you walked in, Billy, when you walked in that door, you know what I thought? I looked at you and I thought, 'That runt! That little runt! Why, I could take him—easy!'"

Usually Garrett said that last line boastfully, and all the listeners (those at least that hadn't heard it a dozen or so times before) would gasp at his daring, at the outrageousness of the idea. But this time he leaned forward, very close to Billy's face, and kind of hissed it at him, spitefully. Bob Olinger beside me chuckled.

Pat waited like that, all leant forward, waited for Billy to say something. But Billy, eyes closed, never twitched a muscle. "Go on, Billy," Pat whispered then, very low, very fast. "Try it, try me. What d'you think your chances are? Grab me, get my gun, get down behind that table quick, before Olinger or Bell get a chance at a clear shot? Or grab me round the neck as a shield, eh Billy? Come on, you'll never get a chance like this again. Open your eyes and look, Billy, I'm real close to you. Probably you'd get an arm round my throat before I could get my shot away. Probably you could, Billy. Open your eyes and see."

Still no answer. Garrett jumped up, clattering his chair to the ground. "Open your eyes, goddammit!" he yelled.

He began pacing up and down the room, very agitated, the bottle in his hand now, talking in fast abrupt sentences between swigs. It was cheap dirt whiskey, and he was going through the bottle fast. "All the times I've had you, Billy, I swear, I've had you in my gunsights. Coming out of the cabin at Tivan Arroyos, standing there blinking in the sunshine. You didn't have your hands up quick enough, Billy. I could have shot you then. You just stood there looking at Charlie Bowdre, all guts and flies, Charlie's body all guts and flies. You didn't have your hands up quick enough. I could have shot you then!" Pat was screaming this; he stopped, took a drink, calmed down a little. "Could have had you in Sumner too, Billy. Two horses coming down the street, you and Tom O'Folliard. Don't think I didn't know which was which, Billy. Don't think I didn't know when I fired!" Another drink. Then sadly, morosely: "You and me, Billy, we go away back."

His ramblings had brought him to the window where he could see the scaffold being built. He stopped there and gazed out at it. "What's the use, Billy?" he asked at last, quietly. "It's all the same stinking life. I kill you, you kill me. A horse breaks its leg in a snowdrift and you kill it. A dog breaks its leg and maybe you take it home and let some kids nurse it. What's the use, what's the stinking use? People talk and their words don't mean anything more than snow. Ever been in the mountains when the snow is falling, Billy? That's something to see. Jesus, that's something to see."

He tilted the bottle high; it was almost empty. "Getting older," he announced. "Dream a lot now, never used to dream. Dream of guns all the time. Mostly they're firing at me." He held the bottle up to the window: about half an inch in the bottom shone dirty gold. "Snow in the mountains," he said. "Jesus, that's something to see."

Without any warning he flung the bottle at Billy's head. Olinger and I shouted and jumped forward, but Billy hadn't moved at all. The bottle missed him by inches, but there was a splatter of whiskey down his face. His tongue moved to lick it in.

Pat Garrett had fallen to his knees in front of him, and was weeping, sobbing uncontrollably. "Billy," he said, just his name, over and over again, "Billy, Billy, Billy . . ."

We were all pretty shaken up by that, I guess, including Billy—though he gave no sign of it at the time. Not as long as Olinger was around. But the next day, when Bob went out for lunch, he was hardly out the door before Billy started.

He opened his eyes first—that's how I knew there was something unusual—then he sort of shivered, all of him, all his body right to the tips of his toes. "Jesus, Bell," he said to me, "did you ever see anything like that?"

It was almost twenty-four hours since Pat's visit, but I knew what he was talking about. "There's no accounting what a man will do when he's liquored up," I said. "Not even Pat Garrett."

Billy said, "I suppose the son of a bitch thinks he's the only person that dreams about guns."

"He's got a job to do," I offered, not really believing it too much, just for something to say to keep Billy talking. "A man doesn't have to like his job."

Billy's eyes flashed at me, like a mirror catching sun. "You like *your* job, Deputy Bell?"

This time I didn't answer him.

"How many men have you killed, Bell?" he asked me.

"I'd kill you, Billy, if I had to. Don't think I wouldn't do it. Don't count on it."

He laughed, as if I'd caught him sneaking candies from a jar. But when he spoke he was serious. "I don't take chances like that, Bell."

There was a moment's awkward silence. He even closed his eyes, as if withdrawing again, then he changed his mind, turned toward me, and said, "Take yesterday, for instance. Pat was right, you know—I *could* have got an arm round his neck before he had a chance to pull his gun. I didn't have to open my eyes to know how close he was. He didn't think I could, of course—thought he could pull the gun in time, stuff it up my nostril or something." Billy snorted contemptuously. "Pat Garrett, drunk out of his mind! Yup, I could have taken him all right. But I didn't. Know why?" He leaned forward confidentially. "Because that pigfucker Olinger wouldn't have hesitated to blow both barrels of his shotgun at me, right through Pat. Shield or no shield, Olinger would have killed Pat to get to me. Now would *you* have done that, Deputy Bell?"

I didn't answer. Truth is, I don't what I would have done.

Billy leaned back, smiling. He'd scored his point; now he wanted to rub it in. "How many men did you say you'd killed, Bell?"

"How many men have *you* killed, Billy?" I countered.

"Oh hell, I don't know. Lost count, I guess."

"The newspapers say nineteen."

"Come on now, Bell, you don't believe what newspapers say, now do you? Take Brady, for instance."

"What about Brady?"

"A hell of a lot about Brady," said Billy angrily. The anger came on kind of sudden, but it struck me as real. "It's Brady I'm supposed to hang for, isn't it?"

"Well, you shot him, didn't you?"

"Maybe," said Billy slowly. "May-be. Guess it's like when the town whore gets pregnant, who's the father? Me and two dozen other people. That's the way it was with Brady. He came down that street that morning, he didn't have a chance. I was behind a water trough in front of him. Charlie Bowdre was up on a roof. Tom O'Folliard was at the hotel window. And at least a half a dozen other McSween men, all over the place. I've heard it said that I stepped out and challenged him, openly, in the middle of the street. I told you, Bell, I don't take risks. We all shot from cover, and we all shot at once. At least a dozen bullets hit him. How come it's me that gets hanged for it?"

"Fine story," I said, "Fine, brave story, shooting a man in the back without warning."

"He deserved it," Billy said calmly. "Now come on, then, Bell, you keep dodging my question. Like a jackrabbit looking for a hole to climb down. How many men have you killed?"

"Four," I told him, which wasn't exactly true. "But that was in the war, mostly."

"I was in a war too," said Billy bitterly.

I didn't bother to contradict him.

"Four, huh? You're probably exaggerating." He looked me in the eyes and I turned away. He laughed. "Fighting for a cause, eh, Bell? Fighting for what you believed in?" He dropped his gaze, and looked at his hands. Looked at them as if they belonged to someone else, someone particularly nasty. "That's the way I felt at first," he said softly. "The Lincoln County War, I thought it really was a war. I mean, I thought there were good guys and bad guys, like in the newspapers. I thought the sides meant something. But it wasn't like that, Bell. They were all just dirty little money-grabbing gangsters. That Tunstall—you know, Bell, I really thought that man was some kind of god, I really did. Turned out he was just a crook with a fancy accent. I killed a lot of men for him, Bell, and I damned nearly got killed myself. Damned nearly singed my balls off, running from that burning house. All for Tunstall, for McSween, for that rabbit-arsed son of a bitch John Chisum!"

All this time, like I said, he'd been staring at his hands. Now he turned to me again, and his voice went high and funny, almost cracked, like a woman's. "He offered me a pardon for all that, Bell. Governor Lew Wallace. He offered to pardon me all the men I'd killed. You think anybody can do that, Bell? Lew Wallace or anybody else? You think anybody can pardon you the men you've killed?"

I looked at him a long time. "No, Billy," I said at last. "I don't think anybody can."

Whatever state he was in, he broke out of it. Another big shiver, and he was changed again.

"Lend me ten dollars, Bell," he said. "Let's play some more poker."

"Sure thing."

He giggled. "Pay you back next month," he said.

I laughed, I guess: what else could I do? I dealt him the cards, keeping a safe distance between us across the table. Outside I could hear Bob Olinger down in the street, whistling some off-key tune. Billy could hear it too.

"That Brady," he said, picking up his cards. "That Brady was a swine, I tell you, he really deserved it. Every bullet. I aimed for his gut, and I hope he had time to feel it proper, before he died. Know how bad he was, Bell? He was worse than Bob Olinger. That's how bad he was."

In the next couple of days we talked quite a lot. It always started when Olinger went out, for a meal or whatever. As long as Bob was there, it was the same old things—Billy sitting with his eyes closed, in that different place he went to, and Bob exhausting his invention for insults and taunts. I don't know what happened between these two when I was out. Once when I came back from lunch Billy's lip was bleeding. None of us said anything about it, though.

Then as soon as Bob was out the door, Billy would pick up the conversation where it had left off, so to speak, as if there hadn't been any kind of break at all. He'd ramble on, one thing to another. I noticed how often he said my name—nearly every second sentence, almost—and once I mentioned it to him.

He laughed. Billy would laugh at anything. "I guess you got kidded a lot, eh, Bell, when you were a kid? Ding dong, and people trying to pull your clapper?"

"Sure did." I grinned. Over the years I'd gotten so I had to grin. It was the only way. "You name it, I've heard it."

"Tunstall now . . ." Billy frowned, trying to recover a memory. "Tunstall had a thing about bells, some Englishman had written. . . . He read it to me once, the phony bastard. I don't remember how it goes."

I told him. " 'Send not to know for whom the bell tolls: it tolls for thee.' "

He opened his eyes as wide as ever I saw them. "You're a remarkable man, Deputy Bell."

"It means everyone's got to die," I went on. "It's a funeral bell he's talking about, and he says there's no point in asking who it's ringing for this time. Really, it's always ringing for you. All of us got to die, sooner or later."

"Yeah but Bell," said Billy, "there's a hell of a lot of difference between sooner and later."

Well, what do you say to something like that? I looked away for a moment and when I looked back he was still staring at me. "Well, I guess you're the one that'd know about that now, wouldn't you, Billy?" I sort of muttered.

Of course I knew what he was trying to do. It had all happened to me before, often enough, in situations like this. They try to get you friendly, play on your sympathy, get you to turn soft on them. Then when you're not watching, bang! At least that's what they think. No one's ever pulled it on me, though a couple have tried. I'm an experienced guard, after all. You don't think they'd pick just anybody for Billy the Kid, now do you?

Billy tried the two standard approaches. The first is the terrible injustice of it all. "What's this building we're in, Bell?" he asked one day.

"Lincoln County Courthouse," I said wearily. I could see the rest of it coming.

"Courthouse!" Billy snorted with laughter. "That's what they call it now, I guess. But you know what this here building used to be?"

"Yes, Billy, I know what it used to be."

But he told me anyway. "Used to be a store, Bell. Run by Murphy and Dolan. You remember who Murphy and Dolan were?"

"Billy, I don't need a history lesson."

"Brady's employers. McSween's competitors. The established

money of Lincoln County. That's where the justice is, Bell, in the moneybags! That's what the courthouse is, Bell, the general store!"

"Aw drop it, Billy. Shut up, will you?"

And the second one is the deprived childhood line. It goes like this:

"That's a mighty fine gun you got, Bell."

"Sure is."

"Must have had it a long time."

"It was my father's gun."

"I never did know *my* father, Bell."

"Tough shit."

There's no way anybody's going to get round me. Olinger now, he hates them all. Maybe he has to work himself up to it, so's he can stand killing them. But that's never bothered me. Hell, I never hung a man I didn't like.

Garrett finked out. I guess that could have been predicted. He called me to his hotel room one morning and when I got there he was sober, which was kind of a surprise. You could still see the shadows of booze, though, under his eyes.

"Gotta leave town for a few days," he announced briskly. "I'm leaving you in charge, Bell."

"Will you be back for the hanging?" I asked.

"Well, of course I will. If I can." So I knew he wasn't going to be.

"What about Olinger?" I asked. "Shouldn't he be in charge?"

"Well, to tell you the truth, Bell ... " Garrett sat down for a moment, and his hand automatically stretched out for the bottle that wasn't there. "I don't completely trust Bob Olinger. You and him, Bell, you balance each other nicely. You're like a pair of horses, one all snuffy and impetuous, the other solid and steady. It makes for good guarding, Bell. Bob keeps him scared and you keep him happy."

I hadn't quite thought it out that clear, but of course he was right. Pat Garrett is a mean, calculating son of a bitch when he's sober.

"But I wouldn't want Olinger in charge," he went on. "Too liable to do something stupid. Olinger doesn't really believe in hanging, you know. He'd just as soon shoot Billy's balls off. But you, Bell—you're a rope man."

I couldn't just let that pass. "Yes, sir," I told him. "And you're a gutless chicken-livered asshole."

Garrett's eyes flicked once, then he stood up slowly and headed for the door. "Interesting anatomical proposition, Bell," he said, and went out.

With Garrett gone, Bob Olinger got worse. I had just enough control over him that when I was in the room he didn't actually strike Billy. But regularly now, when I came back from a meal, there would be bruises on Billy's face, and Olinger would say something like "Fell off his chair again—didn't you, punk?"

Billy stayed impassive through all this, eyes firmly closed, watching the pictures inside.

When I was there, Olinger had to content himself with verbal abuse—long, boring tirades in which he went over and over Billy's past life, vilifying every murder, shouting obscenities about every woman from his grandmother on down, picturing in lurid detail a totally perverted sex life. I tell you, Olinger accused Billy of some things I'd never even heard of.

Occasionally I'd say, "Hey, Bob, give us a rest, will you? I have to listen to that shit too." And then maybe he'd shut up for a while, half an hour or so, before starting in again. I offered to play cards with Billy, which might have got us some quiet, but he ignored me. He talked to me less now. I guess the date of the hanging was getting pretty close in his mind. Certainly Olinger never tired of reminding him.

"Six days now. Then you'll swing high, Billy, high. No drop for you, I can tell you that, no clean drop to snap your neck quick. I been talkin' to the hangman. We got it all arranged. Just a small drop, Billy, won't kill you. You'll have plenty of time to swing. Just gradually choking, you know. You know what I mean? Tongue coming out of your mouth. Turning blue. Real pretty sight."

I was cleaning my gun, trying not to listen. Click, click, the oiled pieces falling into place, perfect machinery, as they had so often before. Under my father's hands. His hands too were like mine, dirty with oil, wiped off on his pants. His hands too clicked the pieces in place, his eyes sighted down the barrel. I used to watch him for hours on end, sitting on the porch at sundown, cleaning his gun.

"You can feel the air being blocked," Olinger was saying. "I know all about this, Billy. Talked once with a fellow that was strung up by a posse, then cut down just in time. Turned out he was guilty after all, and we hung him again six months later. He told me all about it. The air's blocked in your throat, the blood can't get out of your brain, it starts to well up behind your eyes. Eyes pop open. You'll open your eyes then, you bastard, I'll tell you that. You'll open your eyes then."

I put the bullets back in the chamber, one-two-three, four-five-six. Snapped the chamber shut. Click went the perfect machinery.

And a very odd thing happened.

I raised the gun and sighted along the barrel, as usual. Then I held it out at arm's length, my finger on the trigger. And I aimed it at Bob Olinger.

He had his back to me, he was leaning over close to Billy's face, sort of spitting in his ear. He didn't see me at all. And my finger began to tighten on the trigger.

I could see it all happening, and it all seemed to happen very slow. You understand, none of it *actually* happened, but I could see it all in my mind, very slow.

My finger squeezed the trigger so, so gradually. Click, the hammer came back. Poised, its one perfect balance, last moment of innocence, first closing of guilt. Click, the hammer went down. A minor explosion inside the gun.

Now the bullet started on its journey. Up the length of the gun barrel, through that dark opening, into the light. I could see the bullet take its long path across the room, through the air of the room, straight line across strange territory. Confident in its direction, leisurely in its speed. I could see it reach through the air on its way to Bob Olinger.

The bullet completed its journey. It touched his shirt, and the shirt ripped slowly apart to let it through. It nudged the skin and pushed it to one side. It pushed its way into the flesh like a strong man shouldering through a crowd. The flesh collapsed as it passed through. It knocked on the door of bone, then bust it down. The shoulderblade splintered like dry wood.

I could see Olinger's body making its first startled jump and turn, slowly, the face, incredulous, coming round towards me, the mouth opening to scream. And I could see the fountains of blood erupt from the wound, spurt into the air, and splash down onto Billy's face. His eyes were closed. I could see Billy's face, all streaming in blood. It ran down over his eyes. It trickled into his beard. It dripped onto his shirt. His face was completely scarlet. It oozed from the roots of his hair.

And then—and this wasn't in my mind anymore, this is what really happened—then Billy opened his eyes. He had no reason to, but he opened his eyes, and he looked over Olinger's shoulder, and he looked right at me, and he saw me holding the gun, and he saw what way the gun was pointing.

And just like that time before, he smiled.

"Hey, Bell."

It's been an uneasy day. The heat is killing me. Billy didn't say anything when Olinger went out to lunch, and he's been gone three quarters of the hour. I'm sitting by the door wondering about yesterday.

"Hey, Bell."

"What is it, Billy?"

"You remember that card trick? The one with the house of cards that doesn't fall down?"

Sure I remember it. Even though I've seen him do it, I still think it's impossible.

"Want to see how it's done?"

Of course he's up to something, but I'm careful. I come over to the table, take out the cards, and Billy starts. Two cards propped up against each other in a triangle. Two along the side, vertical. Two on top of these two, horizontal, either side of the triangle, form a base to start again. I'm watching closely, but I don't see anything unusual. Billy's hands work quickly, cleanly, unhesitatingly. He has perfect hands.

"Take away that card." He points to one right at the bottom of what is now a four-storey structure.

I take it away. The whole damn thing falls down. Cards scatter everywhere: on the table, on the floor. In spite of myself, I laugh.

Billy stares dumbfounded. "Son of a bitch!" he says. "Hey, let me try that again." And he reaches for the floor to pick up the fallen cards.

"Hold it." Nothing as obvious as that. "I'll get them." So very carefully, keeping an eye on Billy, I bend down and pick up all the cards.

He starts again. The same quick movements as before.

The whole damn thing falls down.

Billy looks furious this time. "Pigshit!" he says.

And this time I'm really laughing. He can't do it! I was right, it is impossible. He really can't do it. "Hey, Billy, why don't you try again?" I say, bending down to pick up the cards. It's impossible, I think, he really ... and I come up facing the gun. My gun. My father's gun. Picked clean out of my holster as I bent for the cards. Bent for the cards that second time, not looking, not thinking. Thinking only, the cards fell down, he really can't do it.

"Sure is a nice gun, Bell," says Billy. "Sure is a beautiful weapon."

His eyes are on me, his narrow cat's eyes. I can't see through them.

And at the same moment we both hear it: the sound of Bob Olinger whistling, down in the street, coming back from his lunch. Billy's eyes flick once to the double-barrelled shotgun by the door.

I get up and start to back away.

Billy raises the gun and points it at me. His eyes are open.

"Please, Billy," I'm saying. "Please no. Don't."

The historical background of "Deputy Bell" is accurate, except that the view of Bob Olinger as mean and nasty is part of the legend rather than the history of Billy the Kid. How Billy did in fact shoot J. W. Bell is a matter of some conjecture: the most widely accepted version is that a friend managed to leave a gun for him in the privy. After shooting Bell, Billy went to the window, called out Olinger's name, waited till Olinger could see him, then carefully shot him in the stomach. The "Canadian reporter" who claims that Pat Garrett never got drunk is of course Michael Ondaatje: see *The Collected Works of Billy the Kid*, pages 28-29. This story is dedicated to Michael, and to Barry.

CHRISTOPHER LEVENSON

Spiritual Exercises

The leg bent
    back
        so far
it hurts,
    the foot flat
        against the floor,
finger and thumb
    gripping the end
        of the pommel
hard.
    "Harder. So." My
        fencing instructor's voice
chooses impatience.
    I submit
        to his correcting hand.
"No, look: like
    this."
        Behind my mask
I sweat tears
    and admire
        a discipline
I have not mastered
    yet,
        prize the
immaculate
    timing,
        balance,
the whole body
    intent
        on its own kind of
perfection.
    Limbering up,
        we sweat
to make it easy.

DAVID HELWIG

Notes for a Ballet

1   *Pas de deux*

Like the iambic alternation of light and dark,
sky and earth, like fire licking the air
and air the fire, the two move
in a duel of arms and legs. The breath,
iambic, in and out, lost in the huge space,
invisible as white birds on a white sky
as they move against the pull of gravity.

There is a story with names, but here
the names are lost.
                      Children fall
from the sky like snowflakes, iambic
as angels and devils.
                      Earth and Sky
move together and apart. Light and Dark
leap and leap.

2   *Finale*

What is the music for the end of the world?
Statements exist, respectable ironies.
The laws of story-telling say climax, resolution,
denouement, catharsis, but every second of living
is a separate and fatal heart attack.

To ever cut the thread is to say too much.

Consummatum est. But it isn't.
Not quite yet; there is no accurate translation
of time into the language of final causes.

Things go on and on being continuous,
yet turning aside for a moment or walking away,
there is always a sad temptation to say goodbye.

DAVID MACFARLANE

Words for two dancers
(for Karen Kain)

And with the war and with her lover dead
she describes slow circles.
Within the music and the silence,
at the border of a forest,
she moves only for the only darkness
and for the unexcited smoke
that climbs from blackened hills.
Her steps are innocent;
it is her hands that push away
and then admit the cries of distant women.
Alone with her uncertain shadow,
she is the only commotion of the darkness.

The shadow is a reflection in the trees.
There is a pool beyond the forest.
The shadow is an echo in the mist.
More certain now,
the shadow dares a step beyond
the forest.
Once free it teaches what begins
before the forest.
She learns the doomsday dance,
the dance of open flowers.
They become the only monument.
Dance is like a wind that finds the perfect tree.

Lines somewhat in the manner of Ovid

I wasted those days, Maria. I am not so reckless with verses.
This poem's a classic and has nothing to do with your eyes.

Older, I will not persist with the madness of praising your perfume.
I insist upon epics and wrestle with subjects of import.

No, not that I have forgotten the grace of your well-oiled shoulders.
I remember the tan you purchased on beaches in Nassau.

Even the visions of Liberty scarves leave me mournful on Bloor St.
Your neck is a silken remembrance I am never without.

And your hair is a golden dilemma my hands still long to resolve.
And moreover, your father's a magnate with interests in oil fields.

The l'air du temps on your thighs would have easily distracted Paris.
Though your thighs are two subjects I have tried for years to forget.

But damn it! If ever you think my devotions less than entire,
I will reveal volumes written in praise of your breasts.

You wintered with athletic lovers in villas rented on Corfu
while I scribbled sonnets in draughty and non Grecian attics.

Not that the means of my poems were ever requited with endings.
Your interests, it seemed, never lay in the field of the arts.

Though Maria, if ever you consider taking an interest in poets,
I will be in this room, doubtless rewriting these couplets.

The routine of significant activity

Since I have taken to writing stories by day
I have come to resent the necessity of adjectives.
I have grown indifferent to exclamation marks.
I am troubled by the conformity of commas.
I question the existence of dialogue.
I am frightened by the space between paragraphs.
I object to the tyranny of titles.
I am opposed to the narrator.

At night I build fires.
The perfect flames always fit
the holes I make in the simple night.
I take great comfort in fires.

WILLIAM LATTA

The Logician as Poet

On beginning this poem
I want you to understand
very clearly
that I intend to say
unequivocally
that all fallacies
whether intentional or
otherwise
must, like the pox,
be avoided
must, like incest
or adultery or killing
one's fellow-countrymen,
not be committed
under any circumstance
if we are ever to get
to the truth of things
as they really are.

I hope that you can see
the logic of my position
very clearly
and that my poem has
affected you strongly.

Now I intend
to end.

TIM INKSTER

The Printer Addresses a Fop

You have given me language
typed on the pages of your manuscript,
you would call it something
else, in that we are agreed:
but your words are caterpillars
splayed lifeless by my machinery
onto the printed page.

Your wisdom is invisible,
I have printed it that way, black
on white vellum. Your genius
reflects nothing, did you know that?
But you can see everything
around your insects, like the sheets
around a spider on a bed.

They are dead, your flies,
yet they take with them, each one
some part of my own hell,
an impression of the type I cast
used and discarded
like so much lead in a hellbox.
So it is, with printers.

Your insects are corpses,
with serifs; my hands are dirty
but not so much with grease,

the embalmer's oil, that is your dirt,
your ink. I sweat
& where two broken tentacles cross
is a ligature, an arrangement of letters

more beautiful than you are aware.

GLORIA OSTREM SAWAI

Mother's Day

Mother's Day was on May 9 that year. On May 6 we had the blizzard and school was closed. On May 7, I was sick. I was sick until May 8 so I missed two days of school: May 6, the day of the blizzard, and May 7, the day I was sick. (May 8 was a Saturday so there was no school that day anyway.) On Mother's Day I found the cat. And on Monday, May 10, everything was back to normal.

I will begin with May 6 because that is the first day of all the days. I suppose I could even start with the night before since I heard later that the blizzard commenced in all its fury around 11 P.M. I, of course, was sleeping at that time and knew nothing of it. But people talked about it for days and weeks and months afterward, so naturally I have quite a clear picture of how it all began.

It began with the wind. Even before I went to bed that night the wind was blowing. The snow had melted early that year, before the end of March, and although fields in the country were still wet and patched with dirty snow, the streets in town were dry and dusty.

Every day we walked to school in whorls of dust and rolling thistles. Saskatchewan, as you know, is one of the three prairie provinces, and spring on the prairie is a dry and dusty scene indeed. It is unlike spring in areas farther south, such as the Southern states in the United States. I've read about spring in these places and seen pictures of it. In Kentucky, for instance, spring is calm and colorful and it lasts longer. In Kentucky there's more foliage, japonica, forsythia, dogwood. All these plants have lovely blooms and the blooms don't develop at the same rate. Thus the colors spread out over a longer period of time. My father subscribes to *National Geographic.*

In Saskatchewan, however, spring is bare. And if I may speak candidly, it is quite lonesome. The lonesome period is between the time the snow melts and the time the grass turns green. (Weeds I should say. We don't have much grass.) The lonesome period is the dry time when the ground is gray, trees (what few there are) are bare, and rubbish, buried for months under snow, is fully exposed. The lonesome period is usually filled with wind. The wind whips up the dust, dead thistles, moldy scraps of paper, whirling them across the alleys and down the streets, with no thought whatsoever to what pleases us.

I was lying in bed when I heard the wind. It rattled the windows, whistled in the chimney. It grew stronger, howling about the house like a great enemy who hated us personally and our home too, down to its very foundation. That's the feeling I got, that it really was an enemy and wanted to rip us right off the ground we'd settled on. I got out of bed and went downstairs to see how my mother and father were taking it. They were sitting in the living room, reading, and didn't seem at all disturbed. My mother looked up at me, her face shining under the rosy lampshade, and said it was all right, just a heavy wind, nothing to worry about. "Crawl back to bed now, sweetheart," she said in a voice that was kinder than usual. So I did, and went to sleep finally, wondering why there was such a thing as wind. Nobody likes it that I know of. No prairie people anyway. And why had God created it?

I do not question the existence of God, as my friend Mary Helm does, whose father runs the Co-op Creamery here in town and who is a Communist. I can't deny what's right there in front of my nose in black and white. But at the same time I do not condemn unbelievers. "Judge not, lest ye be judged," the Scripture says. Nor do I try to convince them. Arguments lead to nowhere. If you tell a blind man the sun is yellow and he doesn't believe you, what can you do about it? Nothing. Nevertheless, although my faith is firm, I wonder sometimes why certain things happen. Like the wind.

In the morning the sky was a whirl of gray and white. The snow was thicker than I'd seen it, and the wind still blowing, whining through the snow. I couldn't see the fence or garage from my bedroom window. Every inch of air was disrupted, uprooted, swirling about. Like refugees, I thought, as I knelt in front of the window in amazement. Like lonely refugees without homes, wandering in the cold, looking for a place to settle, a quiet place where they could put their babies to bed and have some hot tea and visit one another for awhile. But they couldn't find such a place, so they wandered, all in a frenzy, cold and lonesome.

I went downstairs in my pajamas. There'd be no school; that I knew. My father was sitting in the dining room at his desk. He was playing chess, like he does on Sunday mornings and snowy days when he can't work. He plays chess by correspondence since he has no partners here in town. You may have heard of chess players like this. He has a huge map of the world tacked on the wall in front of his desk. On the desk itself is a wooden chessboard, and on a table next to it, little recipe boxes filled with postcards. These cards have been sent to him from his playing partners all over the world. He even plays with one man in South Africa, and he has many games going on at the same time. Every time a player makes a move he sends the move by postcard to my father. Then my father makes his move and sends a card back to the player. Sometimes it takes nearly a month for a card to reach another country, so you can imagine how long one game might last. But my father seems to enjoy this, keeping track of all his partners with little colored pins on his map of the world.

My father is a very intelligent man, I must say, but he is not a man of faith. He does not attend church with me and my mother, not even on special occasions. Even my mother doesn't attend every Sunday. Most of the time it's left up to me to uphold the family in spiritual matters.

My mother was in the kitchen, sitting at the table drinking coffee and gazing out the window at the blizzard. She was leaning over the table, resting her elbows on the white cloth, holding the cup in both hands. Steam curled upward from the cup's brim. The whole room smelled of coffee.

She didn't even notice me come in, or stand there watching. On very snowy days or rainy days my mother abandons all her housewifely responsibilities and sits in front of the window all day, just looking out. We might as well forget about good dinners or a clean and tidy house on such days. She's completely engrossed by storms. In some respects my mother is a bit lazy. Nevertheless, I find her an interesting person. In this day and age it's important, I feel, to observe nature and meditate on all its wonders.

"That's some storm," I said.

"There'll be no school today," she said.

"I guess not," I said.

I went to the breadbox and sliced two pieces from a loaf. I brought out the butter and jam. I knew she was not about to make any breakfast, so I'd do it myself.

I sat down at the table to eat my bread and watch the storm with my mother. I have a good feeling about that day, nothing at all like the days that followed. The blizzard was howling outside. The snow was so high on the walk no one even tried to get out, and the air so thick we couldn't see beyond the porch. But the house was warm, and my mother was enjoying her coffee and my father his chess. Every so often my father would leave his game and come in the kitchen to drink coffee with my mother. I knew they were both having a good day. As the catechism says: "Let husbands and wives love and respect each other."

In the early afternoon the storm ended. The snow stopped, the wind ceased, the sky cleared, the sun shone. And everyone in town shovelled themselves out of their houses. I put on my boots and my new red parka and walked down town between the drifts, clean and sparkling in the sun. I went to see my friend Esther. She was helping her father in the store, straightening tin cans of soup and dusting jars of pickles. We talked about the storm and what we should do for our mothers on Mother's Day. She thought she'd buy her mother a box of chocolates. I said I'd have to wait till Saturday to decide, when I'd have some money. Then I went home. And that night I got sick.

I woke up in the middle of the night. My head was hot, my chest ached, and my throat was sore. I felt damp all over, and weak. I knew I was sick. I crouched under the blankets, shivering with cold and sweating. Finally I got up. I turned on the hall light and walked down the corridor to my mother and father's bedroom. I opened their door and saw them in the light from the hall. They were both sound asleep. My father was lying on his right side with his knees up. My mother was lying on her right side too, with her knees up. She was lying right next to my father, her stomach against his back and her legs fitting into his, fitting right into them like a piece of a jigsaw puzzle. I touched her on her hair, but she didn't move. I touched her on the cheek and she twitched a little. Then she opened her eyes and looked at me.

"I'm sick," I said and walked out of the room and back to bed.

In a minute she was in my room, leaning over me in the dimness.

"Did you say you were sick?"

"Yes."

"Where?"

"All over."

"Here?" She touched my head.

"Yes."

"Here?" She touched my neck.

"Yes."

She turned on the lights. She looked at my face and neck. She looked at the sheets and pillow. They were damp.

"You are sick," she said.

"I know."

She walked down the hall to the bathroom and came back with a glass of water, a washcloth, and a bottle of aspirins. She gave me an aspirin and water to drink. Then she washed my face with the cold wet cloth, and my neck too. She covered me up and brought in an extra blanket.

"You'll be all right," she said. "Don't worry."

I didn't say anything. I just turned over on my side and went back to sleep. In the morning I was still sick. My chest was sore and my head ached. My arms and legs felt damp and heavy. My mother came in again and looked at me.

"I'll make a mustard plaster," she said.

My mother is not an ignorant woman by any means, but she is not a woman of science. She does not read up on the latest developments in medicine as my father does, even though he's only a telephone man. She prefers remedies handed down by her mother and grandmother and even great-grandmother for all I know. Mustard plaster is a case in point. If you're unfamiliar with that old remedy, this is how it works: you make a paste of water, flour, and little powdered mustard. I'm not sure of the proportions, but you don't use very much mustard—it burns. You spread this yellow paste on a piece of cloth cut out to fit the chest it's going on. Then you lay another cloth over it and pin the edges together. You put this on the chest right next to the skin, and it's supposed to do some good—I'm not sure what except warm your chest considerably and make you sweat.

She came upstairs carrying the mustard plaster, holding it in her two hands like a rolled-out sheet of dough. When I saw it I began feeling embarrassed and wished like everything I hadn't gotten sick. I was eleven years old at the time, nearly twelve, and I was beginning to show. I was the only one in my class beginning to show. Ever so slightly I know, but even so I wasn't fond of the idea that someone would see me, even my mother.

"I think I'm feeling better, better than last night," I said. "I don't believe I'll be needing the mustard plaster."

"You'll be up and on your feet in no time with a good strong mustard plaster," she said. She laid the bulging cloth on a chair and lifted the quilt from under my chin, and sheet too. She unbuttoned my pajama top slowly and gently, and I felt myself getting more and more embarrassed. She spread out the fronts of my pajama top, looking at me. Then she lifted the mustard plaster from the chair and laid it on my chest, tucking it under my neck and partway into my arm pits and down to my stomach. She pressed her fingers on it ever so gently and I felt the pressing on the soft places on my chest where I'd begun to develop. I stared at the ceiling and didn't say anything. Neither did she. It seemed as if she didn't even notice, but she must have. I don't see how she could have missed. She buttoned my pajamas again and covered me with the sheet and quilt.

"Have a nice time in bed today," she said. "I'll bring you some magazines to read and some juice."

Maybe it doesn't make much sense to you how I felt about such things at that time. I certainly don't feel embarrassed now. But then I'll be fourteen next month and I'm fully developed. My mother has explained everything to me, about my body and sexual things. So now I understand all that. I have no problems in that line. However, when I was eleven and just starting to develop I felt quite peculiar about it. I didn't want anyone to know. When I was alone I'd sometimes look at myself in the mirror, without my clothes on. Then I'd put on a T-shirt or sweater to see if I showed. I never wore T-shirts to school though. I certainly didn't want everyone gawking. I'd leave the T-shirts to the grade-nine girls—Rosie Boychuck and her group. They seemed to enjoy letting the whole world know they were developing.

Anyway, I had a fairly pleasant morning after that, looking at *National Geographic*s and at the icicles melting outside my window, falling asleep and waking up and drinking juice. If you're not in pain it can be quite enjoyable sometimes being sick.

Then, in the afternoon, it happened. I can't understand even now how my mother could have done that to me. But she did. She came upstairs in the late afternoon and said she would change my mustard plaster. She'd make a fresh batch and after that I'd be finished. She pulled down the quilt and sheet, unbuttoned my pajamas, and lifted the cloth from my chest. My chest suddenly felt icy cold and terribly bare. I pulled my pajama top together quickly without buttoning it and snuggled under the covers. My mother left the room carrying the used mustard plaster, folded like a book, in her hand. I heard her walk down the steps into the kitchen. I heard the cupboard door opening and pots banging. I heard her chatting away to my father about nothing in particular. And I thought no more about it until I opened my eyes and saw him standing in the doorway. My father. My father holding the fresh mustard plaster. My father coming to put the new mustard plaster on my chest. I looked at him and felt my face getting hot and my heart beating faster. Was he actually going to do it? Open my pajama top and see me? And press that bulging cloth against my chest? Had my mother sent him up for that? I felt my eyes sting and I knew I was going to cry. I felt the wetness press against my eyeballs and drip over the edges of my eyes down the side of my head, into my hair. I couldn't say anything. I just lay there and cried.

"You're not feeling well at all, are you?" he said. "It's no great treat being sick. But maybe this will do the trick."

He lifted up the quilt and sheet. He spread open my pajama top. He looked down on my chest. I know he saw my development.

Even though he said nothing, I know he saw. Then he laid the cloth on me, smoothly and firmly, his hands heavy on the roundness there. He buttoned my pajamas and covered me with the sheet. He wiped my eyes with the edge of the sheet and told me I'd be better soon and not to cry and mother was cooking vegetable soup with dumplings for supper.

In the evening I felt better, and on Saturday I was fine except that I had to stay inside all day and couldn't even go downtown to buy a Mother's Day present. My mother told me not to feel bad—if I stayed inside and got completely well by Sunday we could go to church together, to the special service.

On Mother's Day I got up early. I washed my face and combed my hair. I put on my green dress with the long sleeves and white lace cuffs and went downstairs to make breakfast for my mother and father. I set the table with blue placemats Aunt Hanna sent from Denmark. I boiled eggs and made cinnamon toast because that's what I'm best at. My parents were pleased with the breakfast.

After breakfast my father went back to his desk to play chess with someone in India or Yugoslavia. My mother and I went to church.

I do worry sometimes about my father. His indifference to spiritual matters suggests a certain arrogance. And you must have heard what the Bible has to say about that: "Pride cometh before a fall." Of course, my father is not the only person who feels this way. Many people, at least in our part of the province, have no religious faith whatsoever. Men especially. Some men feel that religion is for women and children. And not even for all women. Some women they prefer without any religious faith at all. So they can have fun, if you know what I mean. But if a woman has children and has to take care of things, if a woman is responsible, if she has men and children to take care of, then she should have faith. That's what they think. Well, this kind of argument holds no water whatsoever as far as I'm concerned.

We walked through melting snow to church, our rubber boots black and shining in the slush. When we got inside, Mrs. Franklin and Mrs. Johnson met us at the door and gave us each a carnation, a pink one for me because my mother was alive, a white one for my mother because her mother was dead. She died five years ago. She had sugar diabetes, but it was a heart attack she died from. We pinned the carnations to our coats and walked down the aisle to a middle pew, right behind Mr. and Mrs. Carlson and Jackson, who's one year older than I am.

The text that Sunday was from the Book of Proverbs, written by King Solomon, the wisest man who ever lived, although he had a lot of wives. Mother's Day is the only time it's ever read in church: "Who can find a virtuous woman, for her price is far above rubies."

After the sermon we sang the hymn we sing every Mother's Day. My mother says she could do without that song, but I myself feel it has a lot of meaning. We all stood up. Mrs. Carlson sang in her usual voice. Mr. Carlson didn't sing at all, just looked at the words. Jackson turned around and stared at me a couple of times with no expression.

"Mid pleasures and palaces, though we may roam,
Be it ever so humble, there's no place like home.
A charm from the skies seems to hallow us there.
Which, seek thro' the world, is ne'er met with elsewhere.

Home, home, sweet, sweet home,
There's no place like home,
O, there's no place like home."

That afternoon I found the cat.

I had just come from Esther's house, only she wasn't home. I was on my way to Mary's house to see what she had done for her mother on Mother's Day. I knew it would be something clever because that's how she is. Communists are mixed up in a lot of ways, but they're not stupid.

The cat was in a ditch when I first saw it, a kitten actually, scratching at a little drift of snow and meowing. It was gray and skinny, its voice thin and unpleasant. I leaned over the ditch, picked it up by the fur of its neck as I'd been taught to do, and set it down on the concrete walk. But it didn't go anywhere. It didn't move. It just stood there by my ankle. I walked away and it followed me, meowing after me in its ugly voice. I didn't know what to do, so I scooped it up with my two hands, laid it in the crook of my arm, and took it with me to Mary's house. I stood in the back porch at Mary's house and showed the cat to Mrs. Helm. She leaned against the porch wall, next to the giant-sized pile of newspapers and magazines, and told me I should take it back where I found it.

"In the ditch?" I asked.

"Wherever you found it," she said. "Its owner will be looking for it."

"In the ditch?" I asked. "Will the owner look in the ditch?"

"It may be diseased," she said. "It's best not to bring it in the house." She spoke kindly but firmly. Mrs. Helm is not a cruel person, but she's no lover of cats.

I left Mary's house and went back to ask my mother if we could keep it. She said the same thing as Mrs. Helm. "Take it back where you found it."

"I found it in a ditch," I said.

"By whose house?" she asked. "It no doubt belongs to the people who live near the ditch."

"To Helms?" I asked. "Mrs. Helm can't stand cats."

"Maybe another house," my mother said. "Ask at the other houses. I understand Mrs. Gilbertson has cats. But come home soon," she added. "It's nearly suppertime."

I walked down the street, carrying the shivering kitten in my arms. I began knocking at doors. Everyone said the same thing: "Take it back where you found it." I said the same thing too. "I found it in a ditch." Then they said maybe Mrs. So and So would like to have it. And I'd knock on a few more doors.

The last door I knocked on was Mrs. McDonald's. Mrs. McDonald had always seemed like a very friendly person to me. Whenever she saw me she'd ask about my parents. "How are those fine people?" she'd say. "Your parents are such lovely people." So I thought this might be my lucky chance. Maybe Mrs. McDonald would take the kitten.

"Me?" she asked, standing under the light in her front hall, rubbing her thin hands on the pockets of her frilly apron. "Oh no, honey. I couldn't possibly. As much as I'd like to. Not with my allergy. But aren't you a precious one for caring so. Aren't you just the sweetest little girl, looking out for that poor animal. You are the kindest little thing," she said. I thought she'd said enough, but she went on and on. I stood in the doorway and listened to every word. "You're going to make a very good mother," she said. "Just the nicest mother ever. Look at you cuddling that poor thing. What a sweet little mother you are." I believe she finished right then because she started closing the door, ever so gently, easing me out on the step, still holding the limp and whining cat.

What happened next is what I'm trying to figure out. I've spent two years now trying to figure this out, but I'm not sure I fully understand, even now.

I didn't know what to do with the kitten, so I headed out of town on the dirt road that leads to Goertzen's. It was getting dark and windy and much colder, so I shoved the kitten under my jacket to keep it warm, I pulled the sleeves of the jacket over my bare hands to keep them warm. I felt the cat under the cloth, pressing against my chest, its claws pushing back and forth into the softness there. I bent my head against the wind and stumbled through the ruts, my boots oozing down into the half-frozen mud. I didn't know where I was going, just leaving town with that thin and ugly kitten pushing on my chest, nibbling at me, purring and pressing against me as if I were its home, as if I were the place where it belonged.

When I passed the concession line I looked back and saw the town lit up behind me, all the houses behind me with orange light shining out of windows. I turned and saw the blackness ahead of me, the night, dark and empty as a cave. I tried walking faster through the mud, the cat still clinging to the softness on my chest. The air stuck to my lips and stopped heavy in my nostrils. Suddenly I realized I wasn't going anywhere. There was no place to go. Only Goertzen's, and that was too far—five more miles at least.

I stood in the middle of the road and pulled the cat out from under my jacket. I held it up by the fur of its neck, looked at it by the light of the snow that shone in the ditch at the road's edge, by the light of distant stars above. I saw its eyes glimmering in the starlight, its small kitten eyes looking at me.

"You dumb cat," I said. "You damn cat. You Goddamn cat. You Goddamn stupid cat." Its eyes gleamed. "You don't know anything, do you? Not your father or your mother or even where you come from. You dumb, stupid cat." And I hated the cat. I really did. I hated its matted fur and its loose, sickly body. But most of all I hated it dangling there, under the stars, watching me, waiting . . .

That's when I did it. I jumped into the ditch and shuffled through the snow. I scraped at the snow with my feet and my one free hand. I scraped until I found a rock, until I found two. And then I did it. I laid the cat on the flattest rock, hard and icy. And I did it. I laid it, stomach down on the rock. I spread its legs out and pressed its head against the stone. I lifted the other rock and hurled it down on the cat. It flipped and tumbled off, landing in the ditch. I saw it there, gray and quiet in the snow, its eyes glinting. Then I lifted it up by its hind leg and pressed it again down on the rock. I pressed its head and body with my hand, its fur stiff and icy on my fingers. I raised the rock above my head and smashed it down on the silent cat. I kept smashing it until it was tangled and bloody, dangling on the frozen rock. Then I picked it up by the end of its tail and flung it for all I was worth into the field. I didn't look twice to where I'd heaved it. I just turned around and started back to town.

I saw the lights of town in a distance, the orange lights from all the houses. I used to like going home after dark and seeing those lights. In winter, when it was dark at four, I'd walk home from school and look at the houses with orange light shining out the windows. I'd think of children and fathers going home in the dark. And when they got there, the house would be warm, the supper cooking and the mother setting the table and humming. But that night, walking into town and seeing the lights, it wasn't like that.

When I got home my parents had already eaten supper and were sitting at the kitchen table drinking tea.

"You've been gone a long time," my father said. "Did you find a home for the kitten?"

"Yes," I said

"Oh, where?" my mother asked.

"Some Ukranians took it," I said

"You mean you walked all the way out past the railroad tracks?"

"Only as far as Levinsky's."

"Did Mrs. Levinsky take it then?"

"No," I said. "But Mrs. Levinsky said she knew some Ukranians who live on the other side of the Hutterites. She said they'd take it because they have a huge barn and a lot of other cats and fresh milk and hay, so the cat would be warm and comfortable and have friends. Mrs. Levinsky will take it there tomorrow."

"That was very kind of Mrs. Levinsky," my father said.

"I thought so," I said and went upstairs to the bathroom to wash my hands for supper.

I didn't think about my experience that night. I was too tired. I went to bed early and fell asleep right away. But since then it's been on my mind. I've thought about it now for two years. I still wonder about it—what I did and those orange lights in the houses. I think about this—that there's no place you can go and be sure of things, no house you can enter and not hurt somebody or get hurt. No place. Not anywhere. And how do you take that if you're a person of faith? I know what the Buddhists believe about this. I've studied the Buddhists in the encyclopedia and I understand their doctrines. They believe that if you know you'll do wrong by going places or doing things, then don't go there. Don't do anything. Stay where you are. Just sit. Then you won't sin. That's what the Buddhists believe. But I'm not a Buddhist certainly. I think it's this way—you walk into those houses, knowing all along it's not going to be true or right or everlasting, knowing all along you might get knocked on the head or knock someone else on the head. But you don't think about that. You just step right in. There'll always be some light there, little pieces of it anyway. And you can notice that. You can notice every little piece that's there, even if it doesn't last, even if it fades away like grass.

On Monday I went to school as usual. At recess I met Esther at our special place by the poplar tree and we talked about Mother's Day. I told her I made breakfast and went to church with my mother. She told me her mother liked the box of chocolates and they spent the day at Kobrinsky's. Her family doesn't go to church because they're Jews, not to synagogue either because there aren't enough Jews in our town to have one. They do celebrate festive occasions in their homes, however. Like the Passover. And Mother's Day. At least they do in our town. I don't know if they have a Mother's Day in Israel or not. I know in Japan there's no special day set aside for mothers. Instead they have a Boys' Day and a Girls' Day. But the Scandinavian countries celebrate much the same as we do, at least in Norway, with flowers and gifts. I'm not sure what the customs are in Africa or South America.

But one thing I do know. And no one can argue against this fact, whether he's a Communist, a Christian, or a Jew. There's no nation in the whole world, not a single solitary one, without mothers.

FLORENCE McNEIL

Family Dinner

Our family gathered together
    preserve ourselves
            with ritual
In the middle generation
        we bless the roast potatoes
are aware of our elders
          as fragile china
pass them on tenderly
Admit publicly
      there can be no
            conclusion
          to what we have begun
(privately I wonder
      where is the family
we who are still children among our fragments
        of parents
           the grandfathers all are missing
the sons and nieces who take off our coats
      with such solicitude
the old people who invoke the new suburban moon
        to guide the fishing fleet
speak Gaelic to the unfamiliar city they have lived in
      for fifty years)
Only the smallest children can be safe
      their eyes are still and honest
they do not know how many ghosts already
      hover over our table
and why the chairs set out in orderly fashion
      according to custom
        are always inadequate.

RAY SHANKMAN

Wedding Poem

At my wedding there was no
red haired madman fiddling,
no Uncle dancing with two bottles
of schnaps cradled in his arms,
no Grandmother hiking up her skirts
to dance the Blackbottom;

At my wedding there were 100 plates
invited: how many from our side
how many from that side, arguments
over which is better square tables
or round tables, friends I've never seen
mooching a meal underneath the Circus tent;

A silly photographer who grieved
when the Bride wouldn't smile,
a supercilious Rabbi who droned text
without feeling, a mother whose iron will
never melted before the potential
of Divine Union.

At our wedding we had flowers and tears,
this egomaniac of a Bridegroom indignant
full of passionate conviction screaming
to the guests, "I hope you'll all be as happy
as we are going to be" and a pissed Aunty
shouting back, "we'll wait and see, we'll wait and see."

At our wedding the song ended before it began,
the dance faltered before the mirror
of wilting flowers and tearstained make-up
and the guests, now dead, plotted the marriage course
with deft fingering minds.

MARGARET GIBSON

Aaron

i

Mother. Father. Child.
A trinity.
Broken.
It had to be that.
No more frantic, hard push of
sweaty bodies slippery
within our adult grasping fingers.
Soon you and I were gone
from the other adult.
And I bore you.
But no slippery bodies
sliding between pliable fingers,
sliding like whale oil
could have made you you.

You dunned under my skins.
Dunning.
A Mad Hatter
tick, tock
six-eight time
the human heart beat pocket watch.

My belly was puffed and stretched
like a fat and pale oyster.
My once trim ankles water swollen.
It did not matter.
The days and nights of sitting alone
in a cold flat
the window cracked
like the jagged lash of a whip
would soon end.
I, Margaret, was going to give birth.

Then the cleaving,
the dunning six-eight beat
stopped
within my oyster parts
and was held bloodied and close to my breast.

You did not squall.
"He was always a quiet baby," I was to say in a kitchen-way
as the years passed.
You did not squall.

ii

And now you are five, just five
and have not had much time to be five or four
or anything at all
but yourself.

You are like a lone and beautiful tree
in a riot field of weeds.

You do not hang out with a crowd of kids
but rather
stand back, a little to the side,
and wonder why they do not understand your jokes
or who Dylan Thomas is. You do.
It seems you always did.

Sometimes your caring catches me unaware
Like the day we sat on the hard cold stone steps.
and from a mouth so small and young,
yet old in knowing of difference,
you told me, "Make them play with me, Mommy, I'll buy
                    you a birthday present."
"My love, my love," and we rocked together on the cold,
                    ungiving steps.

I want to tell you from my old age of 29
sitting here at the omnipotent grey machine
the dream machine
the alone machine
that the caring and the wanting to be a wild weed never ends.

Once, weeping, I knelt before you
and cradled
your soft, small head.
I told you that I was sorry,
that I grieved for you, for me,
for all the unright things I had done.
Translucent hand then three patted my arm,
two words: "I understand."
And that made it all worse somehow.

Now at five
you remind me to take my pills
and to phone the doctor when I am crazed
and always you bring my pill bottles
offering them up with renewed hope each time.
Always I swallow the pills and say, "Now I will never be
                    sick again."

I fool no-one.

You are a lone and beautiful tree
in a riot field of weeds.
And you did not squall.

BARRY DEMPSTER

Uncle Claude

it was always over a game
of crazy 8's   around the kitchen
table   the night the size of a
closet   then a part of me would
rise   like the smoke from your
cigarette   drifting across the table
getting mixed up with your hands
in your eyes   there i was   forming
a child around your head.

your cigarette ashes dropped methodically
into heaps in the ashtray   you made
sure of it   same time dealing as
fast as a gambler   cracking jokes
making miracles out of the cards
between your yellow man-size fingers.

i was obsessed with your eyes   the
coils of tight colour   flashing around
the room   your skull of short white
hair   the wrinkles on your forehead
like years unravelling   your prowess
the way   with a smile   you handled
little boys   cigarettes   a pack of cards

now when i see you   too tired after
supper for games   flopped on the couch
like a pillow   old eyes stuck to the
t.v. set   night leaning on your shoulders
i almost forget how big you once were
next to me   how cool with your talent
your affection   the memory gleaming
dull as a quarter moon   as tentative as smoke.

MATT COHEN

Pat Frank's Dream

That winter the snow had fallen early. By late November there
had been a foot on the ground, by Christmas three feet. Now, in
February, the snow entirely covered both the shrubs that in
summertime dotted the hills, and the fences that separated the bush

From the novel *Sunrise*, to be published by McClelland and Stewart.

and scrubby pasture from the few ploughed fields. Between the layers of snow were thin sheets of ice, from times when the temperature had jumped and then dipped. These thin sheets gave support for the smaller animals, even rabbits and foxes. But for the heavier animals it was impossible. The wolves, desperate, travelled in packs, howling close to the houses at night, hiding by day. They fed on deer who struggled and starved in the deep snow; and on occasion they captured sheep and young calves right from the barnyard.

"Even in the winter," Terry Frank had explained, "the deer digs through the snow to eat old grass and leaves. When the snow's deep he can't get at his food, and it's so much work to move that he dies struggling." It had snowed that way one winter before, several years ago, and Pat could remember being towed by his father on a toboggan to see the frozen deer kneeling like ice statues near the back pond.

On this day the sun had a bright hot glare. Nothing alive would freeze in a sun like this. It was rising in the clear sky, promising spring, and its light broke apart on the glittering snow so the whole white rolling terrain was sparked with bits of red and blue. As he lit his cigarette Pat tried to squint the way he had seen the men do, narrowing his eyes against the light and the smoke, and it was at just that moment, out of the corner of his vision, that he saw his first wolf. As he turned full towards it, his hand snaking out for the rifle, it was gone. The dogs, who had collapsed near him when he started to smoke, hadn't even noticed; and for the time he thought that the wolf, and the shadows that seamed it into the edge of the far bush, were only in his imagination.

When he had finished his cigarette he began working his way on the snowshoes again. Though the temperature was low, the hot sun warmed the still air and soon he was sweating in his clothes, enough to open his jacket and the top button of his shirt, and then, finally, to leave his jacket on a tree branch and continue in shirt and heavy sweater. The dogs raced around, barking at whatever they could tree, anticipating his direction. He had never, alone, travelled so far from the house in winter, and the sensation of his increasing distance made him feel tense and independent; he found himself continually clenching the rifle for reassurance and running his hand against his pocket, where he kept his hunting knife.

He had agreed to limit himself to one of the lines, half a circuit. To save carrying he was first walking to the point farthest from the house; and by the time he got there, which involved a trip through the back bush and two miles along the curve of the lake, it was noon and he stopped to eat the bannock and cheese he had brought with him. Twice he had climbed up from the shore to the bush surrounding the lake, and both times had seen dense layers of wolf tracks. "They'll come round you from behind," his father had told him. "You don't have to worry about surprising them."

He threw the scraps of the bannock to the dogs, then rolled himself another cigarette. The heat of the burning tip made the air above it shimmer like liquid glass. Looking through it he could see the whole flat surface of the lake stretching out miles in front of him, so smooth and icy-serene it could have been a giant eye, his father's eye, frozen and buried in earth and rock. And the trees around the lake were like dark green lashes, thick and tipped with snow, so still in the cold air that for a moment the boy forgot about his father, himself, the place he had come from and the place he was searching for, and saw only the lake and the surrounding trees, a sudden oasis that had lived its own life for thousands of years, freezing and thawing, breathing air fishes birds as easily as the passing seasons. And then he came back to himself and wondered if this was how it looked before there had ever been farmers, if Indian eyes had seen the same lake, the same trees, the same liquid movement through smoke and fire.

"The trouble with Indians," Terry Frank liked to say, "was that they didn't understand the plough."

At the first trap he found a rabbit, caught by the leg and frozen. This was a good start—some days they caught nothing at all. He cut the rabbit free and threw it in his sack, already wondering how he would carry his bountiful harvest. But then he followed the line a whole mile back on the upper reaches of the shore before he found the next—a squirrel. Black, its huge tail was fanned out on the ground. It too was frozen dead, its lips drawn back so far it seemed its mouth had been pried open for its spirit to escape. Working the squirrel free his hands got cold and there was the sudden awkward sound of bone scraping metal. At one point he thought he heard movement in the bush. He jumped around, reaching for his rifle and scanning the trees for wolves. The dogs, unconcerned, lolled a few yards away, eyes incuriously closed and tongues laid out against the snow.

The traps had been set out in the hollows of the streams that fed into the lake. In places the drifts were so deep and powdery that the snowshoes sank in and left him floundering, buried to his thighs. Even the dogs grew tired, and where on the way out they had perambulated five miles to his one, now they were content to struggle in the ragged track he was breaking.

The sun shone only weakly through the dense bush, and Pat was alternately flushed and shivering as he worked. The trap line was clearly marked with blazes, but he had never travelled through such deep slow snow; and at each empty trap he grew more discouraged until finally he stopped to roll a cigarette and think about giving up.

He could already see the look of scorn on Terry Frank's face as he came in the door carrying only one small rabbit and one torn-up squirrel. Following the line it would take him three hours to get back to the field where he had left the jacket; by that time it would be dark but not, in the snow, impossible to see his way home. But if he gave up and cut back to the lake he could be back at the house before the sun set.

"Well, dogs," Pat said, "you decide." The two bitch hounds, named by his father Rusty and Red after their colour, looked at him speculatively. Even more than most hounds, they had skulls spectacularly pinched and narrow, and allowing for the thickness of bone, Pat had often calculated that the size of their brains must be about that of a baby's handful of peas.

"Well, dogs, is it home or hunting? Does the early rabbit get the carrot? Will you guide me through the evil forest?"

At the sound of all this human voice the dogs rolled over in the snow to be patted on their bellies.

"Jesus." Pat was thirteen years old, and though Mark was wider and stronger, it was he who was the tall one, the first to be stretching up into the world of manhood. If he went home early with nothing but the rabbit he'd be saying he couldn't do it, that he was still too much of a baby to take the cold and the effort of walking the line. If *he* was sick, Mark would have gone alone; and Mark, he knew, wouldn't have come home empty-handed, would stay outside till his stocky boy's body froze before admitting defeat.

Pat stood up, clapped his gloves together until his fingers hurt, and took the census of his body: feet numb but without twinges of pain, the seat of his pants wet from sitting on the snowy log, cold circles where his wrists and neck were exposed. Nothing that wouldn't get warm or be easy to ignore once he was moving.

In the fall, when these traps had been positioned, it had taken only a few hours to walk the entire circuit. Not only did the snow make it harder to move, it also disguised the numerous deadfalls that had been scattered about by disease, lightning and careless loggers. Sometimes Pat found their tops, gaining good support for his snowshoes; more often he stepped right in front of one, and when he went to lift his shoe found himself trapped and falling forward.

By the time an hour had passed the afternoon sun was beginning to run out. And aside from another squirrel, also too small and bony to be bothered with, he was still carrying the only game he had come up with all day—one rabbit no heavier than a good-sized rock, and one frozen squirrel with its skin ruined.

During the second hour shadows began to block the spaces between the trees. He missed two traps entirely, and a third was empty. He was just about to reconsider going home when he came up to the crest of a hill and saw, in the small valley below, the dark form of a wolf lying motionless in the snow. At first he thought that the wolf was dead, that it had been caught in the metal trap, frozen and straved. He didn't even think about the dogs, who were labouring behind him, until they scented the wolf and began barking and running crazily down the hill.

When at first the wolf moved, Pat thought he must simply be seeing things with fatigue. And then the bush came alive with the weird howl of more wolves, their sudden music twisting him out of himself, making him feel like glass suddenly shattered and thrown across the snow. The dark forms whirled and turned on the charging hounds.

As quickly as Pat had his glove off and the rifle to his shoulder, three more wolves had come out of the bush and thrown themselves at the dogs. "Rusty," Pat shouted. "Rusty. Red." The four wolves were a circle around the two hounds, the black and grey fur blotting out the red. Pat's finger was on the trigger but everything was moving too fast, the shadows of dog and wolf intermingled. His mind, fixed on the confusion, suddenly froze.

And then the wolves were gone.

The dogs lay bleeding in the snow. He ran clumsily toward them, his snowshoes flailing and threatening to send him over on his face.

He was sure the dogs were still alive, that at any moment they would leap up, dance around him with their muzzles poking wet into his neck, their paws pushing off his shoulders. But they didn't move; their bellies and throats were torn open and faintly steaming in the cold air. Frozen in the trap was a small fox, which might have made the whole trip worthwhile had not its hide, too, been ripped apart.

When he got home it was almost six o'clock. Pitch black. His father was sitting by the stove, bottle in one hand and watch in the other.

"Jesus Christ," he said. "I almost got to worrying about you."

"I'm okay," Pat said. Their were lanterns on downstairs but no light from the upstairs bedrooms. "Is Mark asleep?"

"He's at the Kincaids. Gone to see if you were there."

"Sorry."

"You better feed the dogs before you get to taking off your boots."

Pat, without speaking, continued to pry off his rubbers. His feet were so cold he couldn't feel anything in them, not even the pressure of his hands massaging them.

"You heard me."

"They got killed by wolves," Pat said, and kept rubbing his feet. He could already feel the pain starting in his ears, needles edging up from the lobes.

"They did, did they. Them dogs wouldn't make a meal for a goddamned raccoon."

He was drunk, Pat could see, but not *that* drunk. He was still sipping from the bottle, not taking it in the big swallows that made his Adam's apple look like a fish being coughed up by the sea; or at the stage of being so drunk he didn't even bother with alcohol anymore, just boiled coffee and poured it into his belly in a useless effort to keep from getting sick.

Pat took a pair of dry socks hanging from the stove and pulled them gently over his toes.

"What kept you?"

"I don't know. It took a long time." He looked at his burlap bag with the one rabbit. "I didn't get much."

"That's all right," Terry Frank said unexpectedly. "It's a bad time of year. You did good to try."

This made Pat want to cry.

"I remember the first time I went out alone. I was lucky to get back." He smiled at Pat and leaned over to touch him on the shoulder. "You better feed those dogs now. They get tired too."

And Pat, his toes starting to hurt, his shins stiff from a whole day on snowshoes, his hands red and numb, finally started to cry and tell the story of what had happened. At first explaining it all unreservedly but then, seeing the look on his father's face changing from kindness to anger, cut himself short.

"I'm sorry," he finished.

"Sorry."

"I didn't know what to do."

"What did you think the rifle was for? Pissing?"

Pat was silent.

"Well?" His father's voice rising.

"I don't know.'

"Didn't you have it loaded?"

"Yes."

"Well, for Christ's sake, why didn't you shoot?" This shouted.

"I didn't want to hit the dogs." He was still sitting beside the stove, the snow melting through his clothes and into his skin.

"You didn't want to hit the dogs," roared Terry Frank.

His father's face: wide, open, screaming. Pat tipping back in his chair, the words rushing through him, tipping back in his chair feeling so small that when he reached for the rifle against the wall it was only to keep himself from falling into the stove.

'Jesus Christ,' shouted Terry Frank. "Don't grab that thing at me." Which only frightened Pat more, startling him to his feet, holding the rifle across his chest now, his finger slid into the trigger, alive now where it had gone dead before.

"Put that down."

"Don't tell me what to do."

"Put that down or I'll beat the arse right off you."

"Fuck off, shitface."

The sound of the wet wood hissing and whistling in the stove. Of his father's breathing, hoarse and protracted; of his own, high-pitched and gasping as if he had been running the whole day.

"Give it to me."

"Stay away."

"Give it to me."

Backing off from his father, who was edging towards him. Stepping back to the landing and then one by one up the stairs, Terry Frank following, his hand held out. And with each step he climbed, Pat was gradually swinging the rifle from across his belly to point first at the stairs and finally at the belly of Terry Frank. Who followed, just out of reach.

And then he was at the top landing and if he didn't stop he would be backed into one of the bedrooms, trapped.

"Give it to me."

"No."

His father's face: wide, open generous. "I'll let you alone."

"Let me alone now."

These negotiations whispered, his father's mask beginning to slip and dissolve, Pat's eye caught by the empty burlap sack hung over the chair. His finger on the trigger, tense and jumping, his nerves needing the shots that should have been fired in the bush, already anticipating the echoing sound of this one shot fired in the narrow stairway, the sight of Terry Frank exploding backwards in one long last vacant fling.

"Come on."

"No."

Terry Frank's big hand, fast for once, whipping forward to the muzzle of the rifle, but Pat had caught it coming, had spied out the blue eyes surveying the gap, and he was ready, swung the rifle forward. "No," he shouted, everything contracting inside of him as he pushed forward with all his strength, springing as he jabbed Terry Frank in the chest with the muzzle, his weight behind it, sending his father cascading down the stairs.

The noise of his falling was so loud, and the blood racing through his hands so hot, he thought he must have shot him after all. And as the boom and clatter of the falling faded, and his father settled at the bottom of the stairs, the noise of his voice rose. At first Pat thought he was just shouting with pain, and then he thought that he was crying, but finally realized it was neither but only the never-heard sound of his father laughing unrestrained, truly laughing as he straightened himself out, unhurt. And finally he pointed up to Pat, his face scarlet with anger and pride. "You goddamned little bastard, Pat you would have killed me."

FRANCIS SPARSHOTT

The Naming of the Beasts

In that lost Caucasian garden
where history began
the nameless beasts paraded
in front of the first man.

Who am I? they asked him
and what shall I be
when you have left the garden?
Name me.   Name me.

Poverty, cruelty, lechery,
rage, hate, shame—
each stalked past the podium
seeking his name.

Adam stood to attention
unable to speak,
his life too short to utter
what was made that week.

The glum parade stumbles
from risen to set sun
past their dumbfounded patron.
But he knows each one;

and at last a strange dampness
salts either cheek.

That was the language of Eden.
Not Hebrew, not Greek:

in groans, grunts, howls
as the first tears fall
the inarticulate brute
finds names for them all.

Nympharum Disjecta Membra

White under Knob Hill's fluorescent glare
dismembered hens, wing, breast, and thigh,
gutted and weighed are arranged, packaged in plastic,
each bearing her own price,
stacked under glass in the cold case.

Probed by cool stares and appraising fingers
of the jeaned and jacketed or ringed and furred,
in a basket of bright wires
jostling and colliding down the aisles
home to the oven goes the dead meat.

Ranked upon racks over the cased cigars
young women parade the glazed nakedness
of buttock and breast and whatever intimate else
furrowed and furred will sell. They simper dreamily,
spreading their limbs to the hard lens.

Lewd men, bitter with oppression,
lovers of bondage, look: their eyes are not for you.
It was weeks ago, they were hungry and held
in the cash nexus. Proud or ashamed, they smiled,
paid not to scowl or scream in the studio's hot light.

Reflex

The lens may be adjusted
for inner and outer vision
with a simple screw
this calls for a decision
of course there are sharper lenses
will focus inner and outer
into a single scene
but those things cost the earth
                              and
I never felt ready
to give up the earth.

With a gelatine filter
under a dull sky
all colours are softened
in the blue distance
flesh tints turn pale
and the general effect
of faded harmony
like nunnery compline
using it all the time
wins me my reputation
for quiet good taste.

Fiddling with chemicals
was never my style;
processing is arranged
through a local drugstore.

GEORGE RYGA

Beyond a Crimson Morning

An hour from Osaka, the east China Sea is obscured by grey, warm clouds. Ahead of us, under monsoon cover, is Shanghai. The Boeing 707 is spotless. It smells of fresh enamel. Stewardesses, hardly more than children in pigtails, baggy blue trousers and tunics and plastic shoes with white stockings, push a serving cart down the aisle. Their manners with the passengers are cautious, curious, and tentative. The children of new China are no more comfortable with the people of the outside world than we are with them.

The Boeing 707 begins to drop over the east China Sea. Below us, the monsoon clouds are turbulent and grey-white. The setting sun ahead of us throws metallic shadows over the gleaming aircraft wings and motors. The Chinese music on the aircraft intercom system dies down and a faint message in three languages is heard—on arrival in Shanghai all passengers will disembark for dinner before proceeding to Peking.

Shanghai airport is deserted and wet. Parked on the tarmac near the airport building are a half-dozen transport trucks of Soviet design. Behind them, just visible in gathering darkness and mist, are three small prop aircraft. People in blue cloth caps and blue jackets and pants and rubber boots are hurrying across the runways, as if using them for short-cuts on the way home from work. A soldier in green cycles past, slowing to watch us curiously before he vanishes in the rain.

In the evening or night the third world is poorly lit, for electrical energy is scarce. A small group of Chinese people are on the steps of the airport building, waiting for us. Under the large, softly lit portrait of Chairman Mao which graces the wall above the building entrance, they are totally in shadow. We approach and the leader of the group steps forward to guide our delegation inside, where a meal is already in progress for visitors to China who have arrived on a flight prior to ours. . . .

Arrival at Peking airport is late and group morale is low. Customs clearance is cumbersone and slow despite the late hour. Luggage check tags, issued in Tokyo, are mismatched and do not reflect the amount of luggage we have brought. Four items that arrive with us have not been checked properly. Customs officials are cordial but confused. They laboriously line all luggage on the wooden floor of the customs building and, squatting over the pieces, try to match the check stubs.

Our group stands around waiting. Then an argument erupts between Bess and Randy. As if this is the signal they have been waiting for, most group members now move in among the customs workers and begin selecting their individual bags from the floor.

Mrs. Tsu, our translator, is on hand to meet us with a small cluster of young translators and guides. She is a thin, shy country woman. Because of nervousness, she appears to have difficulty with her English, which corrects itself quickly as we gain ease with each other.

"What is the problem? Is there something the young gentleman is worried about with his luggage?" she asks, indicating Randy.

"No," I reply. "They are tired, impatient North Americans. It will be better tomorrow."

I cannot follow how the argument between Bess and Randy developed, or over what. It seems to take the form of two people very familiar with each other who would find it easy to argue over anything. I later learn they have not known each other previously.

"What is your country like? How do people live and think?"

"It would take a year to explain everything, by which time much would have changed and such information would be useless, Mrs. Tsu," I tell her. She laughs and translates her question and my reply to the translators, who are curious but separated from us by an aisle on the bus.

"It is the same in China," she offers.

We are driven to the Peking Hotel. Room allotments have been prepared, and organization of everyone for the night is quickly accomplished. In moments the lobby is cleared and Mrs. Tsu asks if I still have the energy left for a briefing session, I do.

The junior translators are dismissed for the night, and Mrs. Tsu leads me to an isolated table at the far end of the lobby. Waiting for us with a tray of teacups and hot tea are two people from the travel service—Mr. Chou and Mrs. Kwon. He is the younger of the two—a cheerful, energetic, and provocative man of slight stature which strangely fluctuates with his bursts of energy. He is rough-edged but confident. Unlike Mrs. Tsu, he is both peasant and urban dweller. His stride is strong, his voice authoratative, even when he is in error—a leader in training.

But it is Mrs. Kwon who fascinates me and will continue to do so in the weeks ahead. She is the senior leader of this work group. Her age is close to my own. She is thoughtful, considerate, patient, and cultivated—the person who trains leaders in this new society.

This first meeting is a moment for each of us to acquaint with the others. It begins stiffly. Chou presents me with the program of activities for the following day. The program is pored over and discussed unnecessarily. There is concern over possible medical needs of group members. I suddenly feel it is a bad beginning, a strain that could quickly formalize into a ritual. At the same time I am uncertain as to the graces and cultural mores of our hosts.

"Goddamn it, we're guests in your country. Outside of one member who speaks Han and has made an academic study of China and a few middle-class converts to Maoism, we are here and we know nothing of China. But we are here to learn. We can start anywhere in the morning—with a pig farm or nuclear research laboratories. It makes very little difference!"

After the meeting ends, I walk through the hotel and up the stairs to my room. Ol' Bill is asleep now, his things unpacked. My luggage has been placed on my bed. I unpack and have a cold shower. The hotel still has an atmosphere of continental European grandeur, but it is fading and seedy, smelling of carbolic and decaying paint. I dress again and leave the building for some fresh air.

The great boulevard in front of the hotel—the main thoroughfare dissecting the city is abandoned at one in the morning except for state cars performing taxi duties. But these are not numerous, and their gentle beep-beeping horns are like cricket sounds in the night. In front of the hotel the fountain is filled, but it is neither lit nor functioning. The water in the fountain basin is stagnant, and numerous hoses and buckets left near the fountain suggest it is used as a water source for washing hotel buses and cars, which gleam nearby in their parking spaces under elm and poplar trees.

Peking reminds me of Edmonton. The odor of the streets at night, the rustle of northern trees, the low buildings and sense of sprawl. But as I walk a short distance down the poorly lit boulevard, the differences are overwhelming. Unlike Edmonton, this is an ancient city, where fresh brick and concrete are overtaking gloomy shelters of mud, stone, and porous tile. Heavy trucks loaded with building materials are parked overnight beside slender scaffolding of bamboo poles and reeds which surround the gaunt silhouette of new steel framed buildings under construction. Now and then, in singles and small groupings, workers with thermos bottles in their hands pass me in the night. I peer into their faces, but they are in shadow under peaks of blue cloth caps. My leather-heeled footsteps sound on the pavement. Theirs are silent. Tired but elated, I return to the hotel.

In dawn twilight I am awakened by a sound I have not heard before. The beeping of car horns from the night is still there, but under it is a soft rustling. With my eyes shut, I strain to listen and realize it is not the familiar sound of wind or rain. Ol' Bill is still asleep as I get out of bed. He has been sleeping in his pajamas on his covers. He has enjoyed a serene, unrumpled sleep. I give his bed a kick with the heel of my foot. The bed shudders and hums. He is instantly up on his feet, both hands down at his crotch.

The sound I have heard is the sound of thousands of bicycles on the pavement, their rubber tires buzzing as they move twenty abreast, filling both sides of the great street with a sea of humanity on the way to work in factories, offices, and outlying farmlands. Here and there are three-wheeled cycles, loaded with tools, building materials, coal, and sacks of cereals. Of all ages, the men and women cyclists appear lean and remarkably fit from where we watch them. . . .

We dine on rice gruel, tea, and pickled vegetables and seasoned strips of pork and beef. We dine on this so-called "Chinese breakfast" by choice. A Western breakfast of scrambled eggs and bacon, high-gluten bread toast, fruit preserves, and coffee is also available, and many members of our group are to happily return to it after that initial meal. But the first meal is an orientation affair—a getting-to-know-China event which is only partially successful.

Chou, crisp and fresh looking in a freshly pressed white shirt and grey trousers is waiting in the lobby after breakfast.

"Did you eat well?" He asks cheerfully.

"Yes... yes, I did." The atmosphere between us is still touched by caution and some uncertainty. I gesture for him to walk down the lobby with me in the direction of the hotel bookstore.

"In the town where I grew up, Mr. Chou, there was a restaurant—wedged between a blacksmith shop and a lumber business..."

"We have such places in China," he interrupts.

"Yes, I'm sure you do... In the window of this restaurant was a sign which read: 'Eat like a horse for 50 cents. To eat like a man will cost you $1.50'."

He carefully removes his glasses as we walk and, withdrawing a white handkerchief, cleans them. He bites his lower lip thoughtfully, then replaces the glasses.

"It is not like that here. Horses are not allowed into restaurants. I think they are provided with eating places of their own!" He is unable to suppress himself and breaks into a chortling laugh.

We enter the bookstore, which is vacant at this hour of the morning. It is unlike bookstores at home. The displays are attractive and colorful, but the selection of books and prints reveals the strong imprint of revolutionary zeal. Most of the books on display are political or theoretical. There is no escapism. No departure from the serious undertakings of education of the masses. There is also a surprising absence of Chairman Mao's little red book of quotations, which previous travellers to China had mentioned as being very much in evidence after the Great Cultural Revolution of 1968 and subsequent years. I locate and purchase a copy. But it is in an obscure part of the shop, not displayed. The book which I buy is bound in red plastic and shows signs of aging....

On the Great Wall the winds from the Gobi desert are dry, hot, and taste of ashes in the mouth. Grey masonry, bleached by the centuries and polished by wind, glows with a sacred light. Rising to the tops of mountains and snaking down into deep ravines, it makes no compromises with nature, or reason—or a hesitancy in will and determination. The final battlements, girding China like a belt of stone, are not overgrown with vines or shrubs. Crumbling, it is still the treacherous platform of warriors, ready for battle. The curing rack for heroes, exposing their souls to the gales and snows of winter and the burning summer, drying them into leather through which a spear or a compromising argument cannot pierce. Visible even from the moon, it still divides the world between those who have let the past slip out of their hands and memories, and those who cannot—perhaps never will.

The voices of our unit—for we are a unit now—a unit of observers. Diverse, crude, specialized, childish, wise. The voices of our unit are muted now, for despite outbreaks of excitement, even laughter, a great silence imposes itself on the wall. A silence of wind and stars. Of colossal human labor and earth resources frozen eternally into a vigil whose significance is mind shattering.

Hot sand cuts the eyes. I suddenly want to leave the wall. The babble of languages struggling to explain what they do not understand. Ahead of me, in the burning cauldron of desert and wind, is my ancestral homeland. Longing and remorse, hot as a wound, spreads outward from my entrails. Tears fill my eyes, and through the tears the landscape dances and diffuses into horsemen, their sabers gleaming, their voices a shrill metallic cry of battle as their numbers darken the horizon, their turbans in flames as they gallop westward to conquer the steppes of Russia and the scented, soft underbelly of Asia Minor.... There is one rider among them, his eyes glowing, teeth bared to the wind, who will seed discontent into drowsy wide-hipped women in sleepy thatched hamlets thousands of miles away. I want to overtake him as he gallops in service of the mercurial Genghis Khan. I want to embrace him until we both fall to the earth. And if he reaches for his weapons, we will both do battle until I destroy him so I may free myself from the spell in which he has snared me.

"Why do you, who have never handled weapons, fight me with such fury?" he cries.

"You are an animal!" I scream. "A dark animal devouring me from inside since I was a child!"

"If you kill me, you will also die!" He taunts me, then laughs, dropping his arms to his side. Helpless, unguarded, waiting for death at my hands. I sob and run from him...

The road down from the mountains and the Great Wall is steep and twisting. Great metallic mirrors are imbedded in granite on treacherous corners to reflect oncoming traffic. As we approach the lowlands, the roadway fills with peasants leading draft animals pulling carts loaded with vegetables, corn, and wheat. The exchange of commodities is on a primitive economic level. I see the same produce being moved in two different directions. I comment on this to Mrs. Kwon. She shrugs.

"China is an enormous country. It is not an easy or simple task to rationalize transport and communications," she says. "The masses plan and execute their plans wisely. But some things remain unchanged..."

In the lowlands, the road to Peking widens, and the curves are graceful and gentle. Tall poplars, their lower branches stripped, border the highway, their shade cooling the road surface. Half the roadway is now filled with peasants and workmen on foot and on bicycles, going to or returning from work. We progress slowly now, for the human and animal traffic overflows often into the pathway of the bus. The driver is expressionless. The only irritation he shows are the frequent horn blasts he executes when the bus is forced into first gear by the human spillover in front of us. The armed forces are in evidence, in pale green fatigues, working with the population on construction projects in the fields and hamlets beside the highway. The building underway is of irrigation facilities, small factories, and low-rise apartment housing. The heat of the lowlands becomes oppressive, and all windows in the bus are opened. The warm air blowing into the bus smells of tar, harvest wheat chaff, and alkaline dust. Ahead of us, a crowd of younger people fill the road as far as we could see. They are alert, fit, and quick-paced. Over their shoulders they carry hand tools for harvesting grain and soil cultivation....

Today, the valley is seeded to cereals and planted in orchards. A flat valley, the bed of an ancient river, enclosed by gentle mountains to the north and west—the final burial ground of slavery and feudalism. There are thirteen tombs in all, visible across the valley as slight elevated mounds, each now covered in fruit trees. Only one tomb has been excavated and prepared for public viewing. The remaining twelve tombs have been sounded and mapped. Scientific teams who may or may not excavate further anticipate no surprises. But contemporary society has introduced a new anxiety over the future of the tombs. The reservoir for storing irrigation water for the good health of agriculture in the region is now threatening the tombs, for as the water has risen in the holding basins, the increased filtration pressure has resulted in seepage and a rising water table in surrounding land—particularly the land under which the tombs are located. The Ming Tombs are threatened with underground flooding. I found it ironic that in overcoming starvation, new China unknowingly began drowning the desert resting places of previous rulers for whom a society without starvation was unthinkable!

There is no fanfare or information facility at the entrance to the excavated tomb. Only a temporary and simple museum housing some of the art treasures and tools recovered from the tomb. A few workmen, farmers, and the odd militiaman. And the hole in the earth leading down to the tomb.

A slight wind begins to blow from the south. On the wind, the sound of distant meadowlarks. In the fields, workmen clearing irrigation canals. Somewhere in the distance, the opening bars of a folksong, which dies in human chatter and laughter.

The entry to the tomb is through a stoned trench. Flowerpots have been placed along the trench softening the austerity of stone and paving. At the end of the trench, we go into the hillside and onto a stairwell that goes downward to a considerable depth. Although the tomb has been opened for a number of years, there is a stench even at the top of the stairs—a moist, decayed odor of contaminated earth. Ann, one of the older members of our group, leans momentarily against the wall of the stairwell, her hand over her mouth.

"Will you be all right?" I ask her. She nods.

"Yes. You go ahead. I'm not much for going down a grave. Putting off the inevitable, I guess." She laughs then. I take her arm and we walk into the tomb together.

At the bottom of the stairs, a wide passageway now leads toward two thick, heavy marble doors. Each door is a single slab of pale marble, peg-hinged top and bottom and opening inward into the first chamber of the tomb. The walls and vaulted ceiling of this room are made of the same marble. Temporary electric cable and lights are crudely attached under the ceiling and into surrounding rooms.

"When our scientific workers first excavated to the doorway of the tomb, they found the doors sealed from the inside and barred by two enormous marble props fitted into the doors and floor of this room," the monotonous voice of the guide's interpreter intones in the dead air. He continues, "Marble to construct this tomb came from the south of China at great expense and human effort. It is also important to note the doors were sealed by living slaves entombed with the remains of the emperor, his horses, pet animals, household staff, and personal wealth . . ."

The mind boggles at the implication of this.

"How many people were entombed with the cadaver?"

"Hundreds," the guide responds.

We move into the deeper chambers of this underground palace of death. The odor of contained decay is overpowering. I notice Ann has left the group and returned above ground.

"When the tomb was first opened, were you here?" I ask the interpreter for our guide.

"Yes. I was in the work brigade which was first to reach the marble doors. It took great effort to open the doors, sealed as they were from the interior."

"What happened when the doors were opened?" I ask.

"There was a violent rush of air from behind us. A wind howling into the tomb. There were people and animals everywhere, the expressions on their faces still distinct . . . lying where they fell or lay down to die. But when the air of the outside world touched them, they fell into dust, as did the clothes they wore. The skins of the animals also collapsed." His voice is unsteady now. "In a moment, it was all over with. Later we learned the same thing had happened even in the deepest chambers of the tomb" . . .

Bill and I walked until morning. The sunrise finds us in Tian An Men Square, opposite the Great Hall of the People—the parliament buildings of the republic. In the shadow of walls, under the gloomy early dawn light, old men stretch and stab with their fists in a ballet-like series of physical exercises, their eyes half-closed, bodies taut as they weave into and out of martial postures. They are fit for old men, remarkably fit. In another section of the massive square, workers, men and women, are assembled beside a waiting bus. They carry hampers of food, as if they were preparing to leave the city for the day. Elsewhere, a cluster of younger people play badminton without the benefit of a court or net. Yet they are precise, the imaginary outline of their sports facility is understood and respected. I am fascinated when a shot is called out of court and the match ends in each team applauding the other.

We are about to cross the square when a new sound echoes from the square and the masonry of surrounding walls. A rhythmic "clop-clopping." The old man and I stop and peer toward the gates to the square. Suddenly a few thousand young men enter the square from the avenue. They are wearing green baggy trousers and plastic footwear and are stripped to the waist, their faces and upper bodies gleaming with perspiration. Members of the People's Liberation Army, jogging in formation. Column upon column they enter the great square. They are followed by formations of young women soldiers, fully dressed in green fatigues, some with pigtails, others with short-cropped hair. The rhythmic sound of footfalls is thunderous now as they run past the Great Hall of the People, turn at the northern gate, and depart through a narrow side street.

The sun has risen well over the walls and roofs of the city. Its heat is direct and pure, as the night windstorm has swept away the smoke and chemical vapors of the previous day. The warmth of the streets and open doorways has the mild, peppery odor of cabbage being cooked. Children are awake now and emerging outside. They chatter and laugh softly in their unusually high voices, but when they see us—the strangers in their city—they become silent and stare at us, openly and without shyness. Ol' Bill extracts a postcard from his pocket and offers it to a girl of primary school age, who carries a basket of covered food in her hand and has paused to watch us pass. She smiles and shakes her head in refusal. . . .

As we enter another narrow street some chickens are pecking through a dropping of horse manure, watched by a few squatting construction workers who are waiting for their tea to boil on a propane burner, which hisses and sputters and contaminates the air with its acrid smell. Bill clears his throat and coughs. The men watch us walk by, and as we pass, we hear them chuckle softly. Entering the main boulevard, we notice morning cycle and bus traffic has thinned considerably. A traffic policeman sees us approach and blowing his whistle, escorts us across the wide street.

A short distance in front of us, a workman is filling a cart from a pile of gravel that has been stockpiled in a spot left vacant by demolition of a house or small shop. The cart is attached to a drowsing donkey by two bamboo poles which are attached on either side of the animal by a leather harness.

We stand in the shade of a poplar tree and watch as the workman methodically loads shovel after shovel of dry gravel on the back of the open cart. The bamboo poles are rising up the sides of the donkey as the cart becomes overloaded on the rear half over its two rubber-tired wheels.

"Wonder if he's plannin' to lift his donkey off his feet doin' that?" The words are no sooner out of Ol' Bill's mouth than there is a startled twitch to the donkey's ears. And slowly, gently, the harness attached to the two poles raises the donkey into the air. The workman throws another two shovels of dirt on his load before he notices what is happening.

Bill starts to laugh. The workman sees the two of us watching him. He also sees his donkey now suspended a good two feet off the ground. Quickly, he throws his shovel on the gravel pile, then moves forward to stand beside his animal. With one arm he reaches over the donkey's head and pushes downward to put the four feet of the animal where they were earlier. With the other hand he pulls his straw hat low over his eyes. He then places his free hand into his pocket and stares nonchalantly beyond us out into the street, pretending he hasn't goofed; that he is merely resting. . . .

Morning on the Peking subway en route to the Peking Zoo. The pressure of enormous crowds moving briskly onto and off the underground train system. Filling the wide stairs, the entrance and exit gates. Spilling out into the sunny street, their voices a constant, chattering, rather high-pitched sound. Exhilerating, exciting, alarming. Two of the women in our group are overwhelmed. Suddenly conscious of such an overwhelming pressure of people, they freeze. The surging crowds for an instant threaten to separate us into fragments. Ol' Bill moves in between them and, taking them each by an arm, maneuvers them back into tight open spaces, up the stairwell, and down underground to the train.

The authorities have reserved a coach for us. As we approach, on the heels of two new guides assigned to us for the day, these two young people shout instructions to the train crew, who in turn call out to the population of Chinese people waiting to board the underground train in the central station. The waiting commuters graciously make way for us, retreating carefully, lifting their children to their shoulders in an attempt to clear additional space.

The train begins to slow, its brakes shrieking as it approaches the next station. The subway tunnel widens and is dimly lit by wall lamps. I see an enormous steel plate anchored into the concrete wall on our side of the tunnel.

"What is that?" I ask the guide. I assume it is a storage compartment for tools or repair parts for the track and trains. The guide looks closely at me and smiles.

"We are prepared, should our country be attacked with nuclear weapons, to evacuate the populations of our cities underground. The people of Peking would be protected, as would others."

"This underground train system would provide little protection against a conventional bombing, I would think. And how many people could enter it before space and air ran out?" I say.

"The subway is only a small part of the underground defence system—an entrance into it." He speaks with a half-smile.

I stare at him. "I don't understand."

"This is only one passage among many. They emerge many kilometers outside the city—at distant communes."

"In the countryside?"

"Yes."

"How extensive is this underground network of tunnels?"

"Very."

The train begins to move, silently and very smoothly. Another steel door slides past as we enter darkness. I point to the door.

"Yes." He nods before I even ask the question. "Those doors lead off the subway into the network of underground highways. There are other entrances elsewhere."

"How . . . wide are the underground highways?" I ask.

"Wide enough for two large trucks to pass each other." He replies, then leans toward me, his thin face almost cavernous now, his eyes intent. "If you wished to see the facilities, a restricted tour can possibly be arranged."

I sit back in my seat and shut my eyes as I consider the implications of our discussion. A network of underground highways, a secondary system of transportation in times of peace. But at what cost? What slice of the national budget and over what period of time did this exercise absorb the energies of thousands of people? How many casualties had there been from cave-ins and accidents in this earthquake-prone land? The questions tumble through my mind. I am curious, fascinated. . . .

The Temple of Heaven in the first bright heat of the day. We drive toward it through an ancient pine forest. The packed earth beneath the trees glows. Not a blade of grass or ground cover. The pressure of population on recreational facilities shows in this park. No grass can ever sprout to green the packed clay. It is never free of human walkers long enough to enable grass seeds to sprout.

The Temple is now a recreational place for rubber-necking Peking residents, as well as a well-preserved museum from China's past. The circular courtyard surrounding one of the imperial buildings has become a playground for old and young, its acoustical pecularities called "the telephone system" by locals. Two people in different parts of the courtyard, out of sight of each other, place their faces against the wall and speak to each other in normal voices. The sound is magnified and carried by the circular wall—hence, the "telephone." I lean my ear against the courtyard wall. About a dozen different conversations make a singsong cacaphony, interspersed with laughter and coughing from those conversationalists near me who are smoking as they talk.

The pavillions surrounding the temple have been restored and are in good repair. The temple itself resplendent in rusty red, blue, and gold lacquer. Most ancient buildings in China are of wood construction, a puzzling detail when so much masonry is visible in construction of walls and courtyards and tiled roofs. As I run my hand over the smooth columns, a maintenance man moves toward me. He explains the ingenious trussing detail of the roof and ceiling of the building. Then he gives me an elaborate explanation, complete with diagrams he sketches hastily in pencil, as to preparation of the columns. They were turned from great cedars which once flourished in much of the country. After curing for a number of years, the columns were taken to the pavillion and temple sites. Once they were in position, they were carefully wrapped in silk fabric which was sealed with glue and lacquer. Many layers of silk were wrapped around each pillar. They acted as a preservative and as a bond around the cedar wood, preventing it from dying further and splitting. Somewhat like mummification...

Sleep comes with difficulty. The old man in the bed next to mine is also restive. Outside our open hotel windows night insects in the poplar trees whisper and chirp. From the street below we hear the faint tinkle of bicycle bells and the shrill but musical beep-beeping of cars performing taxi duty.

"You thinkin' of money or women?" Ol' Bill asks.

"Neither. I'm trying to sleep."

"Never get to sleep that way." he growls.

"Why not?"

"When I go to bed with a pain in my chest, I think of money or women. Makes the pain go away. If I think of both, I sleep like a baby."

"But you're not sleeping now."

"No, I'm not. I find it hard to think of money or women in this goddamned country. Why's that?"

Although the exchange is playful, Ol' Bill's comments and question hang unanswered and unanswerable in the warm night air. Surrounded as we are by the quiet, proud personal poverty of China, all thoughts of one's own economic assets and liabilities have been put out of mind. Considering it now as we lie staring through the darkness, it seems like a barbaric obscenity. Women are both close and far in men's thoughts. Society is healthy and erotic, but the senses are drawn into a new realignment. A man is conscious of it but unable to discuss it with another man. It somehow seems less important. I begin to wonder if our social urgencies are not as much a neurotic reaction to a hostile environment as they are expressions of love and dedication. The old man seems to be reading my thoughts.

"Seems to me the reason some men think of women all the time is because they're scared of dyin' . . . they got to make one more baby before they go. . . ."

"Sounds to me like the windy theory that a man in prison who gets hung always spurts out semen when he falls through the trapdoor," I say, laughingly. Ol' Bill shifts irritably in his bed.

"Never mind puttin' down what you ain't seen. I was in England durin' the war. Every time there was an air raid an' I took to the streets to keep from gettin' killed I had a hard-on like an axe handle. Later when our unit was sent to Europe into active duty, same thing happened when the shellin' started . . . But what's the use tellin' you all that when you're laughin'. . . ." He turns away from me and pulls the bedcovers up over his head. . . .

Shihchiachuang in the morning, grey slate roofs ancient and parched in the warm light. The train journey from Peking had taken five hours in the evening and into the night. At twilight, dinner had been served in the dining car. Our group is in a good state of animation. Our final morning in Peking had been relaxing and pleasant.

The electrical generator factory is some distance outside the city.

When we arrive in our bus, the rain has become a steady downpour. The driveway and courtyards of the factory are lagoons surrounded by brick and concrete walls of the facility. The bus driver unsuccessfully attempts to park under some protective roofing or beside an elevated sidewalk free of water, but after a few attempts, abandons the effort and apologizes to us through Chou. We disembark and rush through the rain to a gateway, festooned with drooping bunting and inscribed posters welcoming us. In the arch of the gateway, a cluster of workers, their blue tunics wet and clinging to their bodies, wait for us.

The vice-chairman of the factory is a slender, gracious man in his thirties who bears an uncanny resemblance to Chou-En-Lai. One of our women mentions this, and when Chou translates the comment, I notice a confused expression cloud his face. Speaking rapidly, he searches for clarification. Our woman laughs and explains she is complimenting him on possessing an unusual face. We hurry toward the main building in the factory complex, but the discussion has begun on an awkward note. Language is a barrier. The specific nuances of each language are faltering. The tonal delicacies of one language do not correspond to the other, even though we have competent translators of great sensitivity bridging the cultural chasm between our two civilizations. We are to enter a fascinating discussion on this topic later the same day, but for the moment we settle to tea and a briefing with our hosts at the electrical generator plant. Statistics on production, always impressive but meaningless without previous reference, are recited by the administrator with Chou-En-Lai's face. The plant manufactures and sells electrical generators for steam-generating plants all over China. We are the first foreign guests to visit the factory. We are welcome, and invited to prepare any question we might have about the operation of the plant, or further information about the lives and commitments of the workers in the plant. More statistics—a third of the workers are women. The proportion of women elected to administrative posts in the plant is somewhat less than the percentage of employees. When a woman from our group asks for an explanation of this disparity, the vice-chairman assures her the problem is being corrected. A litany then follows of praise for the wisdom and guidance of Chairman Mao, and condemnation of the "capitalist roaders" who threatened China with revisionism prior to and after the Cultural Revolution.

Near the end of the tour of the factory, Hector approaches and, reaching out to me, presses my arm warmly, tears in his eyes. He speaks, but I cannot hear his words above the din of machinery. He points and I follow him. Near the rear entrance to the plant workers are busy installing armatures and monitoring devices on the enormous generator casings in their final stages of assembly. There is an argumentative discussion as we approach. Four young women workers have congregated around a generator and are scolding two male workmen, who sheepishly step back, soldering equipment in their hands. The women examine the wire connections the men have made, then, reaching up, they tear loose one faulty connection after another. The men are embarrassed at Hector and me being near to witness their humiliation. Two of the women workers take the soldering equipment from the men and begin reconnecting the defective work. They are less agressive now as they chide the men. But a point in work discipline is scored. And the determined expression on the faces of the women leaves no room for discussion of mistakes....

I dress quietly and walk out into the streets of Shihchiachuang. Much of the city has been recently built. It has a feeling and an odor of freshness. The people I meet on the street early in the morning have a resoluteness, a sense of singular purpose I have seen in other places where tradition has been thinned out by an overturn of the landscape, where nothing is old enough to deserve or require sanctity. Cities like Puerta Vallarta in Mexico and Vancouver in Canada have that sensation to them. Trucks lumber by loaded with coal and construction materials. Peasants are entering the city with a variety of conveyances loaded with grain and vegetables—farm trucks, horse-drawn wagons steered by drowsy draymen.

I begin to run, happy in the opportunity to stretch my limbs and move blood more quickly through my body. The warm air is dry and refreshing, the new paving even and spongy. A group of students leaving the city for harvest work on the communes—a huge red banner drooping as it is carried by the leading cadres—are marching briskly down the middle of the roadway. As I approach them, they wave and shout a greeting I do not understand.

Rounding a corner, I come face to face with a dromedary pulling a cart, a rider with a bamboo stick mounted on its back. I stop and the animal stops. Moving to one side to let this unusual street traffic pass, I am convulsed with laughter. The rider pushes back his cap and grins. He salutes me by tapping the brim of the cap with his stick, then shouts a high-pitched command at the animal. Slowly, like a heavy truck clutching, the cart and dromedary move on. . . .

The Dr. Norman Bethune military hospital is located in Schihchiachuang. It is a complex of low buildings with no distinctive architecture. But for a Canadian visiting the hospital there is a mood and definition of history specifically tied to Canada, and affecting Canadians. Bethune in China approaches the status of a deity of the revolution. His example of commitment, discipline, and purity of revolutionary zeal is held up as a standard for youth to aspire to.

The dictatorship of the worker and peasant allows little, if any, counterexpression. So the revolutionary new society is both liberated and frozen in a sense of destiny that is political in name but religious in intensity. The creation of myths evolves naturally and in a religious way. It would be doubtful and unrewarding conjecture to suggest a date on which Chairman Mao ceased to be man and was transmuted into godlike spirit. It could not be willed or manufactured, as was attempted crudely and unsuccessfully in the Soviet Union during the days of Stalin's attempts to deify himself.

In China the metamorphosis of flesh into spirit appears to have taken place during the headlong plunge of the revolutionary transformation, when each individual participant ignited and went through baptism in the holy flame. Grovelling beggars became stokers, teachers, doctors. Men and women of great spirit donned the mantels of gods. There was no vote, no consensus taken by bureaucrats, no clumsy concrete statues built to line the highways of the land. The transition from man in simple blue tunic, cloth cap, and baggy trousers to god in the same apparel happened quietly and without fanfare. Bethune was in that sacred circle when the flame of purification engulfed and congealed the man of action into the man of eternity, still bent over a worktable, unaware of the deafening thunder blast which had just rolled over him.

This is Bethune in China. His body the holy glass through which the Chinese people gaze at the rest of us in Canada.

RALPH GUSTAFSON

The Magi

The cheering is always sad to someone.
I saw Canada dismembered. In the streets
The happy hung on trucks,
Some blaring horns,
Whistling girls, drinking from cans.
A bottle smashed in a corner
Of the pavement, sparkling
From the lamppost. Fleur-de-lis
Waved, blue on a white ground.
Someone pissed on the maple leaf.
It was joyous, there was joy.
Lights blinked. The night filled
With joy. The land was dismembered.
Upstairs, statesmen smiled.
Plural mouths spilled precepts, stations
Reached for microphones. Someone
Shot off a Saturday night
Special. Culture was singular.
Prophets spoke with one tongue.
Always there are a few
Who do not laugh.

Country Walking

1

Two humps of snow stood on two fir trees,
The place looked like an entrance to importance,
To a field of white snow, field
As in heraldry, leading nowhere of much
Consequence, a slope with a cottage on it
Shut up for the winter, the roof without icicles,
No one there for a fire. I went between the gates
Of the trees to anywhere. Shadows on the slant
Were purple, prints were in the snow
For no purpose, the denizen apparently
Not caring, going on instinct.
I thought of sophistications, music and poems:
How Liszt solved his fugue
Back into romantic grandeur,
How Yeats shook the desert birds
With emerging beasts of Bethlehem.
The snow was darkening white,
Runnels of shadow unravelling.
It seemed consequence was forgotten.
I looked back then upward, to scuffing clouds.
I went on across the hastening light,
My weight pressing in, leaving
Footprints, a complication into.
Suddenly
Sun slammed through going.

2

The moon is up there with a cart on it,
White-golden. Down here,
Calmly ice on the lake freezes;
The movement of air brushes the cheek
With cold; old Mr. Hall is dying.
There is no concern. Christmastree lights

In places blink green and red
For whatever purposes Eaton's makes of it.
My nose wants to run. Gloves on,
I wait to get home. I want to get home
To my own true love. It is glorious.

Allhallows Eve

Until the dust from the broom came
In the beam from the basement window
The suncast was invisible. It squared
Tangled. The smash on the far wall
Hit cement low down since the sun
Stood over the next house
And the elm at the roadway. Crammed
With dancing dust, anywhere near it
Man sneezed.

                  The ladder was put
Away, halloween was on
The doorstep, the second day All Souls.
Lucifer! he shouldn't have fallen to Satan.
The beam was glorious, dust in it,
Autumn leaves were raked and the bulbs
In, the gates to Eden open,
No one needed to climb walls.

Canada Still Life

The man from Bell-Canada
Buzz-sawed it,
The white birch leaning

Toward their wires
Irrelevant with good buys,
Urgent appointments
For oral cavities.
I meant the pole
To be moved,
The birch up the hill
Busy with permanent matters.

TOM MARSHALL

Summer of 'Seventy-Seven

i

The new country of summer came upon
us only gradually: we began
our day with sunlight and a train journey

from Montréal along the St. Lawrence
to Kingston and its conclave of lilacs
briefly perceived as on a rising wave.

(Each year there are whales in the Saguenay.
White whales meet in the great estuary.
Congregate, being social animals.)

From a longer poem in progress.

McLuhan says: Trudeau has a tribal
mask for a face. An endangered species
brief as whales or lilacs needs a totem

perhaps? The river runs its sunlit course
through many centuries of human change,
masks alter meaning with the centuries,

one hopes. The river offers up islands
for our need, our greed. Wealthy foreigners
inhabit many of them happily.

The new country of summer comes upon
us only gradually, only now
alongside the ageless, shifting river.

ii
June 24, 1977

On St. Jean-Baptiste's Day a carnival
erupts in Montréal: Lévesque's triumph,

magnificent fête nationale, new pride
sealed in fireworks and a rock band's blaring

sound of happiness. So the river waves
that take our vision to the Atlantic

go for a time unheard. A local pride
is sounded, a sense of self-worth long lost

and long overdue. Québec magnifique!

And we who envy you your summertide
rejoice also that a residual

bigotry in both of us may wither
like débris given back to the good earth.

iii
July 1, 1977

The Atlantic beats against the rocks at
Peggy's Cove continually. The huge
textured rocks! Bold stones! Great speckled eggs or
bones of female earth! Glookskap's daughters born
of crash and shock, foam rising in the air
a perpetual fountain. Crash and shock!

We clamber over boulders. We are small
animals at tidal pools. And the eye
moves outward irresistably in salt
undertow. Moves into teeming death, that
ocean overwhelms all differences,
all pride surrenders to that salty pull
and heave, crash and shock of great Atlantic
waves beating perpetually on rock.

iv

Summer's end. I ride air to Vancouver
and back. An earthscape unfolds. Québec will
surely stay autonomous within it?

Forces and charmed particles in movement:
the mindscape of sub-nuclear physics.
I sip my drink over gold-striped flatland.

"A sin against the spirit?" Or mountain,
hills, prairie, sky, forest, lakes, shield: islands
that make one splendid archipelago

ocean to ocean-bursting-with-dolphins?
Endangered peoples surely band and bond
together under one sky and one earth.

There are so many peoples, languages
here present. All embrace locality,
soil. All move uneasily together.

(Monarch butterflies populate Kingston.
Cavortings in the garden of the gods.
Sails gavotte along a thousand islands.)

I hold fast onto a vision in which
we are moving together like lightning
riding forever on rivers of air.

NOTES ON THE CONTRIBUTORS

Don Bailey (1942–   ) was born in Toronto and turned to writing while serving a sentence in Kingston Penitentiary. His published works include a novel and two collections of short stories, most recently *Replay*.

Douglas Barbour (1940–   ) was born in Winnipeg and now lives and teaches in Edmonton. He has published six books of poetry including *Songbook* and *Visions of My Grandfather*. He is editor of *The Story So Far Five*, which will appear in the fall of 1978.

Ronald Bates (1924–   ) was born in Regina, Saskatchewan, and now lives in London, Ontario. He has taught English literature at Uppsala University, Sweden, and at The University of Western Ontario. He has published two volumes of poetry, *The Wandering World* and *Changes*. His poems, translations, articles, and reviews have appeared in a wide variety of journals.

Henry Beissel (1929–   ), Professor of English at Concordia University in Montreal, is the author of *New Wings for Icarus, Face on the Dark, The Salt I Taste*. Among his best-known plays are *Inook and the Sun* and *Goya*. His translations of Walter Bauer have been highly praised.

Robert Bringhurst (1946–   ) was born in California. He came to Canada at the age of five and now makes his home in Vancouver. He is the author of several volumes of poems, including *The Shipwright's Log, Bergschrund, Jacob Singing,* and *The Stonecutter's Horses*.

Jim Christy (1954–   ) was born in Richmond, Virginia, and now makes Toronto his home when he's not travelling up the Amazon or through the Yukon. He has published made-up and true stories in journals (mostly obscure) in Canada, the U.S., and West Germany. A book of poetry, *Palatine Cat,* recently appeared.

Fred Cogswell (1917–   ) was born in East Centreville, N.B., and now lives in Fredericton. After serving in the Canadian Army during World War II he became, although not always at the same time, student, teacher,

234

magazine editor, translator, anthologist, and book publisher. His latest books are *The Poetry of Modern Quebec* and *Against Perspective*. He teaches English at the University of New Brunswick.

Matt Cohen (1942 –   ) was born in Kingston and now lives in Toronto. He has published two collections of stories, *Columbus and the Fat Lady* and *Night Flights,* and several novels including *The Disinherited, Wooden Hunters,* and *The Colours of War.*

Brian Dedora (1946–   ) was born in Vernon, British Columbia, and now lives in Toronto, where he writes and runs his own picture-framing business. His only other published work, *The Dream,* a visual poem, was distributed through Phenomenon Press in Toronto.

Barry Dempster (1952–   ) was born in Toronto and educated in psychology. After a brief career working with emotionally disturbed children, he turned to writing. His work has appeared in numerous periodicals including *Fiddlehead,* the *Dalhousie Review,* and the *University of Windsor Review.* He is editor of the anthology *Tributaries.*

Gail Fox (1942 –   ) was born in Connecticut, but has lived in Canada since 1963 and is a Canadian citizen. She has published five books of poetry, among them *God's Odd Look.* She is the editor of *Quarry* magazine.

Irena Friedman (1944 –   ) was born in the Urals and is still wandering. She obtained an M.A. from McGill and M.F.A. from UBC and is determined to make her living as a writer. Her work has appeared in magazines and anthologies here and abroad, as well as over the CBC.

Keith Garebian (1943 –   ) lives in Dollard des Ormeaux, Quebec. A specialist in Canadian and Commonwealth Literature, he is a free-lance literary critic for the Montreal *Star* and a drama critic for *Scene Changes.* His critical articles have appeared in such journals as *Canadian Literature* and *Modern Fiction Studies.* His poems have appeared in a number of "little mags," including *Quarry* and *Impulse.*

Eldon Garnet (1946–   ) was born in Toronto, where he still lives. He is the author of the lyric books *Angel* and *Asparagus,* and of the epics *The Last Adventure* and *Brébeuf, a Martyrdom of Jean de.* He is the editor of *Impulse.*

Margaret Gibson (1948–   ) was born in Toronto and lives with her son in Scarborough, Ontario. Ms. Gibson's first collection of stories, *Butterfly Ward,* was widely acclaimed and shared the 1977 City of Toronto Book Award. A second collection of stories, *Considering Her Condition,* will be published in the fall of 1978.

John Glassco (1909–) was born in Montreal and now lives in Foster, Quebec. He has published three collections of poetry and *Selected Poems* won the Governor-General's Award in 1971. He has also published several works of fiction and translations from the French, winning the Canada Council Award for Translation in 1975 for *Complete Poems of St. Denys-Garneau.*

Ralph Gustafson (1909–) was born in the Eastern Townships of Quebec. He is the author of over a dozen books of poetry, *Fire on Stone* winning the Governor-General's Award for 1974. His most recent publications are *Corners in the Glass* and *Soviet Poems.* He is poet in residence at Bishop's University near his home at North Hatley, Quebec.

David Helwig (1938–) was born in Toronto and teaches in the Department of English at Queen's University. He has published collections of short stories and poetry and two novels, *The Day Before Tomorrow* and *The Glass Knight. A Book of the Hours,* a new collection of poems, will appear in the spring of 1979.

John Hirsch (1930–) was born in Siofok, Hungary, and now makes his home in Toronto. In 1956 he became founding artistic director of the Manitoba Theatre Centre. Most recently he served as Head of CBC Television Drama.

Greg Hollingshead (1947–) grew up in Woodbridge, Ontario. He went to school in Toronto and London, England, and now teaches at the University of Alberta, in Edmonton. Lately he has been writing stories, some of which have appeared in *Descant, Event, The Capilano Review, The Canadian Forum,* and *The Story So Far.*

Tim Inkster (1949–) is a printer, and the co-owner (with wife Elke) of The Porcupine's Quill, Inc., a printing/bookbinding firm in Erin, Ontario. His published books include *The Topolobampo Poems, Mrs. Grundy, The Crown Prince Waits for a Train,* and *Letters.*

Hans Jewinski (1946–) spends some of his time as a police officer in Toronto. His work has appeared in many small magazines and in such anthologies as *The House Poets* and *Storm Warning. The Magician's Cage Is Bulletproof* and *Poet Cop* are two of his books of poems.

William Latta (1929–), who teaches at the University of Lethbridge, has published poetry and fiction in numerous journals and little magazines, as well as two books of poetry, *Summer's Bright Blood* and *Drifting into Grey.*

Christopher Levenson (1934–) was born in London, England, educated at Cambridge University and the University of Iowa. He held teaching posts in Holland and Germany before coming to Ottawa in

1968. For the past ten years he has taught English and Creative Writing at Carleton University. He has published four books of poetry, most recently *Into the Open.*

David Macfarlane (1952 -   ) was born in Hamilton, Ontario, and is a graduate of the University of Toronto. For much of the past year he has been living in England, completing collections of poetry and short stories. He is presently working on a novel.

T.D. MacLulich (1943 -   ), who is currently a Sessional Lecturer in the English Department at the University of Alberta, has published several critical articles on Canadian literature. His poems have appeared in a number of literary periodicals.

Darlene Madott (1952-   ) was born in Toronto. Her first novel, *Song and Silence*, was recently published by Borealis Press and her short stories have appeared in *Grain, Waves,* and *Antigonish Review.* A classical pianist and artist as well, she is currently in Vancouver working on a second novel.

Joyce Marshall (1913 -   ) was born in Montreal and has lived for many years in Toronto. She is the author of two novels, *Presently Tomorrow* and *Lovers and Strangers,* and of a collection of short stories, *A Private Place.* She has translated seven books from French. Her latest, *Enchanted Summer,* a translation of *Cet été qui chantait* by Gabrielle Roy, was awarded the Canada Council Translation Prize for 1976.

Tom Marshall (1938 -   ) was born in Niagara Falls and now lives in Kingston, Ontario, where he teaches at Queen's University. He is the author of a poetry quartet organized around the four elements. He has also written two critical works (one on A. M. Klein and one on D. H. Lawrence) and a comic novel, *Rosemary Goal.* From 1973 to 1978 he was poetry editor of *The Canadian Forum.*

Florence McNeil (1940-   ) was born in Vancouver. She has taught at various universities including the University of Calgary and UBC. She has published five books of poetry, most recently *Ghost Towns* and *Emily. The Electric Theatre* is scheduled for publication in 1979.

Susan Musgrave (1951 -   ) grew up on Vancouver Island and has spent recent years in Ireland, England, and the Queen Charlotte Islands. Her books of poems include *The Impstone, Gullband* (for children), *Grave-Dirt and Selected Strawberries* (now reprinted as *Selected Strawberries and Other Poems*), and *Becky Swan's Book.* Her most recent collection, *A Man to Marry, A Man to Bury,* will appear in the spring of 1979.

bpNichol (1944-   ) was born in Vancouver, raised in various western cities, and now lives in Toronto. He achieved an early reputation with his concrete poems. He has published novels, poetry, comic strips, records, and essays, most recently Books III and IV of his ongoing long poem, *The Martyrology*.

Joyce Carol Oates (1938-   ) was born in Lockport, New York and since 1967 has lived in Windsor, Ontario, where she teaches English at the University of Windsor. Her most recent book is *Night-Side*, a collection of stories; a new novel, *Son of the Morning*, will appear shortly.

Al Purdy (1918-   ) was born in Wooller, Ontario, and lives in Ameliasburg when he isn't wandering or serving as writer in residence. He won a Governor-General's Award for *Cariboo Horses* in 1965. *A Handful of Earth* is his most recent collection of poems.

John Reibetanz (1944-   ) lives in Toronto and teaches at Victoria College. Until recently, his writing has been primarily critical rather than creative, consisting of articles on modern poetry and Elizabethan drama, and a book on *King Lear*. The poems in this volume are part of *Ashbourn Changes*, a sequence of dramatic monologues now nearing completion.

George Ryga (1932 -   ), who was born in Deep Creek, Alberta, now lives in Summerland, B.C. He has been published in a variety of forms from songs to TV documentaries. His novels include *Hungry Hills* and *Ballad of a Stonepicker*. He is probably best known for plays such as *The Ecstasy of Rita Joe* and *Paracelsus*.

Gloria Ostrem Sawai was born in Minnesota and grew up in Saskatchewan and Alberta. After several years of home-making and teaching (in Canada, the U.S., and Japan), she earned an M.F.A. from the University of Montana in 1977. She is presently teaching writing courses in the Faculty of Continuing Education at the University of Calgary. Her work has appeared in several American periodicals.

Stephen Scobie (1943-   ) was born in Scotland, came to Canada in 1965, and now lives in Edmonton. He has published several volumes of poetry, a critical study of Leonard Cohen, and a scattering of short stories. A book of poetry, *McAlmon's Chinese Opera*, will appear shortly.

Ray Shankman (1940-   ) was born in Toronto. He has taught at Lakehead University (Thunder Bay) and at the University of the Negev in Beersheva, Israel. He now teaches English literature and Bible at Vanier College in Montreal. His poems have appeared in a number of little mags.

Kenneth Sherman (1950-   ) has travelled extensively through Asia. His poems and short stories have appeared in *Waves*, *Jewish Dialog*, and an anthology, *Now We Are Six.* His first book, *Snake Music,* will soon be published.

Raymond Souster (1921–   ) was born in Toronto and still lives there. He is a writer by avocation, bank accountant by necessity. His last book of verse was *Extra Innings* and he is preparing a manuscript of new poems under the working title *Hanging In.*

Francis Sparshott (1926–   ) was born and raised in England and has been teaching philosophy at the University of Toronto since 1950. As well as writing two books of poetry, he has published a lot of philosophical prose, including *An Enquiry into Goodness, The Structure of Aesthetics,* and *Looking for Philosophy.*

Guy Vanderhaeghe (1951 –   ) was born in Esterhazy, Saskatchewan, and is now a student at the University of Regina. His stories have appeared in the *Chelsea Journal* and *Grain.*

Miriam Waddington (1917–   ) was born in Winnipeg and now lives in Toronto, where she teaches literature at York University. She has published nine books of poetry, the last two of which are *Driving Home* and the *Price of Gold.* As well, she has written a critical study of the poet A. M. Klein and has edited *John Sutherland: Essays, Poems, Controversies* and *The Collected Poems of A. M. Klein.*

Rudy Wiebe (1934–   ) was born in Saskatchewan and has lived in Edmonton since 1967. He has written five novels, including *The Temptations of Big Bear* and *The Scorched-Wood People,* as well as short stories, essays, and film and television scripts. When not writing, he is professor of English and Creative Writing at the University of Alberta.

George Woodcock (1912–   ) was born in Winnipeg, Manitoba, lived in England for a number of years, and returned to Canada in 1949. He is the founding editor of *Canadian Literature* (1959) and is the author of some forty books. His most recent works include a study of Thomas Merton and a collection of poems, *The Kestrel.* He is now working on his autobiography.

Morris Wolfe, the editor of *Aurora,* writes a television column for *Saturday Night,* a column about books for *Books in Canada,* and teaches film history at the Ontario College of Art. He is also the editor of *A Saturday Night Scrapbook, Toronto Short Stories* (with Douglas Daymond), and *The Best Modern Canadian Stories* (with Ivon Owen).

THE NEXT ISSUE OF AURORA WILL BE PUBLISHED
IN SEPTEMBER, 1979.

If you wish to submit, the contest rules are as follows:

• You may make one submission in one or more
of the four categories: short story, poetry (no more
than ten poems), prose non-fiction, and excerpt from a
longer work-in-progress.

• You may only submit work that has not been
previously published or broadcast.

• Closing date for submissions is January 15,
1979.

• All submissions should be accompanied by a
stamped self-addressed envelope and be sent to:

> Aurora 1979
> Doubleday Canada Limited
> 105 Bond St.
> Toronto   M5B 1Y3